CHAMPION SPORT

BIOGRAPHIES

MARADONA

CHAMPION SPORT

BIOGRAPHIES

$\frac{1}{10}$

10

MARADONA

LIAN GOODALL

W

Warwick Publishing Inc.
Toronto Los Angeles
www.warwickgp.com

To Deborah, Bob and Lou. Thanks for taking a hike and
supporting me in many other ways.

© 1999 Maverick Communications

We acknowledge the financial support of the Government of Canada through the Book Publishing Industry Development Program for our publishing activities.

ISBN: 1-894020-53-7

Published by Warwick Publishing Inc.
162 John Street, Suite 300, Toronto, Ontario M5V 2E5
1300 North Alexandria Avenue, Los Angeles, California 90027

Distributed in the United States and Canada by Firefly Books Ltd.
3680 Victoria Park Avenue, Willowdale, Ontario M2H 3K1

Cover and layout design: Heidi Gemmill
Editorial Services: Joseph Romain
Cover Photo: AP/Wide World Photos
Inside Photos: Page 51 Stan Behal, Toronto Sun
     Page 52 Michael Peake, Toronto Sun
     Page 53 Stan Behal, Toronto Sun
     Page 54 Greig Reekie, Toronto Sun
Printed and bound in Canada.

Table of Contents

List of Figures

Factsheet

Diego Maradona

Born October 30, 1960 in Avellaneda, Argentina

1976 — starts his professional soccer career with Argentinos Juniors

1978 — selected for Argentina national team but dropped from World Cup finals

1980 — moves to Bocas Juniors team

1982 — sold by Bocas to Barcelona team; injures ankle in game against Bilbao

1984 — is sold to Naples, Italy, team ("Napoli") for record amount

1986 — competes with Argentina national team in World Cup in Mexico; makes controversial Hand of God goal; Argentina wins World Cup against West Germany

1987 — leads Napoli to win Italian League title

1988 — with Napoli wins UEFA Cup against Stuttgart

1990 — with Argentina national team makes it to World Cup finals

1991 — fails drug test and is suspended for 15 months

1992 — attempts comeback with Seville, Spain, team

1993 — is dropped by Seville; returns to Argentina to play with Newells Old Boys

1994 — fails drug test for ephedrine during World Cup and is suspended again for 15 months

1995 — rejoins Boca Juniors

1997 — fails another drug test; announces his retirement from soccer

Introduction

Argentina's Diego Maradona is famous as one of the greatest soccer players of all time. For more than two decades his star illuminated the world of soccer.

Soccer buffs consider this mid-fielder to be legendary. If you like soccer, you can't think about the game without different pictures of "Number 10" popping to mind. We see Diego, a young upstart with the Argentine Boca Juniors, running down the field, leaving older, more experienced players far behind. He pounds the ball into the net to help his team win the league championship in 1981.

Soon after, there he is again, a young man triumphantly hoisting the World Cup in 1986. His dancing black eyes are full of the pride of victory his extraordinary talents have brought the Argentine national team.

Then at the 1994 World Cup, we witness a stronger, more experienced player, fighting for control of the ball, almost thigh to thigh with Nigeria's Michael Emenatoat. Diego has brought many exciting moments to the game of soccer. The magic feet of this stocky, 5-foot-5 mid-fielder have scored astounding goals that will never be forgotten.

Maradona has inspired a new generation of soccer players to try and play the sport as well as their mentor. He has also set an example with the management of his career as a professional. He has shown soccer players important ways they could control the commercial, money-making side of their careers.

Diego's story is remarkable. He was brought to national attention before his tenth birthday — a child prodigy. At just under 16 years of age he became the youngest player in football history to play a first-division match. He has been bought for record-breaking amounts of money and played for clubs in three different countries: Argentina, Spain and Italy. He has also participated in four World Cups, and is ranked third for the number of World Cup minutes played. During this time he made goals and assists of stellar quality.

As a young boy Diego's star began to shine from his childhood home in the slums of Argentina. With courage and determination he steered a course so that his star shone brightly for all the world to see.

With his fame, came exposure to many opportunities. not all of these were good. In fact, some of them were dangerous and destructive. While brilliant on the field, off the field Maradona has made some bad personal choices which affected his career. Three drug-related suspensions probably contributed to his decision to leave the game.

By the time he retired in 1997, Diego Maradona's star had shot across the sky, leaving behind it a brilliantly shining trail of soccer greatness.

Chapter 1

Childhood of a Star Born in the Slums

In Eva Peron Hospital in Avellaneda, Argentina, on Sunday, October 30th, 1960, a little boy was born. One day he would be adored by millions as the greatest soccer player in the world. But as he lay in his mother's arms, a baby, no one suspected that there was magic in his tiny feet. The mother and father named the baby Diego Armando Maradona, a name that one day would be on the lips of millions.

The happy parents thanked God for the safe arrival of their first-born son. To father Chitoro and mother Dona Dalmo Salvadora Franco (known as Tota), children were very important. Chitora and Tota were not rich people. They had come from poor families with native Indian and Italian immigrant roots. They had grown up in mud and dung huts covered with reeds in a country village called Esquina. Conditions were poor and life was difficult in this small village. Diego's parents did what most country people were doing in

Argentina at the time. Looking for a better life, they moved to the capital city of Buenos Aires.

Almost half the population of Argentina lives in the seaport of Buenos Aires. They work near the docks or in factories, like Diego's father did. Chitoro got a job in a factory where they crushed bones to make bone meal, which is used in fertilizers. Tota found work as a servant in the home of rich people. With these jobs the parents tried to make enough money to feed their children.

They lived in a shantytown in a suburb called Villa Fiorito. Chitoro built a little shanty using whatever he could find: pieces of metal, cardboard, and bricks. This was to be the Maradona family home for some time. When he was born, Diego already had three sisters. Eventually there would be eight children, three of them boys, all growing up in the tiny shelter. Their grandmother also lived with the family and their Uncle Cirilo lived nearby.

What the Maradonas found when they came to Buenos Aires wasn't glorious. Life in Villa Fiorito was very difficult. The family banded together to help each other survive. Diego's family cared for and guided him from day one. His mother and his grandmother were his first teachers. His father and his uncle were his first soccer coaches.

Soccer, which is called football outside of North America, has been around for a long time. Various games involving kicking a round object have probably existed as long has humans have existed. One of the earliest records of the game is a law banning soccer-playing from the streets of London, England, in the 1300s.

But although it's been with us since ancient times, the rules for the game varied from place to place. The game we know today as soccer only really took shape in the 1800s. In 1846, a set of formal rules for soccer was set up at Cambridge University in England. Having a set of rules that everyone agreed upon made it easier to have matches between communities, towns, and countries. These competitions made it an entertaining sport to watch as well as play.

One of the great things about soccer is that it requires so little equipment. To play a game, all you really need is a soccer ball. This also made it a very easy game to transport. As people travelled, they brought soccer with them. They taught the game to the people they met in new lands. In this way, the formal game of soccer spread from continent to continent. Today it is one of the most popular team sports in the world.

British sailors introduced soccer to Argentina in the early nineteenth century. Since that time, it has grown in popularity to become the number one sport in the country. Many Argentines play on some kind of team. Others simply enjoy picking up a ball and playing an informal game. When they can, Argentines like to watch matches on television. In fact, Argentines are crazy about soccer.

Living in a country where soccer fever was a common malady, it was only natural that Chitoro Maradona and Uncle Cirilo loved the game. They had played on a local team in the village of Esquina where they had grown up. Uncle Cirilo had helped his team, San Martin, win a local championship in 1952. People had noticed how well he played. His nickname had been *Tapon* or "The Plug" because of the way he stopped the ball. Now much older, the two brothers were still very interested in soccer. They couldn't help hoping that a Maradona might one day be a great soccer star.

Diego's father and uncle helped the little boy develop an interest in the sport. It was Uncle Cirilo who gave the lad his first soccer ball. Growing up a poor child, Diego remembers he "never had many toys." The first ball he received was "the most beautiful present" of his life. His uncle presented him with the leather ball on his third birthday. The tiny tot fell asleep clutching it, perhaps dreaming of the journeys they would make down the soccer pitch together before crowds of fans screaming in the stands. Soon, Diego was happily kicking the ball around the dusty soccer fields of the slum.

Whether you're rich or poor, playing soccer can give you a great feeling. Being in control of the ball gives a soccer player a taste of power. Running down the field inspires a sense of freedom, almost like flying. You don't need much equipment and you don't have to be rich to play this sport. All you really need is a ball and a bunch of friends.

Most boys in Villa Fiorito played soccer, but most boys couldn't play like Diego Maradona. He began to develop amazing ways of handling the ball that others couldn't imitate. The people in the neighborhood saw that the boy could really kick! The word began to spread that the Maradona boy was something special.

The word from Villa Fiorita reached the ears of some important sports people. When he was eight years old, Diego was given the opportunity to join a special soccer team called Los Cebollitas. A neighbor arranged a meeting between the young slum kid and the Los Cebollitas trainer, Francisco Cornejo. Cornejo was impressed by the dribbling talents and control the small boy displayed. He could see that the little boy had a rare gift. Right away Cornejo asked him to join the Los Cebollitas.

Cebollitas is a Spanish nickname for children, meaning "little onions." This team developed young players with potential and encouraged their education at the same time. Diego and his family knew that he was being given an exciting and important opportunity. They also knew that although he wasn't like most of the boys his age who played soccer, talent wasn't enough. There was a lot of work ahead if he ever hoped to advance to the next level, let alone become a soccer star.

The little boy dreamed of being a great player like his heroes, Argentina's Bochini, or the Brazilian, Pele. He was thrilled to wear the same sweater number as Pele — Number 10. In choosing Diego to wear that number, the coaches of Los Cebollitas were also challenging him. Number 10 is usually given to the best scorer. Now the young boy had to work toward fulfilling the reputation of the number on his sweater.

So began years of hard work, when everything in Diego's life would revolve around the sport of soccer. Each night after Señor Maradona returned from work, he took his son to practice with Los Cebollitas. On the field, the new Number 10 did his best to impress his coach. Cornejo was important as the first person to shape this natural talent and introduce the boy to discipline. Cornejo liked the way that Diego applied himself to become a more skilful player.

Cornejo's job was to help the boy become the best soccer player possible. But he was concerned that the lad was small for his age. Popular sports philosophy of the time thought that special medicines and vitamins were the best things to help bodies reach their maximum growth potential. Whether it was through this part of the regime the team doctor put him on, or simply improved nutrition, Diego's body did become stronger.

Within a few years Diego had honed his ball-handling talent to the point where all kinds of adults were paying attention to him. When he was only 10 years old he was executing ball tricks between halves at major soccer games. The boy would go out on the field all by himself to show fans his kicking feats. It seemed his feet could perform stunts that no one else could. Fans couldn't get enough of this curly-headed boy with the dark brown eyes and the magic feet. When he came on the field, zigzagging the ball, or bringing it to the top of his head from a back spin before letting it fall onto his chest — the crowds went wild! They almost wouldn't let him leave the field.

The young prodigy even went on Argentine national television. He performed before the camera, balancing an orange or a bottle on his foot for a long time. Diego soon became known in Buenos Aires, and even in other places across the country. He must have felt very excited after his stadium and television appearances. Fame must have seemed very close.

However, at home in the shantytown, the glorious applause of the crowds quickly faded into the dim light of poverty. The reality of the Maradona family's life was less than glamorous. There was no running water in the little shanty. Curtains, not doors, separated the three tiny rooms. Diego's father worked 10 hours a day in poor conditions in the bone meal factory to try to make their lives better.

As the eldest son, young Diego strongly felt that he needed to help his family by earning some money. He tried several things to earn a few coins. He would travel to the city and hang out at train stations, opening taxi doors for people in the hopes that they would give him a tip. Another thing he did was collect cigarette packages. Then he would carefully separate the paper and silver foil of the wrapper. It took a long time to collect enough silver foil to sell, but every bit of money counted to a little boy growing up in the slums.

Diego dreamed of helping his family so that one day they would be rich. He realized that if he became a famous soccer player, he might achieve that goal. He set his sights high, deciding that not only would he achieve personal excellence, but that one day he would help his team win a League Cup and even the World Cup.

His desire to rise above poverty became stronger as soccer introduced him to the world of people who were better off than his family. On one trip in 1973 his team traveled to Chile. There they stayed in a luxurious five-star hotel. An ecstatic Diego got as much enjoyment as he could from this privilege. He even had room service bring him his breakfast in bed. This treatment was quite a contrast from his life in shantytown. The pampering seemed to have a good effect on him. Later that day he scored four goals for his team.

Diego continued to play hard, showing his commitment to his club. Los Cebollitas became a successful team, largely thanks to young Number 10. In 1973

Los Cebollitas were runners-up in Argentina's Youth Championship. The next year they won the contest. Thirteen-year-old Diego's contributions to his first team made a big difference, as they would to several other teams in his career.

As his strength and power increased, so did his reputation as a dribbler and brilliant scorer. It seemed his career was going the way he wanted. But as a teenager, Diego showed some emotional characteristics that he could not seem to change even as he grew older. Sometimes he lost his temper on the field. Once a referee expelled him from a game. His advisers hoped that such a talented player would learn to control his impulses as he matured.

As Diego moved into his teenage years, the time came for him to graduate from his first team. One first-division club, River Plate, had already expressed a desire to work with Diego when the boy was only 12 years old. Now, at age 15, he received a special birthday present from another first-division team, the Argentinos Juniors. They gave him a key — the key to his own apartment! The apartment not only had bedrooms, a kitchen and a bathroom, but was big enough to fit his whole family. It was located in a nice neighborhood called Villa del Parque.

This must have been very important to the son of a family living in a tiny shanty with only three rooms altogether and without running water. It didn't take

Diego long to decide to play with the Argentinos Juniors. He was to play with this team for five years, between 1976 and 1981.

Taking the apartment key in his hands, and signing a contract, Diego was about to become a professional soccer player. He knew that he was stepping in a direction that might lead to a better life than that of his parents. A few sportsmen in the world made fantastic sums of money. If he worked hard enough, one day he might live in a big house. If things went well for him, he would never live in a shanty or have a job working in poor conditions for little pay. His career was beginning to take him away from Villa Fiorito.

Diego Maradona would never forget the years of his childhood spent in poverty and the lessons of strength and survival that growing up in shantytown had taught him. But now, he had a chance at securing his dreams for himself and his family. A starry-eyed teenager, Diego knew he had the talent and didn't doubt that he had the courage and self-discipline to make himself a great soccer star. Confidently, he prepared to show his new team that he was ready to play.

Chapter 2

Rising Star in Argentina (1976–1982)

In the fall of 1976, the curtain was about to rise for Diego Maradona. The Argentine world of professional sports was going to meet the person who would change sports history. Diego played his premier professional match 10 days before he turned 16 on October 30, 1976. It must have been exhilarating, and a bit scary too, knowing that at 15 years of age he was about to become the youngest person in history to participate in a first-division match.

Diego was nervous. To make things worse, in the game against Talleres from the province of Cordoba, the Argentinos Juniors were losing 1–0 when manager Montes sent the novice player on the field. Everyone in the stands was yelling. They wanted their team to win. What could this new player do?

Running out onto the field in front of thousands of screaming people, Diego's stomach churned. Yet, once his feet connected with the ball, the magic took over.

He remembered his coaches' advice to "enjoy yourself," and began to play soccer as only he could.

He was unable to turn the score around and his team lost. Still, he had reason to feel good about his introduction into professional soccer. The fans were excited about the new talent that had joined their team. The sports reporters wrote about the "joy" with which the young player handled the ball. Some people criticized the other team members who they thought hadn't really helped the new player. Whatever the comment, after that day all of Argentina excitedly watched the young man with the magic feet.

Among those who saw Diego's notable performance was the coach of the Argentine national team, Cesar Luis Menotti. Menotti was impressed with the young man's play in the game against Talleres. When the player was just 17, he was invited to join the Argentine national team as a substitute. This was fantastic news for Diego. Every soccer hopeful in Argentina wanted to be on the World Cup team. At World Cup time, the strongest players from different clubs join together to form what their compatriots hope will be the best team in the world.

The 1978 World Cup was especially exciting for Argentinian soccer fans because the tournament would be taking place in Argentina. Sixteen teams from around the world would meet in their country to battle for soccer's most coveted prize. Everyone was expecting great things. Argentines hoped to see their side take the trophy on home ground. Diego badly wanted to be a part of this extraordinary action. Furthermore, if he was chosen as one of the final 22 members of the national team, he would be the youngest player ever to play in a World Cup.

Eagerly, the midfielder went to practice with some of Argentina's best. Coach Menotti scrutinized the player carefully. He included him as a substitute in some international matches and watched him play other games with the National Youth team. In the end, Menotti decided that the teenager was too youthful, both physically and mentally, to play in the finals.

Diego wept bitterly when he heard the news. Argentina went on to defeat the Netherlands and win the World Cup without his aid. Although he was happy about his nation's victory, the young man was terribly disappointed that he hadn't been able to play.

But with the encouragement of his family and friends, he stuck with the game. Because of his success at soccer, the family's lifestyle had changed from poverty to one of affluence. In the new apartment they had many timesaving conveniences that had been unknown in the shantytown.

Señor Maradona had been able to give up his factory job. Now he used his time to help his eldest boy with his career. Sometimes after a match the elder Maradona would sit in front of the television with his famous son. They would watch the game and analyze the play with the goal of improving his style.

When Diego hit a low spot in 1978 after being prevented from playing in the World Cup finals, the entire family decided that they weren't going to let him stop playing. They knew how important soccer was to him. They let the boy know that one day his turn would come.

The young man, too, recognized that soccer was his life. Even though he hadn't been able to play with the national team, he had been selected. He realized that many more opportunities lay ahead if he continued to strive for them. Determined to improve and get out of his rut, Diego worked hard. A few days after his disappointing news about the World Cup, he was back at his training, kicking the ball with a vengeance. He scored three goals to help the Argentinos Juniors beat a club from Charait.

Diego knew that becoming a soccer star at a professional and international level was not easy. He trained all day long and tried hard to please his advisors. He felt that he had to do his best on the field — even when he was injured. Sometimes when Diego hurt himself, the doctor would give him painkilling injections so that he could get back into the game quickly. Then he would be back out kicking the ball, sometimes before his body was really ready. The quick snap back into play after these injuries would gradually take its toll on him physically. But Diego knew that a soccer player wasn't worth much if he wasn't playing. The only way to be a player was to play — at any cost.

So play he did. The commitment to training Diego showed in late 1978 and 1979 paid off. The strength in his powerful legs grew. His style matured, aided by the international exposure he was beginning to get. He participated in some friendly games with teams from other countries. This was another level of soccer. Often the young man faced older, more experienced players. He was also coming across techniques and strategies different from those he was used to in Argentina.

But Diego seemed to adapt to these challenges. In Scotland in 1979 he danced around three Scottish players to score and win 3–1. The Scottish press sang the praises of the young midfielder. They even compared him to Brazilian soccer great Pele. People all over began to see why Argentina was becoming so crazy about their young hero. The world saw the first glimmer of Diego's star rising in the international sky.

It seemed that his star might shine brightly, very brightly indeed. In 1979, Diego captained the Argentine team at the World Youth Cup in Tokyo, Japan. He was determined to do well and he played incredibly. A Brazilian journalist wrote that "not since Pele" had the world seen such a fine player.

In the qualifying match, Argentina beat Peru 4–0. They went on to play the Soviet Union and win the World Youth Championship Cup. Observing these games, the Japanese greatly admired the stocky and powerful midfielder. Diego had a whole new set of fans in another country and on another continent.

Back at home in Argentina, jubilant crowds filled the streets, chanting his name. Not only was Number 10 a national hero, but he had the honor of "Best South American Player" bestowed upon him in 1979 and again in 1980.

While Diego was developing from a novice player to a professional one, he was also growing from a boy into a young man. Like many young men, he was interested in different girls, but Diego met one special young woman named Claudia Villafane. Claudia would one day become Diego's wife. Claudia first met Diego's mother in the neighborhood supermarket. When the family matriarch found herself short of change to pay for her groceries, the slight, teenaged girl in line behind her offered to lend Tota the money. Later, Tota sent her eldest son to repay the loan. It didn't take long for the two to become romantically involved, much to the delight of their families.

Although Claudia would often help support Diego from then on, they would not marry for a number of years. Over much of that time the press accused the soccer player of having other girlfriends and romantic affairs. Diego was a young man glittering with stardust, and many young women were attracted to him. He in turn was easily seduced by a dazzling life.

His life changed after he became a professional soccer player and his lifestyle shifted gears too. He bought his parents a new house and provided friends and family with apartments. Diego had fulfilled his dream of improving his parents' lives. Although he was still only a teenager, he soon owned his own huge house, with many rooms, maids' quarters, and a swimming pool.

He also liked to spend his money frolicking with his friends in Buenos Aires at night. His reputation for wild adventures began in his teenage years and would only escalate as he grew older. Diego couldn't seem to resist exploring the thrills and temptations the streets offered after dark.

While his active nightlife took up some of his energy, most of his daylight hours were still spent on the soccer field, training. He divided his time between his social activities and his job. With this sort of schedule, Diego began missing more and more school. Before long he abandoned his secondary school studies.

Diego was no longer a school boy. He had a professional, full-time career as an athlete. As a soccer star, he also had to become a businessman. Well-known athletes can make a lot of money from promoting different products. Companies like to have their products associated with popular, successful people, because then consumers think of their products as popular and successful as well, and want to buy more of them.

As he grew famous, many companies clamored to have Diego represent their products. He had to decide which ones could use his image in their advertising. He also wanted to create his own line of products. He didn't want other people to take advantage of his star status.

To do all this, Diego needed a manager who would represent him fairly in business deals. He made an important connection when he met Jorge Cyterszpiler, a young man with administrative experience. When they first met, Jorge would buy the soccer player pizza and pop. At that time, the young midfielder didn't have much money, but Jorge could see that he had lots of talent. Not only did they become friends, but soon Jorge became Diego's first manager.

Their company launched its own Maradona merchandise. A little Diego doll and other items came onto the market. Maradona Productions also signed deals with some large, well-known corporations. Diego's face was used to promote Coca-Cola and Puma sporting goods. Over the years he did advertisements for soap, toothpaste, and many other items. It must have been a funny feeling for the young man to know that kids were playing with a toy that looked just like him, or brushing their teeth with a certain toothpaste just because their hero used it.

A few times the star refused to associate with certain products because he did not believe in them. For example, he would not sign with a cigarette company because he didn't smoke. Nor would he help advertise wine because he knew the dangers associated with drinking. Later in his career he wouldn't work for Nike, the sporting goods company, because at that time he didn't feel comfortable supporting an American manufacturer. Diego wasn't always interested in just making money. Sometimes other factors influenced his decisions.

The money that Maradona Productions made became an important source of income for the player. As Diego's business manager, Jorge's goal was to have the "the first company ever devoted to promoting the image of a footballer." This company also provided an example for other soccer players, especially those in Argentina. They were not used to thinking of themselves as businesspeople in this way. After Diego began his own company, other players realized that they, too, needed to have control over how their images were used. This was an important change in the world of soccer.

While he was one of the first soccer players to retain control over his business affairs, Diego seemed to have little choice over how his image was used on the political scene. More than once in his career, politicians would use his prominence to boost their favor with Argentines. It worked much the same way as it did for commercial products. Consumers bought more Coca-Cola when they saw their favorite athlete drinking it. If a politician could be seen at Diego Maradona's side, the soccer player's fans might see that politician in a more favorable light.

Even though he was only a teenager, and probably not even terribly interested or informed about politics, it didn't seem to matter. The people in power wanted Diego Maradona on its side. The government knew how popular the star was with the people. If they could show that Argentina's Number One soccer player believed in the government, then they would have more support from Diego's many fans.

Diego lived in Argentina during a period of political turmoil. In 1976, the military took control of the government. The dictatorship of Generals Videla and Lami Dozo, and Admiral Massera had ruled harshly. Thousands of people who the government suspected belonged to guerilla groups disappeared and were presumed murdered.

Within a few years this regime would topple. In the meantime it was interested in getting the approval of soccer's brightest star. Politicians made sure they were photographed congratulating Diego for his team's success at the World Youth Championship.

There were reports that people connected with the military pumped funds into the Argentinos Juniors so that the club could afford to pay Number 10's generous salary.

The government tried to make themselves popular with Diego and his fans by shortening the star's draft period. In Argentina, all males 18 years of age had to do an obligatory military service. In this case, the government made sure that the young man was drafted for only a short period of time. Officials told him that he could serve the country better as a soccer player. The theory was that as long as Diego Maradona was playing soccer, the people would be involved with watching sports. They might pay less attention to the worrisome events unfolding in their country.

What did the teenager think of all this? A short military service must have meant a lot to him. Like most people, he simply wanted to see his country do well, but he wasn't sure exactly how this should happen. After all, he was a soccer player and unschooled in the area of politics. He may have been unaware of the government's shameful treatment of many people. Diego didn't make the best choice in directly or indirectly letting his popularity prop up a corrupt political regime. Perhaps he really had no choice.

Diego's political, social, and business ties were far more complicated than they were for most people his age. He had a lot to cope with as a famous soccer star and wealthy young man. Yet, in the early 1980s he was only a few years older than he had been when Coach Menotti of the Argentine national team had voiced concerns about his immaturity.

Such a high-profile life in sports held advantages that were also disadvantages. For example, Diego loved his fans, but he also felt that they expected too much from him. Sometimes people wrote to him, asking for favors, gifts, or money. When he was playing, he knew that his fans were waiting for him to score miraculous goals. But when he had the occasional "off" day, he sensed that the same people turned on him.

Throughout his career he would often feel tense with the stands full of crowds chanting his name. The constant attention paid to him by fans and the press, and the pressure to succeed on the field, got on his nerves. It seemed everybody wanted something from him, and all he wanted to do was play soccer.

Already at this time in his career, Diego was taking holidays to escape such pressures. He would go to his parents' village, Esquina, to relax in the quiet atmosphere. But the occasional holidays did not seem to be enough to bring him peace of mind. The pressure continued to build up, like steam under a volcano. Sometimes it burst through and a nasty young man appeared through the cracks. One day a young fan jostled the star. Diego responded by punching him. He received a suspended 15-month sentence for this action. Another time he returned late from a holiday. Coach Menotti suspended him for a time.

The player's behavior shows that he may have been exposed to more than he could handle too early in life. Connecting with the black and white soccer ball was the one thing in life that constantly made sense in the young star's spinning world.

On the soccer field, real magic existed for Diego as he scored goal after goal after goal. As the reputation of the power in his left foot grew, other clubs vied to have Number 10 play for them. In 1981 the Argentinos Juniors loaned him to the Boca Juniors for a year.

The Boca Juniors play in a stadium called *La Bombonera* (the Candy Box). The stadium is located in a working-class community of Italian descent near Buenos Aires' dock land. The Boca Juniors thought of themselves a working-class team. Their arch enemies were the River Plate, a team they considered to be snobs. Sometimes the clashes between the two teams became very heated.

Diego had several professional and personal reasons to be eager to play for the Boca Juniors. Their supporters were mostly workers of Italian descent. His mother's family had Italian roots. Furthermore, the kid from the slums always identified himself with the working class. Another thing that made Diego happy about the new deal was the fact that the Boca Juniors were one of the best teams in Argentina. The young player needed a victorious club to propel his professional career along.

Right away he seemed to fit in with the team. The year he joined the Boca Juniors, the team won the Argentine League title, with many thanks to the new man. Boca Junior fans went wild! They adored their new star. It seems that the Boca Junior fans and the midfielder formed a special bond. Fan Leandro Zanoni says that Boca followers will never forget "that rainy night in 1981 where Diego, with a memorable play, scored against [opponents] Fillol and Tarantini. ... With this magic he won everybody's love." The Boca Juniors would be an important team to Diego throughout much of his career. The team colors — yellow and blue — are often identified with him.

When Diego helped win the title, he said simply that he had played his best for Antonio Labat, an elderly parking attendant. Antonio must have felt honored to be noticed by the best soccer player in Argentina.

At age 21, Diego was playing with an incredible amount of power. He had a very creative style, moving so that those trying to stop him were fooled time and time again. Not only did he make brilliant goals on his own, but he worked with his teammates, enabling them to score points too. It's not surprising that soccer clubs outside Argentina were now becoming interested in getting Maradona to play for their teams.

With the news of a deal in the air, once again the politicians tried to interfere with Diego's career. In 1982, the government decided that the famous young soccer player should help them. This was the year of the Falkland War. Although the Falkland Islands lay off the coast of Argentina, Britain controlled them. The new dictatorship of General Galtieri took up arms against Britain, disputing the ownership of these islands.

To dispel the people's worries about the war, the government tried to emphasize the good things happening in the country at the time — such as soccer. As before, the government tried to link itself with Argentina's Number One soccer star. Now the question was whether or not he would leave his native land and go abroad to play soccer. The government insisted that Diego was a national treasure and that he would never leave Argentina.

However, the Argentine clubs and even the government realized that they could not afford to keep this treasure. Diego was no longer the teenager who had been kept from playing in the 1978 World Cup finals. Now he was being recognized as one of the best players in the world. He desired and deserved the opportunity to develop his skills by playing on soccer fields in other countries.

All this meant that Diego Maradona's skills were worth a lot of money — more money than the government and Argentine teams could afford to pay. It was time for Diego to step out onto the international scene.

At 22 years of age, he was in many ways a wild horse — right down to his long, flowing mane of hair. No one loved him more than the fans who fondly nick-named him *El Pelusa*, "the Straggly-Haired One." The people in the stands identified with the kid from the slums. They loved it when he scored a goal and ran across the field, throwing victory punches into the air or thanking God.

Diego had come a long, long way from the shanty-town in Villa Fiorito. Now he was a businessperson and a sports hero. Because of this he had achieved his goal of helping his family. He continued to help these people who made him the happiest.

While soccer was the other thing in life that made him happy, his role as a sports hero was not always easy. With it came pressure: from fans, from the press, from meddlesome governments, from businesspeople, from the training schedule, and from taking pain medicines to help him recuperate quickly from injuries. Already, the difficulties of his profession were beginning to affect him.

On the other hand, Diego's teenage years had been thrilling. He had the satisfaction of knowing that he was very successful in his chosen field. Already he had captained a winning team, been the youngest player in the world to play on a professional soccer team, and helped his club take a league title.

And there were still many exciting events that would happen in Diego's career. In 1982, Maradona would leave his homeland for a time to seek opportunities in the wider world of international soccer. But whenever he would return to La Bombonera, yellow and blue smoke would still billow in his honor, as overflowing crowds chanted their adoration.

Maradona's Career Landmarks, 1975–82

1976 First-division debut, Argentina Juniors. Youngest player in football history to play a first-division match.

1977 Full international debut for Argentina

1978 Excluded from the World Cup finals by Coach Ceasar Menotti

1979 Captain of the Argentine team, winners of the World Youth Cup in Japan

1981 Wins Argentine League title with Boca Juniors

1982 Sold to Barcelona, Spain

Chapter 3

Star High in the International Sky (1982–1989)

When Diego Maradona joined his new team in Spain, he must have felt very important. Barcelona bought the player for a record-breaking amount of money. The Boca Juniors and the Argentinos Juniors reportedly sold him for $7.3 million. Diego's paycheck amounted to more than $50,000 per season. People nicknamed the deal the "Maradollar." Diego also held on to merchandising rights, which meant that any money made from advertisements using his face or name would go to him.

Diego's new club was different from the Boca Juniors. The stadium he played in was large. The team he worked for had one of the biggest fan clubs in the world. His new teammates seemed impressed with his style and were eager to imitate his tricks.

But in this world of sunshine a few clouds were already appearing. Until his family joined him, Diego felt very lonely in the large house he had purchased in Barcelona. He filled his spare time by visiting night clubs and going to parties.

It is even said that he experimented with drugs for the first time in 1982. If that's true, it may be that he was just trying something new and perhaps attempting to fill an emptiness. If he had been a drug addict, it is doubtful that he would have participated in an anti-drug campaign for the city of Barcelona. But the warning lights were flashing. His drug use would later cause him much grief, and the problem began in Barcelona.

A good deal of his personal unhappiness ended when his family travelled from Argentina to join him in Barcelona. But other problems did not go away. Some of these were physical. Diego contracted hepatitis (an infection of the liver) early in his stay and had to miss some games.

Later in 1983, he suffered an injury due to a foul in a game against Bilbao, Spain. His tendons were so badly hurt that the doctors put three pins in his ankle. Unhappy with the treatment that the Spanish doctors were giving him, the star insisted that his old doctor be brought from Argentina. With the encouragement of Dr. Olivia, he soon threw away his crutches.

Not everyone felt that the advice of this doctor, a man who was to stay with Diego for a long time, was the best. It was said that Dr. Olivia steered the star in the wrong direction by having him take on a "tough man" stance rather than follow the cure prescribed by the other doctors, which involved rest and giving the injury time to heal.

While physically disabled from time to time, Diego also felt himself being mentally worn down by the attitude of the fans in Barcelona. People were not really sure of how the new team member would perform on the soccer field. After all, he was not a great international star when he arrived in Spain in 1982. The deal with Barcelona had been made before the 1982 World Cup competition and Diego was to play with his national team before moving to his new home.

Argentina was one of the 24 teams to compete in the 1982 World Cup. The competition took place in Spain and some games were played in Barcelona. For some Spainards it was their first opportunity to see the new Barcelonan forward play. And, unfortunately, Diego did not make a very good impression on them.

It was the first time the young man fully participated in a World Cup competition, and Diego had some disappointing experiences. For example, when Argentina played Italy in Barcelona, Diego was marked by a guard called Claudio Gentile. Gentile, who was nicknamed "Qaddafi" after the leader of Libya, kicked the Argentine's shins and knees without mercy.

Diego later said that "in all my career I have never suffered a marking like that of Gentile." Gentile com-mented that "soccer is not for ballerinas; soccer is a thing for men." The Barcelonan press put headlines on their articles about Maradona that called him *Mini Dona* — "Little Lady." They implied that Diego was too delicate for the rigors of international soccer.

Perhaps such comments fuelled the young man's anger and inspired him to be more aggressive in his next game. Five minutes before the end of a game with Brazil, Diego was expelled for a foul. It was a particularly nasty foul, which one writer remembers as "a pointless psychopathic assault." It also didn't help the team, and Argentina lost the match 3–1.

In light of his rather unimpressive behavior at the World Cup, it was understandable that the Barcelonan fans did not immediately embrace their new player. Instead, they waited to see what he would do for their team.

Things started out well enough, with Diego making several important goals for the club. In the first season, Barcelona took the Spanish title. In 1983, a goal Diego scored with teammate Schuster helped the team take the King's Cup against their rivals, Real Madrid of Spain. When he returned from his ankle injury in the New Year of 1984, Diego immediately scored two goals to lead Barcelona to victory over Seville (Spain). Number 10 scored 22 goals in the 36 league games he played for this team.

But he also turned in some poorer performances. Fans were terribly disappointed when Barcelona was eliminated from the 1984 European Cup-Winners Cup. Diego didn't play well at this match, blaming the painkilling injections that he was given to help him finish the game.

When Barcelona and Bilbao squared off, Maradona displayed childish behavior. The last time he had played this team, Diego had received his ankle injury. Still angry, it didn't take him long to enter into what became a huge fight with the Bilbao players. The Spanish king, Carlos, was in attendance at the match. The Barcelonans were disgusted with Diego's lack of respect.

They also did not approve of Diego's after-hours shenanigans in their city at night. Argentines might have occasionally frowned at his behavior and criticized his play, but they would always have a deep love their national soccer hero. Barcelonans had no such attachment.

They were not impressed with Diego as a person or a player. Had he played brilliantly all the time, they might have had more affection for him. As it was, the club had paid a huge sum for the new man. Barcelona did not find what they wanted in Diego and Diego did not find what he was looking for in Barcelona. Sadly, he remembers his Barcelona experience as one of the "unhappiest periods" of his life. Both sides decided a change would be best.

In 1984 Diego moved to Naples, Italy, to play for the Napoli team. Barcelona received about $13 million for the trade and Diego $6.4 million. But more than the money, the trade gave him the fan support he had lacked in Barcelona. During his time in Italy, Diego Maradona would play the best soccer of his career. His professional star was to shine its brightest.

On July 5, 1984, the day the 24-year-old soccer player appeared at the airport, the citizens of Naples showed him how happy they were to see him. Crowds were so frantic with joy that a double had to be hired so that the real Diego could arrive at his destination. Balloons and fireworks greeted him. A beaming Number 10 walked triumphantly into the San Paolo stadium where 85,000 fans rose to their feet, applauding wildly. He greeted his new adoring masses in Italian with *"Buona sera, Napolitani."* The crowd roared.

This was only the beginning of the "Maradona fever" that would grow to a frenzy during his time in Naples. Perhaps the people were so excited because their new soccer hero strongly identified with the working class, and Naples was a working class city. Maybe it was his mother's Italian ancestry. Whatever its source, it would have been hard for Diego, or anybody else, not to respond positively to the love the Italian people showed him. In return for their support, he was to give them some of the best years of his soccer life.

Diego settled in and got to know his new country and its people. He had an audience with the Pope, the head of the Roman Catholic Church. Most Argentines and Italians practice the Roman Catholic religion. The soccer player was honored to visit the person who held the highest position with his church. He also acted as an ambassador for UNICEF, the United Nations foundation for children. He played some charity matches with his brothers, Hugo and Lalo, for this organization.

Now a very famous man, Diego was invited to many parties and gatherings. At one he met a woman called Cristiana Sinagra. Although they did not marry, it seems Diego fell in love with her for a short time. Cristiana would name her son Diego Armando, a boy who grew up loving soccer.

As seemed to be his pattern, sometimes Diego connected with the wrong people. Members of the Mafia (an organized society of criminals) began courting the star, who attended parties held by the Camarra family. Through such ties he had easy access to illegal drugs. It would be revealed later that his drug addiction was growing at this time. People around him, such as his teammates, later said that they didn't know anything sinister was happening to Diego. Although it didn't seem to be directly affecting his soccer career, his growing cocaine addiction was lying under the surface, waiting to explode into his professional life.

Despite these growing problems in his private life, at this point in time Diego was doing extremely well on the soccer field. In his first season he impressed the people of Naples as the top goal-scorer of their team, with 14 goals in 30 matches. In one match against Lazio, he scored straight from a corner kick and another time from mid-field!

In the 1985–86 season, he continued his strong show. When Diego scored in Naples with a free-kick against the team from Juventus, the team won 1–0. It was the first time in 13 years that they had defeated their enemies. The whole city celebrated.

Diego had matured over the last few years as a player and his style had become more refined. He also had a better understanding of international tactics. This would become apparent in his most famous performance — his astounding play that brought the Argentine national team the winners' trophy at the 1986 World Cup.

He took time off from his club activities to travel with the Argentine national team to Mexico. There, at his second World Cup, Diego scored two goals that will never be forgotten. One is remembered because of its notoriety and the other because of its sheer brilliance. No one will ever forget how the Diego's instincts to win guided him to send the ball into the net with his hand. It is also a soccer legend how he kicked the ball past the entire English defense to place another magnificent goal.

Argentina played against England in the quarter finals of the 1986 World Cup. With the Falkland War still fresh in everyone's mind, tension ran high when the teams representing these two nations met on the field.

Diego's reputation at that point was so great that British coach Bobby Robson felt Argentina didn't have a hope of winning without him. He warned his players that Number 10 had to be stopped at all costs.

At half time neither team had any points. But a few minutes into the second half, Diego spotted the ball flying down the outfield. He dashed after it, and found himself faced with the English goalie, Peter Shilton. The Argentine, at five feet, five inches (1.65 metres) was half a foot (15 centimetres) shorter than the English man. But as they jumped toward the ball, Diego leapt the highest. He used his hand to bat the ball into the net. The English players protested against the illegal touch of the ball. However, the referee did not see the play. He admitted the goal.

Diego's only desire was to see his team win the match. Instinctively, he tried to do this in any way he could. It was the referee's responsibility to decide whether or not to allow the goal. Although the English team protested and television replays clearly showed Diego's action to be illegal, the goal went down in the books as a legitimate point. Maradona attributed this success to inspiration from the heavens. Thus the "Hand of God" goal entered the annals of soccer history.

There will always be debates among soccer fans about the goal. But there is little doubt that the next goal Number 10 scored was purely brilliant and due to his shining skill alone. Beginning in the Argentine end of the field, he dribbled up alone through the entire English defense. His foot only touched the ball seven times, astoundingly keeping the ball with him as he ran nearly 66 yards (60 metres) in 10 seconds. His adversaries thought he had lost control of the ball. In fact, he was simply tricking them into believing that, before sweeping it away again. Once more, Diego flipped the ball past the English goalie, Shilton, to score.

The excitement was incredible! To this day it is remembered as one of the greatest World Cup goals and commemorated by a plaque in the Mexico stadium.

Argentina won 2–1 against England thanks to Diego Maradona. The English team went home humiliated. When the Argentine team played Belgium, an "acrobatic pirouette" by their hero sent the ball into the net for a 2–1 win. They went on to the finals against West Germany. Number 10 did not score in this game, but worked defense so well that his teammates were able to place three goals to the Germans' two. Argentina was the winner of the 1986 World Cup!

After the victory, Maradona kissed the World Cup and held it high up in the air. He was the hero of the tournament and the king of soccer. He had scored five goals in seven games and showed the world some of the best soccer it would ever see.

His fantastic soccer play did not stop after the World Cup victory. Returning to the Italian League in 1986–87, Diego did some beautiful work. He scored one point in a game against AC Milan by passing two defensemen and shooting from the goal kick line. He led Napoli to take the Italian League title, scoring 10 times in 29 matches. Not only was it the first time Napoli had won the title, it was also the first time that a team from Southern Italy had beaten a Northern Italian one to do so.

The next year Napoli had a difficult beginning. They came up against Inter Milan for the Italian League title. Inter Milan had strong German players such as Andreas Brehme and Lothar Matthäus, which made for an unbeatable team. However, in 1989 Napoli rallied and won the United European Football Association (UEFA) title in Stuttgart, Germany.

The Italian people celebrated the victory long and passionately. It was the first time that Italy had received this honor. Everywhere blue and white decorations fluttered. Songs were written about the hero who brought them the victory. His picture appeared on gigantic murals in the city. One depicted a baby

Diego being cradled in the arms of a saint. Some showed him as the king of soccer. Others claimed that the city of Naples had three attractions: the Bay of Naples, Mount Vesuvius, and Diego Maradona.

It seemed that Diego could do no wrong. He was a hero in both Argentina and Italy. No one would ever forget how his magic feet had brought Argentina a World Cup and Napoli the Italian League and UEFA titles. His star had climbed incredibly high, blazing over the world of soccer.

Maradona's Career Landmarks, 1982–89

1982   Plays for Barcelona, Spain

1984   Traded to Napoli (Naples, Italy)

1986   Leads Argentina to a gold medal victory at the World Cup, Mexico

1987   Napoli takes the Italian League title

1989   Napoli wins the UEFA (United European Football Association) title

Diego Maradona cases a loose ball during an exhibition game in Canada in 1996.

Diego Maradona and Ben Johnson go through their paces. Johnson, the Canadian sprinter who lost his Olympic gold medal after a drug scandal, was Maradona's trainer in the early '90's.

Soccer great Maradona bows to the media before an exhibition game.

Maradona, right, laughs it up as he pokes fun at 'pregnant' Pasquale (Pat) Fiocala, president of the Toronto Italia team, in Toronto, Canada.

Chapter 4

Star Ablaze
(1989–1994)

Diego was now the king of soccer and the hero for thousands of people all over the world. But in 1989, a new decade and Diego's thirtieth birthday approached. In an incredibly short time his life would completely unravel.

In 1989, his relationships with people went through some changes. He fired his old friend, Jorge, and hired a new business manager, Guillermo Coppola. He married his long-time companion, Claudia Villafane. They already had two young daughters, Dalma and Gianina, by the time they tied the knot in a lavish Buenos Aires wedding. Number 10 was settling down with his own family.

Diego was returning to Argentina more frequently. In 1989 he went to Esquina for a holiday, stating that he was never going back to Italy. He was trying to empty his mind of all the pressure he felt was building up back in Naples. Despite his recent success, he thought his relationship with club officials and fans was not going well. He felt that the entire city of Naples was turning on him. He was concerned that his family was being affected by the negativity he sensed.

Although he was considered a great man, Diego was just a person and it seems he exaggerated what people thought. Sometimes he had trouble knowing the difference between his real friends and his false ones.

His feelings of persecution increased with the events that unfolded in 1990. At this time the Italian police were cracking down on the underworld. Diego had connections with the Italian Mafia. There were photos showing him at their parties. Maradona's response was that the police were using false witnesses and setting up situations to try to gain evidence to convict him of drug charges.

It's understandable that this legal battle would occupy a lot of his thoughts. It also brought the public's attention to the growing suspicion that their hero was involved with drugs. All of this would come tumbling down around the soccer star soon enough.

Despite his growing personal troubles, Diego had the incredible ability to put them behind him and zero in on the soccer ball. Once he was out on the field, his skills showed why he held the crown as the soccer king of the world. In the winter of 1990, he prepared to captain Napoli to its second league championship. To get ready for this event, he cut down on the cortisone treatments he had been receiving. He also trained very hard.

The work paid off when Napoli had its revenge against Inter Milan, the 1988 winners of the championship. The hero of Naples dedicated the win to someone very important to him — his father. The Neapolitans celebrated the victory that *El Pibe De Oro,* their "Golden Boy," had helped bring them.

With the second Italian league win, it seemed that all was going well in 1990. In this year, Diego was named "sports ambassador" for his homeland. It was also a World Cup year and the player was going to represent his country for the third time. To add to the excitement, this time the World Cup would be held in Italy.

The World Cup action in Italy produced some confusing sentiments for some Italians. Their loyalties were divided. As in many countries, there are regional rivalries in Italy. People in the northern part of the country often have opinions and beliefs that differ from those of people in the southern part of Italy.

Napoli is a southern team, and soccer fans from northern Italy had no love for Maradona, the man who captained the southern team to win the Italian League title. At the World Cup, northerners sometimes whistled and booed when Diego, playing for Argentina's national team, appeared on the field.

Fans from southern Italy and Naples felt different-ly. They loved their own Italian national team, but they also loved their hero, who was now playing for Argentina. It was Diego who had brought their local club to greatness.

The northerners felt the Naples fans weren't being loyal enough, and the southern fans didn't take kind-ly to the northern fans' treatment of their soccer idol. Things only got worse when Diego tried to defend his fans, saying, "The Italians are asking Neapolitans to be Italian for a day, yet for the other 364 days in the year they forget all about Naples. The people do not forget this."

Perhaps Italian businesspeople were among the few who knew where they stood. They believed in the power of money. They pinned their hopes on Maradona to bring crowds of people to the country, all eager to see what would happen in the Argentine's third World Cup. Would it be as exciting as in 1986?

As the World Cup action heated up, Diego assisted teammate Claudio Caniggia to bring victory to Argentina over the favored Brazilian team, placing them in the quarterfinals. The Argentines then went on to qualify for the semifinals. This game was to be played against Italy in Naples.

On July 3, 1990, seventy thousand spectators gath-ered at the San Paolo stadium. The hearts of fans must have been beating quickly the day Italy played

Argentina. Their blood brothers played on one team. Their adopted son captained another.

The air in the stands vibrated with tension. Italian goalkeeper Walter Zenga played a record 517 minutes without conceding a World Cup goal before Claudio Caniggia's header got him. The score was tied 1–1 at the end of the match. Schillaci had scored for Italy and Caniggia for Argentina. A penalty shootout had to be called. Everyone either held their breath or screamed. What would the next few minutes bring?

Maradona took the penalty shot. When Diego's foot touched the ball, the goalie guessed wrong. The ball flew into the net. Diego had scored the penalty! Argentina took the victory. They were to go to Rome for the finals.

The championship game promised exciting soccer. Argentina had faced Germany four years earlier to win a World Cup. West Germany not only wanted revenge against Argentina, but were also motivated by the fact that if they took the trophy, they would be three-time World Cup winners.

However, the game was played without much panache. Two Argentine players were sent off for foul play. One soccer writer called it "a brutal, graceless affair, arguably the worst, most ill-tempered final in the history of the competition." German Andreas Brehme placed a penalty kick to make the score 3–2. West Germany had won the World Cup for the third time.

Diego Maradona was terribly disappointed that he wasn't to win his second World Cup. The former World Cup hero wept. Then, to his anger, some of the people in the stands booed during the Argentine national anthem. Were these Italians who were mad that Argentina had beat their team? Were they Northern Italians, unhappy that the Argentine had captained a Southern Italian team to take the Italian League title? The jeerers may have been discontented fans showing their disapproval of the poor show of sportsmanship in the final. Whoever they were, Diego was very upset with their reaction to the Argentine national anthem. The 1990 World Cup was a fizzle compared to the glory of 1986.

Furthermore, it seemed that the relationship between Naples' Golden Boy and some of his fans had turned sour. On his return to club soccer after the World Cup, Italians were complaining that Diego was no longer a boy at all, but that he was showing his 30 years. In the Italian championship that year, he scored only six goals, all on penalties. He missed some matches. He arrived late at some training sessions. The midfielder blamed injuries and stress for his problems, but the public remained skeptical. Suspicion was growing that a drug problem was making their hero a tired, poor performer.

The problem came to a head when team doctors gave him a random drug test in March of 1991 after a game between Bari and Napoli. The test results came back positive for cocaine.

In disgrace, dazed and confused, Diego returned to Argentina. Things immediately got worse. In April he was charged with possession of cocaine after he had been found asleep in a friend's apartment. He awoke, not knowing where he was and asking for his wife, Claudia. The public was horrified at how far their star had fallen and how quickly.

The repercussions were swift. The Fédération Internationale de Football took strict action. Diego received a 15-month suspension from his job as a professional soccer player. Then he had to face an Argentine court on separate charges. The judge gave him a 15-month suspended sentence for cocaine possession.

Diego swore on the heads of his children that he had not taken drugs to enhance his performance. He said that "as a sportsman, ... I have never betrayed the principles which inspire a loyal and correct sporting activity, in which I have participated with energy and passion."

It seems he was just looking to have a good time. But he had taken drugs and his drug problem had put his personal and professional life in a shambles. Not long ago he had been king of the soccer world. Now he had to decide what he was going to do.

Soccer was Diego's life. It had been his reason for living since he was a little boy and provided his livelihood. He had to beat his problem and get back on the field. He turned to his supporters — his family and friends. The list of people he was to turn to in his time of need had changed. Gone were some of his new "friends" and bad influences. Instead, he was encouraged to see old teammates from his early days of soccer. Carlos Menotti had coached the player back in 1978 and again in Barcelona. Now he called to offer his support. Diego's first manager, Jorge Cyterzpiler, also wanted to help his old friend.

Claudia stood by her husband in these difficult days. When he became fed up with two counseling sessions each day, Claudia understood. She supported his decision to stop such exhausting mental work.

Diego tried to improve his mental and physical health. He started a diet and exercise program. And of course, it wasn't long before Diego was back on the soccer field. He just couldn't stay away. There, he tried to recapture the good things in his life — the joy of playing with fans cheering him on. He played a charity match and kicked the ball around informally with the Boca Juniors. By the end of his 15-month ban he eagerly jumped at a chance to return to professional soccer.

He knew he couldn't return to Italy where everything had gone so wrong. So he decided to accept an offer from Spain, this time to play for Seville. Diego moved to his third international home and began his new job.

It must have been difficult for him to come back to professional soccer. Unfortunately, Diego wasn't to find the greatest circumstances in his new situation. The Seville team was not the best in the country. It wasn't even in the position where it could work toward taking a championship. It had one great player — but that player couldn't make up for a whole team, especially when he himself was not in the best of shape. The midfielder was still overweight. He was unable to fit into the very strict schedule that the manager tried to force on him.

Diego's world was very fragile and it wasn't very long before once again things fell apart. He hadn't abandoned his late-night celebrating. The press, who followed him constantly, accused him of getting the entire Seville team to party late into the night. The people of Seville didn't find him a serious soccer player. They were questioning the social and professional worth of this man, an aging player and a recovering drug addict.

The end came when his manager, Bildaro, removed him from a match in June 1993. Shortly after, the two men engaged in a violent argument. Although the pair later made up, Diego's time with Seville was over. He left saying, "I'm only going because they don't love me."

From his childhood Diego's incredible soccer skills had gotten him a lot of attention and admiration. Over the years, he had grown used to the adulation of his fans. It was important for the star to be loved. He seemed to draw energy from it. So, naturally, he returned where he had felt the most love — to his parents in Argentina.

Depressed and dazed from his continuing drug ordeal, Diego and his mother and father went for a holiday. They returned once more to the quiet village of Esquina. Perhaps there he would have a chance to regroup his thoughts while retreating from the busy world. Showing the strength of a kid who had grown up in the slums, Diego decided that he was not going to abandon the thing he loved the most — soccer.

From this point on, there is no question that Diego's playing, as well as his behavior, was erratic. While his personal life was a mess, his soccer playing teetered between hits and misses.

In October 1993, an Argentine club bought out his contract for four million dollars and promised the player a large monthly salary. The team, called the Newell's Old Boys, was begun by students with British roots in Rosario.

Diego was once again playing in the land where he was adored as one of the greatest Argentines ever. His new fans presented him with a plaque to commemorate their love for him. Their supportive comments read: "May Our Lady of Rosario protect you as a man and as an idol and may today's miracle provide an example of faith, hope and charity. Welcome back to life!"

However, like Seville, Newell's Old Boys was not the best team in the league, and unlikely to become so. Diego alone could not bring the club a title. In fact, he did not stay there very long. He only played seven matches with them. He missed too many training sessions and was soon sacked.

But despite his apparent indifference to training, Diego wasn't ready to give up his life's work. He was still enthused about playing soccer. He returned to captain the Argentine national team and worked hard in preparation for the 1994 World Cup. He helped Argentina qualify against Australia and looked forward to more great play. The next World Cup was where he hoped to make a glorious comeback.

Before the World Cup, in February 1994, the ugly part of Diego reappeared. Perpetually perturbed by the press, he intentionally fired an air rifle at some of reporters. Charges were pressed. Eventually he received a two-year, 10-month suspended sentence. This upset state of mind pursued him during the 1994 World Cup games.

People around the world eagerly awaited to see Argentina's magic Number 10 play in the 1994 World Cup games in the United States. Soccer fans were ready to forgive his past problems. They just wanted to see some good action on the field. The hero of the 1986 World Cup did not disappoint them; he gave a strong showing of the skills that had brought him there.

In the first match against Greece, the soccer king added more bright jewels to his crown. He made a lovely goal, shooting from outside the penalty area to place the ball just under the cross bar and in the net. He ran toward the television cameras, full of power and joy, seeming to shout, "Here I am! I'm still Number One!" Argentina won 4–0. The 34-year-old player was into his fourth World Cup, and glory seemed his for the taking.

In the next match, against Nigeria, Diego made a wonderful assist that allowed teammate Claudio Cannigia to put the ball in the net. Argentina won 2–1 and was favored to take the Cup.

Then, tragedy struck. Diego Maradona tested positive for ephedrine, a performance-enhancing substance banned by FIFA. Stunned, Diego cried at the news he was disqualified. He claimed he was not entirely to blame, that his doctor had given him something, and he had taken it, not realizing it was against the rules.

The rest of the Argentine team was unable to collect themselves after the horrible news. They lost against Bulgaria and then Romania. The soccer world seemed to be in shock. Thousands of people from the

US to Italy expressed their disbelief that their best-loved player could be involved in another drug scandal. Twenty thousand people in Bangladesh demonstrated against the Argentine's suspension.

It was difficult for the people of many nations to believe that the charges might be true. Anyone can make one mistake, they reasoned, and the man had paid his dues for that. But how could he have possibly become involved with drugs again? People were shocked and shaken. The power and energy and everything that was beautiful about Diego's soccer playing seemed tainted. His star was falling.

Diego's response to his removal from World Cup play? "They've cut my legs off."

Maradona's Career Landmarks, 1990–94

1990   Napoli wins the Italian League title

1991   Suspended for 15 months by the Italian League after testing positive for cocaine

1992   Plays for Seville, Spain

1993   Obtained by Argentine team, Newell's Old Boys

1994   -Sacked by the Newell's Old Boys
-Named captain of the Argentine team at the World Cup in the United States
-Tested positive for "ephedrine," a performance-enhancing drug, at the World Cup

Chapter 5

Falling Star (1995–1997)

Diego returned to Argentina in disgrace after he tested positive for banned substances at the 1994 World Cup.

The drug the player had tested positive for was not a "pleasure" drug, like cocaine. It was a performance-enhancing drug that had been administered to him by his doctor. He was not entirely to blame for the fact that he had taken this drug. This was supported by the FIFA ruling. Diego received a 15-month suspension from international play and a fine of 20,000 Swiss francs. Cerrini, his medical supervisor, also received a 15-month ban and a fine of 20,000 Swiss francs.

Cerrini had already been involved with a performance-enhancing drug scandal in 1989, before he entered the soccer star's employ. In his work with Diego, Cerrini used weight-reducing supplements as part of a program to help the player get fit and trim. The drug the Argentine captain tested positive for, ephedrine, was not an illegal drug in the United States. It was sold at drug stores as a diet aid. However, it was a substance that had been banned by FIFA.

In the case of the 1994 World Cup drug charge, Number 10 may have been unaware of what he was taking. However, Diego was an adult who needed to take responsibility for his part in the problem. Perhaps he should have asked more questions. It also seems that he generally accepted energy-giving drugs as something that would help him get back into shape quickly.

Sometimes, athletes don't fully understand what is going on in their health programs. Diego had been given "special medicines" by his advisors since he was a little boy. As a child he had been too young to understand what he was taking. As he grew, drugs that made his body stronger or helped him heal more quickly were part of his career, like training or public appearances.

Of course, he was not the only athlete to have been in this situation. There are now many instances in different sports where men and women have been found to use drugs and dangerous or illegal medical treatments in hopes of improving their performance. The case of Canadian sprinter Ben Johnson made everyone aware of how widespread the use of performance-enhancing drugs had become in sports. Johnson was stripped of his Olympic gold medal in 1988 and suspended for his use of anabolic steroids. The 100-metre runner was then banned from the Olympics for life for his use of the drugs in 1993. Johnson's case is an example of the decisions athletes must make. The promise of being "the best" is a tempting one.

The organizations that regulate different sports recognize that performance-enhancing drugs have become a serious issue. They want people who participate in sports to make the best of their bodies' natural ability, unassisted by chemicals. In the eyes of those who govern sports, the penalty for such "magic cures" is a severe one. Since 1978, FIFA has worked to develop more rigorous drug testing of soccer players. China looked at the problem and decided to impose a four-year ban from sports for anyone caught doping. Many other countries established strict rules against any sort of drug use.

Diego's case and others like it should serve as a warning to young athletes. Firstly, it seems old-fashioned hard work is still the best way to improve one's skill. Secondly, athletes should be aware of anything they are taking and should make it their business to know about the person who is administering the medicine. Doctors can be helpful, but their advice should be carefully considered and sometimes researched. In the final analysis, it is the athlete who suffers for agreeing to inappropriate medical treatment.

Ephedrine was a performance-enhancing drug, but Diego was unquestionably tied up with other types of drugs as well. In 1996, he talked about his drug-taking habit. He admitted that as a young 22-year-old in Barcelona he had tried cocaine because he wanted to "feel alive." It was not long before he had become a terrible addict, unable to stop himself from using the drug. Diego tried to hide his habits from his teammates and family.

He later admitted that using drugs doesn't "make you strong. It makes you weaker, starts killing you gradually." It has been speculated that the player's drug use has negatively affected how he acts in public and on the soccer field. Some said at times it has made him aggressive and paranoid.

Because he was a rich soccer player, Diego became exposed to drugs. But the decision to take them was his alone. Next, he had to decide to clean up his bad habit. Over the next few years he tried several things to meet this goal. He went to different drug clinics, including one in Switzerland in late August 1996. A psychiatrist who worked with the player there said that his client wasn't a drug addict, but a man who sometimes cracked under the burden of worldwide fame. Professor Harutyan Arto Van noted that Diego had "a profound desire to break the vicious circle" of drug-taking.

Diego offered to serve as a volunteer in the Argentine government's anti-drug campaign, thinking that his personal experiences might stop young people from taking drugs.

Throughout this time, he kept up his interest in the sport of soccer. He realized that there were other avenues to explore related to the game besides playing it. He gave a speech at Oxford University in England about the sport. He tried to coach some teams, but this wasn't where his talents lay and it didn't work out.

Not being allowed to play soccer professionally was, for Diego, like having his legs cut off. He badly needed to play. As soon as his suspension ended in 1995, he signed with the Boca Juniors. He played an exhibition game with them against the South Korean national team on September 30, 1995.

When he went back to Argentina to play with the Boca Juniors in October, his fans showed their support by turning out in droves. Sixty thousand people filled La Bombonera. They sang loud songs, threw confetti, and set off fireworks to mark the return of their hero. Blue and gold banners streamed down from the stands. Diego appeared, sporting a goatee beard and a blond stripe in his black hair. Although he was a little chubby, he retained his characteristic style on the field. The Boca Juniors won 1–0 over Colon.

Any opportunity to play interested Maradona. During 1996 he performed in Toronto, Ontario, Canada, where one of his brothers, Lalo, and his nephew, also named Diego, were on a team.

Sadly though, neither therapeutic cure nor work seemed to be effective in his fight against drugs. He couldn't stop his addiction, nor could he seem to control it. On August 24, 1997, a test was carried out after a game against the Argentinos Juniors. The result was the third drug-related ban of Diego Maradona's career.

Diego was obviously shattered about the ordeal that cut short his latest comeback. He cried during a telephone interview. He said that the soccer pitch "is where I feel happy" and that it was difficult to deal with his addiction.

In this interview, it seemed that he was blaming other people for trying to get him off the field. He decided to fight the drug charge. His lawyer, Jugo Wortman Jofre, told Judge Claudio Bonadio that Diego's urine sample had been switched with someone else's. The judge decided that an investigation should be carried out.

The legal proceedings over the next few months were very complicated. Coppola, Diego's manager, was jailed for trafficking in cocaine. But then the judge, Hernán Bernasconi, faced an investigation, accused of having had the cocaine planted in Coppola's apartment. The repercussions went as high as the office of the President of Argentina. Before the scandal erupted, President Carlos Menem had asked the world-renowned soccer player to help him with his re-election.

Diego was allowed to keep playing during the confusing investigation. He "unexpectedly" turned up for a Boca Junior practice, wanting to play. However, because of a leg injury he was kept out of the Boca games.

To keep in shape during 1997, he hired Canadian sprinter Ben Johnson as his trainer at a rate of $1,000 per day. Diego knew that Johnson had been the fastest man in the world, and apparently wanted his advice on how to regain his power.

But Diego's interest in playing professional soccer seemed to be fading. In March 1997, he refused to play for Boca because they were sponsored by Nike. He apparently objected to the white stripes Nike had added to the usual Boca uniforms. The player had his own contract with Puma, a German sporting goods company. This might have affected his decision. Or it may have been that he was starting to think he couldn't face another comeback. Certainly his fans were wondering if at age 36 Diego was going to play soccer at all.

The question was soon answered. The Argentine judge decided that there was no evidence to support Diego's claim that his drug-test urine sample had been switched with someone else's. Just before his thirty-seventh birthday, in October of 1997, Diego Maradona informed the world that he had decided to retire. He made the announcement "with all the pain in my soul." Just before his birthday he said that "tomorrow will be my saddest birthday," but he had promised his father that he would give up professional play.

The curtain had come down on his career as a professional soccer player. His star had traveled, a brilliant, streaking meteor speeding across the sky, before falling. However, Diego's fantastic record will continue to illuminate the pages of the history of soccer for many years to come.

Maradona's Career Landmarks, 1994–98

1994 Returns to Argentina after the World Cup and serves a 15-month suspension for doping

1995 Signs with the Boca Juniors

1997 -New drug scandal erupts
-Announces his retirement from professional soccer

1998 Television commentator at the World Cup in France

Conclusion

Diego Maradona may have retired in 1997, but it seems that as long as he walks on this planet he will need to be involved with soccer. In the summer of 1998 there was still talk of him joining a team somewhere in the world. Other sources said that he might give coaching another try.

He remains attached to the world of soccer through television commentary. In the summer of 1998 he attended the World Cup games in France. It must have been especially exciting for him to see Argentina face England once more. People eagerly awaited the outcome of this "rematch." While the aging star sat in the sports commentators' box, a new Number 10, Ariel Ortega, ran down the field. But everyone was still talking about the thrilling 1986 Argentine victory in which Diego was the hero.

To his delight, once again his country's team defeated England at the World Cup. The former captain of the Argentine team said that he "knew the game against England would be difficult, but my heart told me we were going to win." He followed the Argentine team through the rest of their matches. He provided colorful comments for television audiences, until Argentina was eliminated by the Netherlands in the quarter finals.

Watching the play, he might have seen himself as he once was in some of the new stars at the 1998 World Cup. He remembered what it was like to be full of unrefined talent, powerful, enthusiastic, and as yet untouched by the cares brought by fame. For Diego the vibrant zest and energy on the soccer field translated into brilliant goals. But off the field, the same quality, uncontrolled, led him to make rash and ill-considered decisions. His recklessness took him down the regretful path of drug addiction, a sad fact that eventually ended his time on the soccer field.

Before his retirement, Diego was the best player on the soccer pitch. He captained two teams, one in Argentina and one in Italy, to glorious titles. In the 1986 World Cup in Mexico, he scored "the greatest goal in sports history."

Glossary of Soccer Terms

advantage rule — allows a referee to disregard a foul if stopping the play would take away an advantage held by the player who was fouled against.

back heel — kick made using the heel of the foot.

ball — The ball used in regulation soccer is round, 9 inches (22.5 centimeters) in diameter. It is usually made of leather.

banana shot — shot that curves through the air (like a banana!).

blindside run — run on the side of the field opposite to where the action is taking place.

center/cross — kick from the side of the field toward players positioned in front of the goal.

checking — moving away from an opponent to create space and receive a pass.

chip — passing or shooting technique that allows a player to kick the ball over an opponent.

corner kick — method of putting the ball into play after the defending team has put the ball in its own net. A member of the attacking team kicks the ball back into play from the quarter circle in the corner of the field.

dead ball — ball that is out of play.

dribble — running with the ball, keeping it close and controlling it with small kicks.

drop ball — way in which the referee restarts the game after it has been stopped, usually after an injury has occurred. The referee drops the ball between two players. The ball can only be played once it has hit the ground.

field — area where soccer is played, also called the pitch. It must be rectangular, with a length of no more than 130 yards (120 metres) and no less than 100 yards (90 metres), and a width of not more than 100 yards (90 m) and not less than 50 yards (45 m).

FIFA (Fédération Internationale de Football Association) — governing body of international soccer, founded in 1904, and based in Zurich, Switzerland.

first-division club — an elite professional soccer team.

free kick — a kick at the ball awarded to a team that has been fouled against. Different types of free kicks are awarded depending on the severity of the foul. A direct free kick may be directed toward the opponent's goal. An indirect free kick must be directed toward another player.

goal kick — method of putting the ball back into play after a goal has been scored by the attacking team. A member of the defending team, usually the goalkeeper, must kick the ball from anywhere inside the goal area. The ball must pass outside the penalty area around the net before another player can touch it.

linesman — assistant to the referee. There are usually two linesmen at a game. They move in an area along each touchline and indicate when a ball is out of play, and which side is entitled to a corner kick, goal kick, or throw-in. They also signal when a team wants to put in substitute player and will tell the referee about any breach of the rules that the referee may not have noticed.

man-to-man marking — defensive tactic in which a player is responsible for guarding a particular opponent.

midfielder — the center player on a soccer team.

offside — rule designed to keep attacking players from taking up advanced positions near the opposing goal. In general, players are offside when they are nearer to their opponent's goal line than the ball, unless they are in their own team's half of the field, or are not nearer the goalkeeper than two of their opponents, including the goalkeeper. This only applies when the ball is kicked by teammates, not the opposing team. An indirect free kick is given for an offside offense.

own goal — a goal scored by a player against his own team.

penalty kick — awarded to the attacking team after certain types of foul committed by the defending team within its penalty area. The penalty kick is taken from the penalty spot, 12 yards (11 metres) from the goal.

red card — signal used by the referee to indicate he is sending a player off the field for bad conduct.

referee — official in charge of all aspects of a soccer match. He or she makes sure no rules are broken, and awards points. The referee's decisions are final.

throw-in — method by which the ball is returned to play after going out of bounds. A player from the team that did not touch the ball last throws the ball out from the spot where it went out of bounds. The player must throw the ball from behind and over his head.

touchline — line marking the field of play. If all of the ball moves beyond the touchline it is considered out of play.

World Cup — most important international soccer tournament, held every four years. Also the largest single sporting event in the world. Only the team from the host country and the previous World Cup winner are guaranteed spots in the contest. A long series of qualifying matches takes place to determine other competitors. Teams from 32 countries competed in the 1998 World Cup held in France.

yellow card — signal by the referee cautioning a player for repeated misconduct. If a player receives a second yellow card, he then gets the red card and is sent off the field.

Research Sources

Books and Articles

Bell, Jack. "Corner Kicks." *New York Times,* 6 February 1998, C4.

Burns, Jimmy. *Hand of God: The Life of Diego Maradona, Soccer's Fallen Star.* New York: The Lyons Press, 1996.

"Diego Maradona," *New York Times,* 10 September 1997, B14.

Fodor's South America. Edited by Fionn Davenport, et al. New York: Fodor's Travel Publications, 1997.

"Football's Pride, Footballer's Fall." *Economist,* 7 February 1994.

Kennedy, Kostya. "U.S. Beef." "Scorecard." *Sports Illustrated,* 24 April 1997.

"Maradona Resurrected," *Sports Illustrated,* 16 October 1995.

"Maradona's downfall," *Economist,* 23 November 1996.

"Risotto alla Maradona," *Economist,* 30 June 1990.

Robb, Bob. Interview with L. Goodall, Elora, Ontario, Canada. 14 October 1997.

Sims, Calvin. "A Drug and Sports Scandal Swirls Near Argentine Chief." *New York Times,* 15 October 1996, p. A16.

———. "To Argentines, Judges Are Often Biggest Lawbreakers." *New York Times,* 19 August 1997, p. A8.

"This Week's Sign that the Apocalypse is Upon Us." *Sports Illustrated,* 30 June 1997.

Vecsey, George. "Soccer's Little Big Man." *New York Times Magazine,* 27 May 1990.

Web Sites

"A Tribute to Maradona." [http://www.geocities.com-Colosseum/1862].

"Argentina — World Cup Pedigree." "BBC News and Sport." 2 May 1998. [http://www.bbc.co.uk/hi/english/world_cu].

"England v Argentina history," "World Cup, 1998." [wysiwyg://4http:///www.itn.co.uk].

"Ephedrine: Super Power Trim." [http://www.all-natural.com/superpt3.htm].

"Global sport — Maradona hires Ben Johnson as Trainer", *The Indian Express,* 24 June 1997. [http://www.expressindia.com].

Hawkes, David. "Maradona: San Diego," "Bad Subjects", Issue #35, November 1997, [http://end.hss.cmu.edu.].

"Maradona inks deal with Boca Juniors," Medias. 27 April 1997. [http://www.worldcup.fr].

"Maradona in talks with Spanish second division club, news reports say." [http://www.cfra.com/1998/07/27/50520.html].

"Maradona gets suspended sentence," *The Hindu.* 14 June 1998. [http://www.hinduonline.com/hindu/daily]

"Maradona looses twice in Argentinian Court." Associated Press. [http://sportszone.com/soccer]

"Maradona "not an addict"', "Sport", "The Irish Times on the Web", 17 August 1996. [Times.com/irish-times/paper/1996]

"Maradona's manager says drink may have been spiked." Reuter Information Service. [http://www.soccersite.com/news/]

"Maradona, Oct. 30- 1960- Argentinian soccer player," "Current Biography,"The H.W. Wilson Co. [http://www.Hwwilson.com/soccer].

"Maradona returns after 15-month absence", The News and Observer Publishing Co. Associated Press. [995/oth/soc/feat/archives/092195/soc36077].

"Maradona returns to practice with Boca Juniors," soccersite. [http://www.soccersite.com/news].

"Maradona says he's retiring... again," Media South America, 29 October 1996. Netplus.

"Maradona to go off the field and into the classroom," The News and Observer Publishing Co., Associated Press. [995/oth/soc/feaet/archives/101895/soc45080].

"Maradona to remain quiet, agent says." Agence France-Presse. [http://www.soccersite.com/news].

"Maradona's urine sample too small for drug-related DNA test", Associated Press, 7 October 1997. [http://www.soccersitestar.com].

"Maradona will no longer play in Argentina," 29 September 1996. Nando.net, Associated Press. [http://www2.nando.net/newsroom/ap/oth/19].

"1978: Argentina," "World Cup USA 94: Soccer History Page. [www.fifa2.com/wc94/wcinfo/history].

"Premios Konex 1990: Deportes." [http://www.fundacion-donexcom.ar/maradona].

"Republica Argentina — Secretaria de Turismo." [http://www.sectur.gov.ar/g/info.htm].

"Ricardo Bochini." [www.geocities.com/Colosseum/2773].

"Site Offical del Club Atletico Boca Juniors." [http://contenidos.ciudad.com.ar/boca/tapa.htm].

"Soccer Idol Sheds Tears," 3 September 1997. The Irish Times. [http://www.irish-times.com].

"Sports Drugs: China makes supplying banned sports drugs a criminal offense", 29 August 1995. The News and Observer Publishing Col, Reuter Information Service. [http://somer-set.nando.net/newsroom/sport].

"Toronto Franchise to be called Shooting Stars." [http://www.npsl.com/news/stars.]

"U.S.A. 1994." [http://.geocities.com/Colosseum/1862/usa94].

"We could have done more to help Maradona says team mate," 3 October 1996, "Rete@News-rassenga stampa." [http://www.tin.it/ret/en/14/93].

"World Cup history." [http://soccer.yahoo.com/wc98].

Zanoni, Leandro. "The pride to be fans of Boca Juniors," [http://www.geocities.com].

This is a general account of the history and architecture of Crusader castles in the Kingdom of Jerusalem, County of Tripoli and Principality of Antioch between 1099 and 1291, the years during which the Crusaders had a permanent presence on the Levantine coast.

The book opens with a discussion of previous studies of the subject, and of fortification in western Europe and the Middle East before the Crusades. Subsequent chapters discuss the various types of castles built by the Crusader settlers, siege techniques and the ways in which castle builders tried to counter the improving technologies of attack, and the castles built after the disastrous defeat at Hattin in 1187 such as Crac des Chevaliers and Margat. Extensive use is made of contemporary chronicles to show the reasons why castles were built and how they were used in peace and war. The book is fully illustrated by photographs, drawings and plans, and contains a comprehensive bibliography.

CRUSADER CASTLES

CRUSADER CASTLES

HUGH KENNEDY

University of St Andrews

CAMBRIDGE
UNIVERSITY PRESS

PUBLISHED BY THE PRESS SYNDICATE OF THE UNIVERSITY OF CAMBRIDGE
The Pitt Building, Trumpington Street, Cambridge, United Kingdom

CAMBRIDGE UNIVERSITY PRESS
The Edinburgh Building, Cambridge CB2 2RU, UK
40 West 20th Street, New York, NY 10011–4211, USA
10 Stamford Road, Oakleigh, VIC 3166, Australia
Ruiz de Alarcón 13, 28014 Madrid, Spain
Dock House, The Waterfront, Cape Town 8001, South Africa

http://www.cambridge.org

First published 1994
Reprinted 1994, 1995
First paperback edition 2000
Reprinted 2001

Printed in the United Kingdom at the University Press, Cambridge

A catalogue record for this book is available from the British Library

Library of Congress Cataloguing in Publication data
Kennedy, Hugh (Hugh N.)
Crusader castles / Hugh Kennedy.
p. cm.
Includes bibliographical references and index.
ISBN 0 521 42068 7 (hardback) ISBN 0 521 799139 (paperback)
1. Castles – Latin Orient. 2. Architecture, medieval – Latin
Orient. 3. Military architecture – Latin Orient. I. Title.
NA1465.K44 1994
725′.18′09560902–dc20   93–37701 CIP

ISBN 0 521 42068 7 hardback
ISBN 0 521 79913 9 paperback

CE

CONTENTS

For Xana, with love
to remind her of Syrian days

ILLUSTRATIONS

All the photographs were taken by the author.

FIGURES

ACKNOWLEDGEMENTS

My thanks go to many people who have helped and advised me in the preparation of this book and made it even more enjoyable. I am very pleased to have the opportunity to thank those who have enabled me to travel in the Levant over the last thirty years, to my parents who encouraged me to go, to the Cassels family who first introduced me to Crusader castles in 1964, to Professor Yoram Tsafrir and the Institute for Advanced Study at the Hebrew University of Jerusalem whose invitation made it possible to visit many of the sites of the Kingdom and to Martin Randall Travel for enabling me to re-examine the castles in Jordan. I would also like to say how much I have appreciated travelling companions who have provided friendship and moral support while visiting obscure heaps of stones in hot and dusty places, to Sheila Taylor who risked life and limb climbing the outlying parts of the castle at al-Habis in Petra, to Lizzie Llewellyn and Maurice Howard for companionship and encouragement in Syria. I must also say a special thank you to my daughter Xana who pursuaded me to complete the climb to Bourzey when the spirit was willing but the flesh getting a bit weak, and who provides human scale for the great needle in the moat at Saone and in other photographs. My thanks also go to Katharine, for the loan of photographic equipment. I should also acknowledge the friendly welcome I have received from so many of the local people in villages and castles throughout the area; whatever the political problems, the friendliness of the people has always encouraged me to return.

I owe a very particular debt to the group of scholars producing such important work on Crusader monuments at the British School of Archaeology in Jerusalem, to Richard Harper the Director and to Andrew Petersen for discussion of Judin and other monuments. Above all in this respect I must stress the debt I owe to Denys Pringle, now of Historic Scotland, for advice and help way beyond the normal limits of academic cooperation and for being extraordinarily generous with photographs and unpublished articles. None of them is responsible for the errors and eccentricities of this work but without their help it would certainly be the poorer.

The extracts from William of Tyre are taken from the translation by Babcock and Krey. In some cases I have supplied the Latin equivalent of technical terms and made some minor alterations on the basis of the new edition by R. B. C. Huygens.

I would also like to express my gratitude to colleagues at St Andrews University: to Robert Bartlett and John Hudson for advice about the *De constructione*; to the Photographic Unit who have been so efficient and friendly in preparing the photographs. I could not have revisited Syria or hired cars in Israel without the financial support of the Honeyman Trust of the University of St Andrews and I am very grateful to Bill Pagan for making this possible. I would also like to thank William Davies of Cambridge University Press for his support and advice. Last but not least I want to thank my wife, Hilary, for loving encouragement and tolerance of the monomania which has to afflict authors in the final stages of preparing a book.

A NOTE ON NAMES

Like the naming of cats, the naming of Crusader castles is a complicated problem. Most sites have at least three names, an Arabic one, a Crusader French one and a Crusader Latin one. Some, like Sidon, also have conventional English names while others, like Crac des Chevaliers, have French names which date from the nineteenth century. In general I have preferred Crusader French names but this does not solve the problems entirely. Crusader scribes were untroubled by the need for consistency: the word for castle itself is variously chastel or chastiau while the little keep I have called Calansue (Arabic Qalansuwa) is also recorded as Calanchun, Calanson, Calanthone, Calanzon, Calenchun, Calenson, Calenzon, Calenzun, Calumzum, Kalenson, Kalensuu and Kalensue in Crusader sources, and each one is as correct as any other. Sometimes I have used alternative names to avoid confusion: Kerak in Jordan I have referred to by the modern Arab name rather than the Crusader Crac to avoid confusion with Crac des Chevaliers. Bourzey was probably the Crusader Rochefort but I have used the Arabic to avoid uncertainty. This has led to a certain arbitrariness in the choice of names but I am not convinced that there is any satisfactory alternative and I hope readers will bear with me.

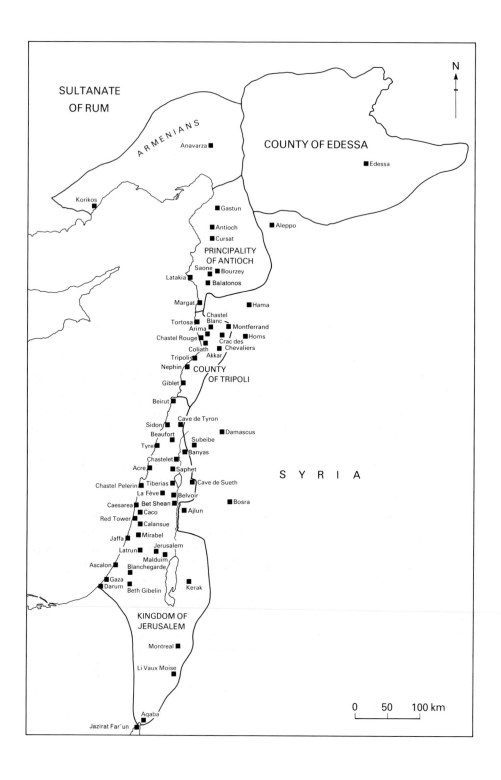

N

SULTANATE
OF RUM

A R M E N I A N S

Anavarza ■

COUNTY OF EDESSA

■ Edessa

Korikos ■

Gastun ■

■ Antioch

■ Aleppo

■ Cursat

PRINCIPALITY
OF ANTIOCH

Saone ■ ■ Bourzey

Latakia ■

■ Balatonos

Margat ■

■ Hama

Chastel
Tortosa ■ Blanc

Arima ■ ■ Montferrand

Chastel Rouge ■ ■ Homs

Coliath Crac des
■ Chevaliers

Tripoli ■ Akkar

Nephin ■ COUNTY
OF TRIPOLI

Giblet ■

Beirut ■

Cave de Tyron

Sidon ■

Beaufort ■ ■ Damascus

Subeibe ■

Tyre ■ ■ Banyas

Chastelet ■

Acre ■ ■ Saphet

Chastel Pelerin ■ Tiberias ■ ■ Cave de Sueth

La Fève ■ ■ Belvoir

Caesarea ■ ■ Bet Shean ■ Bosra

Red Tower ■ ■ Caco ■ Ajlun

■ Calansue

Jaffa ■ ■ Mirabel

Latrun ■ Jerusalem ■

Malduim

Ascalon ■ Blanchegarde ■

■ Gaza

■ Darum Beth Gibelin ■ ■ Kerak

S Y R I A

KINGDOM OF
JERUSALEM

Montreal ■

Li Vaux Moise ■

Aqaba ■

Jazirat Far'un ■

0   50   100 km

PROLOGUE TO THE STUDY OF
CRUSADER CASTLES

THE memory of the Crusader occupation of the Levant did not die when the last Franks were driven from the Holy Land in 1291. The ideal of crusading remained alive into the fifteenth century and revived, in a rather different form, with the sixteenth-century wars between the Habsburgs and the Ottomans. Memories of lands held and lost were kept alive in Du Cange's *Lignages d'Outremer*, and the Cartulary of the Knights of St John survived as a witness of the properties they had once held. Even today there is a titular king of Jerusalem.

Nonetheless, acquaintance with surviving Crusader monuments was increasingly rare. The pilgrims of the late Middle Ages were concerned with finding the Holy Places not the traces of Frankish occupation, and the travellers of the seventeenth and eighteenth centuries, when they noticed ancient monuments at all, devoted their attention to Roman antiquities. It is especially frustrating that we have no detailed descriptions of Crusader castles before the Palestine earthquake of 1837 which did such damage at Chastel Pelerin and Saphet and the contemporary campaigns of Ibrahim Pasha in 1840 which resulted in extensive damage to Sidon, Chastel Pelerin, Saone and Antioch among others.

The scientific examination of Crusader castles was pioneered by Emmanuel Guillaume Rey (1837–1916). Rey's work was the product of a growing French interest in the Crusades in the first half of the nineteenth century. This had been stimulated by the publication in 1822 of Michaud's *Histoire des Croisades* and in 1829 of the same author's *Bibliothèque des Croisades* which included translations of Arabic chronicles by M. Reinaud.[1] The availability of Crusader texts improved further with the publication of the *Recueil des historiens des Croisades* under the auspices of the prestigious Académie des

Inscriptions et Belles-Lettres, which began in 1841 though it was not finally completed until 1906.[2]

The study of the Crusades became at once a scientific discipline and a patriotic duty, since, of course, the vast majority of the Crusaders came from France and French interest in Syria was rapidly growing. Disputes over the protection of Christian churches in the Holy Land had been the ostensible reason for the outbreak of the Crimean War in 1854. Concern about the fate of local churches reached fever-pitch after Christian–Muslim violence in the Lebanon and the massacre of Christians in Damascus in 1860; the press called for Syria to be occupied by the French and the government of Napoleon III showed considerable interest. In this climate, a scholar who showed how lords from Champagne, Burgundy and the Ile de France had once ruled in Syria, and had, furthermore, left magnificent castles to prove it, was sure of a ready hearing.

The other important intellectual influence was the growing interest in medieval archaeology and warfare. The Emperor himself caused a replica trebuchet to be constructed to investigate the power of medieval artillery. The principal authority in France was the architect and historian, Eugene-Emmanuel Viollet-le-Duc (1814–79). Both as scholar and as restorer, he presented his ideas with clarity and conviction (even if he did not show the restraint and self-questioning now considered desirable in these callings), and he drew like an angel. In his *Essai sur l'architecture militaire au moyen-âge* (1854)[3] Viollet-le-Duc had produced the first sustained discussion of the development of medieval fortification from late Roman times to the fifteenth century, complete with plans, line drawings and discussions of siege warfare. Castle studies were now scientifically respectable and had an intellectual framework in which to develop.

The first important work on the Crusader archaeology of the Holy Land was de Vogüé's *Les Eglises de la Terre Sainte*, published in the same year as the massacres of the Christians, 1860.[4] The Marquis Melchior de Vogüé (1829–1916), scion of an ancient and distinguished French aristocratic family, was an elder contemporary and friend of Rey's. His work showed that a number of churches from the Crusader period survived and that their architecture was based on medieval French styles, affirming the antiquity of France's position in the area. De Vogüé went on to produce his *Syrie centrale* in 1868 in which he revealed, for the first time, the great richness of late antique architecture to be found in the interior of Syria.[5] He later became French ambassador to Constantinople and Vienna but he never lost his enthusiasm for the Crusaders: in 1873, as ambassador to Constantinople, he secured French possession of the fine twelfth-century church at Abu Ghosh[6] and later became one of the founders and editors of the *Revue de l'Orient Latin*.

Rey's life is something of a mystery. Henry Bordeaux, writing in the 1920s, found that he had already disappeared almost without trace.[7] He seems to have been a gentleman of means with aristocratic pretensions and properties around Le Mans and Chartres, where he was a member of the local Societé Archéologique. How he became interested in the Crusader east is quite unclear but he travelled extensively in the Levant as a young man. There is a hint that he had government support but he may well have been simply a private scholar. He made three journeys to Syria between 1857 and 1864, visiting almost all the major fortifications except those in the lordship of Oultrejourdain. He developed twin interests in Crusader genealogy and military architecture which were to last all his life. In 1869 he produced his edition of Du Cange's *Familles d'Outremer*[8] and so laid the foundations for the study of Frankish genealogies, and in 1871 he published his *Etudes sur les monuments de l'architecture militaire des Croisés en Syrie et dans l'ile de Chypre*.[9] Looking at this ancient volume, it takes something of an effort of imagination to realise how pioneering a work it is. Viollet-le-Duc's *Architecture militaire* is innocent of all knowledge of Crusader fortification. Rey had virtually nothing to go on except a few narrative accounts of medieval chroniclers and pilgrims yet he identified, planned and drew almost all the most important monuments including such complex structures as Margat and Crac des Chevaliers. Of course much of his work has now been superseded: the proportions of some of his plans, like Saone for example, are clearly wrong, and excavation has revealed much more about Chastel Pelerin than he was able to guess. Yet some of his drawings, like the section of the keep at Chastel Blanc for example, have never been surpassed for elegance and clarity and he preserves details long since gone, like the appearance of Crac des Chevaliers before the Syrian villagers occupied it. When Deschamps began his investigations at Crac in 1927, he and the architect François Anus, with whom he was working, used Rey's drawings as their starting point and designated the towers with the same letters as he had.

He never returned to Syria but went on to write his *Les colonies franques de Syrie aux douzième et treizième siècles* (1883),[10] part history and part gazetteer, another pioneering work, and continued to produce articles on Crusader genealogy and lordships until 1900. After that he seems to have retired into rural obscurity. He never held a formal position or membership of any prestigious academy. Profound deafness following an accident increased his isolation and his death in 1916 was not noticed in any obituaries, but his work survived to inspire subsequent generations of scholars in France and abroad long after the writings of his more honoured contemporaries were forgotten.

The late nineteenth century saw a considerable amount of survey work, mostly in Palestine. In the main, these surveys were more interested in the biblical and classical past but Crusader remains were recorded where they occurred. The most far-reaching of these was C. R. Conder and H. H. Kitchener, *The Survey of Western Palestine: Memoirs of the Topography, Orography, Hydrography and Archaeology* (1881–3).[11] As the catch-all subtitle suggests, this was intended as a general survey of the area. In the 1870s and 1880s, Charles Clermont-Ganneau (1846–1923) produced a considerable volume of work on Crusader remains, including a fundamental account of masonry marks.[12]

In 1895 the Swiss Orientalist Max van Berchem (1863–1920) and his companion Edmond Fatio undertook an expedition to northern Syria covering the area between Aleppo and Tripoli. The stated objective was to acquire inscriptions for van Berchem's *Corpus inscriptionum arabicarum* but, besides being a brilliant epigrapher, van Berchem also had an enquiring mind for archaeology and history. As well as recording the Arabic inscriptions found at many Crusader sites, including Crac des Chevaliers, he also published a wealth of more general archaeological detail and some important Arabic texts describing the eventual taking of these castles by the Muslims. The discussions of Crac des Chevaliers and Margat, as well as smaller sites like Coliath, are still of considerable value.[13]

In 1909 T. E. Lawrence (later famous as Lawrence of Arabia) visited many of the Crusader castles of Syria on foot, though he never visited Oultrejourdain: ironically, in view of his later military exploits, he only failed to reach ʿAmman in Oultrejourdain because of 'the unthinking activity of some local Bedawin in tearing up the Hedjaz railway'.[14] His *Crusader Castles* (now republished with an excellent preface and additional notes by D. Pringle) was only an undergraduate dissertation. It is full of ideas and opinions, notably on the relationship between Crusader castles and those in western Europe (which he knew from lengthy bicycle trips around France in the previous two years). He stressed the western nature of Crusader architecture and discounted Byzantine or Muslim influence. The photographs are interesting but the plans are all based on Rey or the unpublished sketches of Pirie-Gordon. As an undergraduate dissertation it is excellent, and tribute to both the intelligence and endurance of its author. To be fair to Lawrence, he never intended it for publication in its present form so it would be wrong to place much emphasis on its scholarly imperfections.

The next major boost for the study of Crusader castles was provided by the establishment of the French Mandate in Syria in 1921. This led to the setting up of a French administration in Syria and Lebanon with an antiquities service. It also meant that archaeologists could count on government support, up to a point, for supplies, equipment and aerial photography. The mandate may not have been a happy period politically but it saw an unparalleled explosion of archaeological activities, among them the excavations at Ugarit and Byblos, the aerial survey of the Roman desert frontier by Poidebard and the study of the antique villages of the limestone plateaux of the north by Tchalenko. Crusader studies too benefited from this interest, especially as the presence of Franks in the area in the twelfth and thirteenth century could give a sort of legitimacy to their presence in the twentieth.

This activity was presided over by a pupil of Clermont-Ganneau's, René Dussaud (1868–1958). The classic figure of an old-school French academic with his close-cropped hair, toothbrush moustache and gold-rimmed pince-nez glasses, Dussaud had begun his career as an engineer but, after a visit to Smyrna, had become fascinated by the antiquities of the Levant. He travelled extensively in Syria before the First World War and returned to Paris where he eventually became head of the Department of Oriental Antiquities at the Louvre. Here he constantly encouraged expeditions to the Middle East and, in 1920, he was one of the founder editors of the periodical *Syria* in which so many of the results of this activity were published. In 1927 he published his *Topographie historique de la Syrie antique et médiévale*,[15] a fundamental contribution to historical geography.

The first major publication of Crusader antiquities was a direct result of this patriotic urge: 'The war of 1914–1918', wrote Deschamps, 'brought our troops to those shores where so many good Frenchman had previously fought.' In this spirit, General Gouraud, the first Haute-Commissaire in Syria and Lebanon, invited Camille Enlart to record the Crusader monuments. Enlart (1862–1927) had the right qualifications. Apart from his work on medieval French architecture, he had, in 1899, produced his *Art gothique et de la Renaissance en Chypre* which had showed how French art had spread in the Eastern Mediterranean. Enlart investigated the ecclesiastical monuments of the Crusader Levant which were published as *Les Monuments des Croisés dans le royaume de Jerusalem: architecture religieuse et civile* (1925).[16] He had intended to move on to cover the military architecture as well but in February 1927, at the height of his powers, he suddenly dropped dead in a Paris street.

Only a few days later, Dussaud entrusted the task of completing Enlart's work to a pupil of his, the young Paul Deschamps (1888–1974) who was to be the greatest of all students of Crusader castles.[17] Deschamps had been educated in the Ecole des Chartes and had specialised in medieval French art and architecture. He had never, it seems, taken any particular interest in the Middle East before but by December of that year he, the architect François Anus and an army officer called Frederic Lamblin, who acted as photographer, were ensconced in a small and bitterly cold chamber in a tower of the inner court at Crac des Chevaliers. Here they remained until March, exploring, drawing and photographing: Lamblin's pictures of Crac in the snow survive to show how bleak it was.

Deschamps' mission was to investigate all the castles of the Crusaders and he began with the finest of them. Crac became a much bigger project than he had previously anticipated. Since Rey had visited, a village of some 500 people had been established inside. While the basic structure remained largely intact, the villagers had destroyed much of the crenellation and the vast underground vaults were almost completely full of rubbish. Anus and Deschamps began clearance work on a small scale but it soon became apparent that this was a major undertaking. Fortunately two army inspectors came to look at the work with the result that General Gamelin assigned a detachment of sixty Alawite soldiers of the Armée du Levant, commanded by a French lieutenant called Poussin, to help with the work; in the old photographs, they stand there smartly in their shakoes, military tunics and long puttees, probably completely mystified about the purposes of their labours and the mad ways of the foreigners. The work was continued when Deschamps returned from France again in the spring of 1929 when he had another season with Anus and Lamblin. Numerous discoveries were made as a result of the cleaning, including wells and ovens hitherto completely covered. There remained, however, the question of the villagers whose houses prevented any overall appreciation of the architecture. Inevitably too, the building and extension of the houses was damaging the fabric of the castle.

In 1929 the Haute-Commissaire Ponsot suggested to Deschamps that the castle should be taken under the care of the French Administration des Monuments Historiques. With the support of Dussaud in Paris and a motion in the French Senate, Crac was finally ceded to France on 16 November 1933 and placed in the charge of the Beaux-Arts. The State of Lattakia, from whom the purchase was made, was paid a million francs to compensate the inhabitants. The villagers were then moved out and a work force of 120 spent two years cleaning up and restoring the fabric. The castle, meticulously restored, joined Palmyra, Baalbek and Qal'at Sim'an among the great tourist attractions of the French Levant. As Deschamps wrote in the spirit of the time, 'Crac des Chevaliers, which is so closely linked to the history of our country, should attract numerous French [visitors] because of the memories it evokes.' All these arrangements came to an end with Syrian independence in 1946 but the castle remains much as they left it, in a sense a memorial to both the crusading Franks and the twentieth-century French.

An equally impressive memorial is Deschamps' book *Le Crac des Chevaliers* (Paris, 1934) which formed the first volume of his trilogy *Les Châteaux des Croisés en Terre Sainte*. With Anus' meticulous plans and drawings, Lamblin's photographs and Deschamps' careful descriptions, it has claims to be the finest monograph ever produced on a single medieval castle.

Deschamps did not restrict his investigations to Crac des Chevaliers. In 1929 when he was still busy at Crac he visited Beaufort in Lebanon, Chastel Pelerin in Palestine and Kerak in Jordan, where Anus produced the first accurate plan of the castle, a plan which has served as the basis of all subsequent ones. In 1936 Deschamps made another extensive trip accompanied this time by the architect Pierre Coupel (1899–1983); with the aid of sixty-five soldiers from the Chasseurs Libanais, led by Commandant Bigeard, they cleared much of the inner court and donjon at Beaufort. Deschamps left Syria in 1936, never to return, but Coupel remained in Syria until 1946, making new discoveries at Saone and undertaking extensive repairs at Chastel Blanc (Safita) where the great tower was in serious danger of collapse.

Deschamps produced two further volumes. The first of these, *La Défense du Royaume de Jerusalem* (Paris, 1939), deals with a number of major castles, including Kerak, Subeibe (which he believed to be Crusader) and Beaufort, where his descriptions and plans record a building which has probably been mutilated beyond recognition by recent military activity. He also recorded the two cave castles at al-Habis Jaldak and Tyron but many lesser monuments were not noticed and, for all its interest, it remains a very partial record. It was not until 1977, three years after the author's death, that the final volume, *La Défense du comté de Tripoli et de la principauté d'Antioche*, appeared. It was almost forty years since Deschamps had visited the castles he describes and the descriptions lack the clarity and immediacy of his earlier work. Some sections, like the plan of Margat, are confused and inadequate, there is no plan of Akkar, and the description of Bourzey clearly shows that the author had never visited it. He compensates for this thinness by producing a long historical section on the northern Crusader principalities. Despite its shortcomings, however, the work remains fundamental and the discussion of the major monuments at Giblet (Byblos), Chastel Blanc and Saone are of the usual high standard.

Deschamps remained a Parisian all his life. He examined the Crusader castles as he might have done the châteaux of the Loire. He seems to have had no interest in Muslim fortifications of the period and obviously felt that the independent Syrian Arab Republic was not a congenial place to work in; for men like Dussaud and Deschamps, the loss of the Syrian Mandate must have meant the end of so many of their dreams, but his observation, his scholarship and his enthusiasm remain unsurpassed.

Perhaps because the surviving monuments were so impressive, neither Deschamps nor his contemporaries under the French Mandate undertook any archaeological excavation of Crusader sites (except incidentally at Byblos, where the excavator, Dunand, was largely concerned with the ancient city). In Palestine, where the castles were much less well preserved, the Department of antiquities of the British Mandate government sponsored an excavation at Chastel Pelerin, conducted by C. N. Johns between 1930 and 1934.[18] Chastel Pelerin had been severely damaged by natural causes and the activities of Ibraham Pasha who removed much of the masonry. Earlier commentators, including Deschamps, had been unable to make much of the interior. Johns' excavations recovered the foundations of an elegant polygonal chapel and he also explored the small town outside the castle, but from the point of view of the historian of military architecture the most important result was the reconstruction of the main defences which shows just how much can be learned by careful exploration of apparently ruined and formless lumps of masonry. Unhappily, Johns was never able to produce a full publication of his researches which would certainly have amounted to a significant monograph.

The Second World War saw the end of this very productive period in the study of Crusader castles. In independent Syria there was little money for archaeology and Crusader studies were not really a priority even for what there was. Only Gabriel Saadé produced important articles on Bourzey and the 1188 siege of Saone. In Israel, however, an active school of Crusader historians developed under the leadership of Joshua Prawer. This school is much concerned with Crusader settlement of all sorts (rather than purely with military architecture). The most important new discoveries were made with the excavation of the castle at Belvoir by the Israel Department of Antiquities between 1963 and 1968. This revealed a very much more complex structure than the rather simple enclosure imagined by Deschamps[19] and others. The emergence of a wholly unsuspected castle showed that the military architecture of the first kingdom was more developed than many had imagined and a single excavation proved the theorists wrongs.

Recently the most important advances in our knowledge have come from the archaeological explorations including the surveys of the smaller castles of Oultrejourdain by Luigi Marino and others.[20] The most important of these have been the excavations conducted by the British School of Archaeology in Jerusalem, led by D. Pringle and R.P. Harper. This work has concentrated more on the surveying and recording of minor structures than on the excavation of major monuments but the results have been extremely impressive. Pringle's excavation at Red Tower and the survey of the surrounding Crusader remains in the lordship of Caesarea show just how extensive are the traces of Crusader occupation and how much can be learned from the careful excavation of an apparently unpromising site.[21]

After more than a century of investigation, there are still many areas which invite further investigation. There is certainly more to be learned about the smaller castles of the twelfth-century Kingdom of Jerusalem. The same also applies to the County of Tripoli. Political problems in Lebanon have prevented any comprehensive investigation but it is clear from notices in the older sources (Rey, van Berchem and Deschamps) that there is a considerable number of sites which are probably the remains of small twelfth-century castles and we may find a pattern of occupation not unlike the settlements being revealed in the Kingdom of Jerusalem. Another area where more research will undoubtedly yield important results is in the study of siege warfare.[22] Forty years ago, R. C. Smail held that military techniques changed little in the crusading period and siege warfare as such did not merit a separate chapter in his *Crusading Warfare*. Recently C. Marshall in his *Warfare in the Latin East, 1192–1291* has devoted more space to the subject but, again, without discerning much development. A radically different point of view is put forward by P. Cheveddin, basing his work on newly discovered Arabic sources. He suggests that the end of the twelfth and the beginning of the thirteenth century saw a radical improvement in the capabilities of medieval artillery which in turn led to marked changes in castle building. If this is correct, then the Crusader castles of the thirteenth century will need to be re-examined.

With the exception of the castles of medieval England, Crusader castles have been subjected to more intensive research than any other area of medieval military building. This is partly due to patriotic and romantic enthusiasms but partly too to the nature of the material. In a sense, Crusader castles are more purely military than their western counterparts which served as residences and administrative centres as well. In the Levant, castles had to be able to defend themselves against the most advanced siege techniques of the day and both thought and energy were devoted to improving them. Castle builders in western Europe could usually afford to take a more relaxed view and take into consideration non-military factors. The castle scientifically designed as a fighting machine surely reached its apogee in great buildings like Margat and Crac des Chevaliers.

We also have unique literary sources to people these monuments. It is true that we lack accounts and other administrative documents: we shall never be able to find out how many masons were employed or how much crossbowmen were paid as we can in England. On the other hand, we have chronicle accounts of how castles were used in warfare which have no parallel in the west in this period. Latin chroniclers like Fulcher of Chartres and Arabic ones like Baha al-Din and Abu Shama show castles in action but it is above all the work of William of Tyre which is so valuable. He describes the building of castles and what the builders hoped to achieve by their labours, and his vivid accounts of sieges and assaults bring to life the physical dangers and psychological stresses of castle warfare. If we want to understand these monuments, we must interrogate, as far as possible, those who constructed and used them, and the study of Crusader castles provides a unique opportunity for doing so.

It may well be objected that this study amounts to the celebration of an ancient and discredited imperialism and that modern scholars are heirs of those Frenchmen who sought a justification for present policies in the Crusader past. This is not the sense in which this book, or other modern scholarship, is offered. The writer who investigates, and even celebrates, the achievements of the Crusaders does not in doing so suggest that they are a model to be emulated, any more than the Arabs who rightly extol the palaces and gardens of al-Andalus are seriously claiming that they should reconquer Spain and Portugal. There is something fascinating and frequently moving about forlorn and failed enterprises, those 'old, forgotten, far-off things and battles long ago', however perverse they may now seem. It is impossible for me to stand on the windswept battlements at Crac des Chevaliers, climb to the remote crags of the fortress overlooking Petra or explore the magical stillness of the deserted valley by Bourzey, without feeling a potent mixture of admiration and nostalgia which breathes excitement and emotional commitment into scholarship.

2

FORTIFICATION IN THE WEST AND EAST BEFORE THE FIRST CRUSADE

THE men and women who came on the First Crusade and subsequently settled in the Levant came from areas which were already rich in castles and all of them would have been brought up in or near one.[1] When they set about constructing fortifications to secure their new domains in the east, it was natural that they should draw on the experiences of their homelands.

In early medieval and Carolingian times, fortifications in western Europe had for the most part been public or group strongholds, built for defence by and protection of comparatively large numbers of people. The most obvious examples of these were the Roman walls, which still encircled many of the small cities of the time. The legacy of Roman military architecture in the west was much more obvious to eleventh-century men than it is to us today and they did not have to look to North Africa or the Middle East to see examples of the classical tradition; they only had to look at the walls of Senlis, Le Mans or Pevensey to see high stone walls with projecting towers ranged at intervals along them.

New fortifications were also constructed in these centuries. In many cases these were promontory forts, where the man-made defences cut off a natural promontory, either on the coast, or overlooking a river valley or simply on a spur of a hill. Frequently such promontory forts were defended by one or more earth banks and ditches but stone walls were not unknown.

From the early seventh century these large-scale fortifications were gradually supplemented and replaced by castles with a much more restricted perimeter, built to house the lord or castellan and his immediate household and designed to be defined by a very small number of soldiers. These new-style castles took a wide variety of forms. The best-documented and most studied ones come from western France, especially Normandy, where M. du Bouard and his colleagues have subjected them to a detailed investigation, and England. Eleventh-century Normandy saw the development of two distinct types of castle, the motte and bailey and the enclosure castle, which could be a ring-work or a promontory fort. These castles were, almost without exception, constructed in earth and crowned with a wooden palisade. The relationship between the two forms is a matter of some dispute but it seems likely that the motte became common only in the mid-eleventh century around the time of the Norman conquest of England and perhaps as a consequence of it.

Although few people from England joined the First Crusade, the castles of the Norman Conquest are of considerable interest because, like the Crusader castles in the Levant, they were built by an alien, occupying military aristocracy in a hostile environment. The invaders seem to have introduced all the various forms of fortification known in their continental homeland. There were halls defended by earth embankments of greater or lesser strength (Castle Acre, Chepstow), and motte and bailey castles (York, Carisbrooke, Hen Domen and numerous others). Another common pattern in the earliest days after the Conquest was the enclosure castle: there are the excavated earth promontory fort at Castle Neroche, subsequently converted into a motte and bailey castle, and, in stone, the early enclosures at Richmond, Ludlow and Rochester where the great keeps so distinctive a feature today, are twelfth-century additions. There were also, of course, the two great tower palaces raised by the Conqueror himself in London and Colchester but these were exceptions without either parallel or progeny.

South of Normandy, in Anjou and Poitou, the emergence of castles took a different form, that of the great stone tower, either square or oblong in plan and decorated by flat or semi-circular buttresses. Traditionally the earliest of these is said to be the example at Langeais constructed by Fulk Nerra in 994 but in plan this is more like a hall than the classic donjon which seems to appear at Montbazon in 1017. The great stone tower became the characteristic fortification of these areas, spreading north into Normandy and England in the twelfth century.

Other areas had their own distinctive traditions of military architecture. Many of the original settlers in the Kingdom of Jerusalem came not from western France but from Lotharingia in the northeast and areas linked by ties of vassalage or alliance to the house of Bouillon either side of the modern French–Belgian border. If we try to determine the types of castle being built in these areas in the late eleventh century, we find a very different picture from Normandy. Mottes are virtually unknown and stone keeps, where they do occur, do not have the dominant role we find in Anjou and Poitou. The best-preserved castles from Lotharingia are all on natural elevations, hills or ridges and use the terrain as an integral part of their defences.

The castle at Bouillon itself, family home of Godfrey and Baldwin I, the first two Crusader rulers of Jerusalem, has been much rebuilt since the eleventh century but the site shows that it extended along a ridge overlooking the river Semois. A study of four castles along the Meuse valley between Nancy and Metz, Vaudémont, Mousson, Prény and Dieulouard,[2] shows that all four of them were built on ridge or hill-top sites above the river valley. Unfortunately it is very difficult to date the existing remains with any confidence but we can probably make some observations about their design at the time of the First Crusade. They are all enclosure castles varying in size from Vaudémont, which is about 500 m long by 250 m wide at its greatest extent, to Dieulouard where the existing perimeter is less than 100 m across. All four had donjons as the centre point of their defences and in the case of Vaudémont, Mousson and Prény these donjons were part of an inner citadel, separated from the main area of the castle by ditches or an inner wall. The best preserved of these donjons is the one at Vaudémont, the so-called Tour Brunehaut, which is rectangular and without buttresses and probably dates from the late eleventh century but might be earlier.

Further evidence can be found in a study of castles in the Liège area.[3] Two of these, both belonging to the bishops, the neighbours and rivals of the house of Bouillon, are of special interest. Chèvremont, about 10 km to the southeast of the city, was a large enclosure castle, about 5 hectares in area, with a central strong point, though no donjon, and square towers along the outer perimeter. It is noted from the eighth century but seems to have been destroyed in 987 and not rebuilt. In the eleventh century we can see a different style of castle at Franchimont, built on a hill-top to replace a low-lying Carolingian palatium at nearby Theux. Eleventh-century Franchimont is much smaller and more compact than nearby Chèvremont, an oblong enclosure no more than 54 × 26 m with a projecting donjon at one end. This donjon is of three stories, the middle one of which provided the principal accommodation, and has no buttresses. The water supply was provided by a cistern in the centre of the court. While the donjon was important, it does not seem to have dominated the other buildings as the donjons of the west of France did and it was only one element in a compact courtyard plan.

Other areas of France show a similar variety of plan. In Champagne, with its flatter and more open landscapes, eleventh-century fortified sites are divided between mottes in low-lying areas and spur or ridge castles where they were possible.[4] In Provence, mottes, little enceintes and spur or ridge castles are also known from this period.[5]

Another land which should concern the history of Crusader castles is the Norman Regno of southern Italy and Sicily, not only because the Normans here, as in England, were alien conquerors imposing their will but also because Normans from southern Italy were the main settlers in the principality of Antioch. At present, however, little is known of early Norman castles in this area: scholarly attention has concentrated on the garden palaces of the twelfth century around Palermo and on the magnificent castles built by Frederick II in the early thirteenth century. In most cases the Normans used existing fortifications, especially in towns, but there are some small Norman castles with stone donjons. A small-scale investigation of three sites in Sicily suggests that some of these were quite simple structures.[6] There were earth mottes in a recognisably Norman style (Petralia Soprana) while elsewhere a rock platform was shaped into a sort of motte carved from the living rock (Sperlinga). A substantial motte, now crowned with a later round tower, was built by Robert Guiscard at San Marco Argentano near Cosenza.

Even a brief survey of this nature shows clearly that the Crusaders who came to settle and build in the Levant had experience of a large number of different castle types in their homelands. Furthermore, they were used to adapting designs to local terrains. They needed no eastern masters to show them how to build a curtain wall along the crest of the ridge or to separate an inner redoubt by walls and ditches from an outer bailey. But this did not mean that they had nothing to learn from eastern techniques.

The walls of Constantinople must have presented an overwhelmingly impressive spectacle to the arriving Crusaders. Even today in their dilapidated state they show the scale and logic of late antique military science and when they were complete with counterscarp, ditch and outer wall, all dominated by massive height and towers of the inner wall, they must have been even more imposing. We know too that the leaders of the First Crusade saw these walls, but whether they were influenced by them when building their own fortifications is another matter. The scale was too vast for the needs and resources of the early twelfth century. Furthermore, the main part of these walls was more than six centuries old and the engineers who had designed and built them were long since gone. Eleventh- and twelfth-century Byzantine military architecture was very different in scale and achievement.[7]

The Crusaders soon acquired bitter experience of other Byzantine fortifications. From 6 May to 19 June 1097, the army of the First Crusade had besieged the city of Nicaea, then in Turkish hands but protected by defences built when the city was under Byzantine rule. The city walls were about 5 km long, a single line (at this time) with frequent interval towers projecting boldly from the curtain. Though much of this length must have been very thinly garrisoned, the Crusaders could make no real headway. When they attempted to undermine one of the towers, the result was a fiasco and the damage easily repaired. In the end the garrison gave up hope of relief and surrendered peacefully to the Emperor Alexios Komnenos and the Crusaders had to rely on his generosity for supplies and money.[8]

Even more discouraging were the walls at Antioch which kept the army at bay from 20 October 1097 to the beginning of June 1098, a long, hard winter siege which was the crisis of the First Crusade and almost led to disaster.[9] The city walls, which have now almost completely disappeared, had been built in antiquity and restored by the Byzantines after they had retaken the city in 969 when the citadel on Mount Silpius, overlooking Antioch, was constructed. While it did not boast triple lines of defence like the Theodosian walls of Constantinople, the wall was high and supported by numerous square and polygonal towers in which the defenders could live and from which they could overlook the attacking army. The Crusader army could make virtually no impact on these defences and the city only fell through treachery when a member of the garrison allowed the Franks to erect ladders by night against a section of the wall and climb in. Again the Crusader army had been shown the military value of Byzantine fortifications.

Like the walls of Constantinople, the extent and scale of the fortifications of Antioch were a product of late antique planning, not of contemporary Byzantine practice. From the seventh century the Byzantine empire underwent a number of major transformations, one of which seems to have been a dramatic decline in the population and size of cities. The vast defensive scheme of late antiquity were no longer appropriate. Especially in Anatolia where Muslim raids threatened the security of rich and poor alike, the population had come to group themselves around fortified citadels usually perched high on hills or ridges, to which they could retreat in times of trouble. One of the best surviving examples of these is the citadel at Ankara rebuilt in the early ninth century.[10] It crowns a steep ridge on whose slopes the medieval settlement clustered and it consists of an upper and lower bailey sharing a common wall on one side. There is no donjon but the most noticeable defensive features are the frequent and massive interval towers which project boldly from the walls. Many of them are constructed with re-used antique masonry and they come in different shapes, mostly square but there are also round and prow-shaped examples.

There were also Byzantine castles which were later adapted by the Crusaders for their own use. The Byzantine reconquest of Antioch and the mountainous areas of northern Syria which are bounded by the Orontes to the east, the Homs–Tripoli gap to the south and the Mediterranean to the west from 969 onwards led to a spate of castle building to secure the newly won areas. Little of this building survives and still less has been explored but it seems that the Byzantines concentrated on establishing small but well-fortified strong points, similar in area and scale to the small perimeter castles of western Europe in the eleventh century.

In Antioch itself, a new citadel was built on Mount Silpius, high enough above the city to be almost detached from it. This has never been properly surveyed but from both the existing plans and personal observation it seems to have been a modest affair, relying on inaccessibility as its main defence.[11] It does not seem to have been the main residence of the Byzantine governors but a place of last resort. There was another Byzantine fort at Bourzey, overlooking the marshy plains of the Orontes. The Byzantine redoubt here is very ruined but seems to have consisted of a small rectangular enclosure with square projecting towers at the corners.[12]

At Saone, the Byzantine fortifications were more extensive.[13] The Byzantine fortress here consisted of a central redoubt, now much ruined, which was roughly rectangular in shape and about 30 × 40 m. This commanded the highest part of the spur on which the castle is situated. It was protected by at least two curtain walls which crossed the spur on both east and west. These curtain walls are strengthened by small, solid towers, some square, some polygonal, which extend from it. There may even have been a further curtain wall to the east where the castle spur broadens out to join the main bulk of the mountain, protected by projecting round towers. While each of these fortresses had a Byzantine redoubt at the centre, it is clear that the Crusaders did not think that the Byzantine fortifications were adequate. In both cases the Crusader work is on a much larger scale and rubble masonry is replaced by larger shaped blocks, which are, in the case of Saone, very finely worked. It is noticeable too that the projecting towers are much more substantial, with large internal chambers and numerous openings. The Crusaders may have learnt something from their predecessors in these cases, but they certainly brought new ideas of their own.

A more substantial early twelfth-century Byzantine fortress can be found at Korikos, at the western end of the Cilician plain. Recent research[14] suggests that this was constructed in the first decade of the twelfth century by the Admiral Eustathios on the orders of the Emperor Alexios Komnenos at a point where his dominions bordered on those of the Franks and Armenians, and that its architecture reflects Constantinopolitan influence rather than local practice. It occupies an almost flat site beside a small harbour and opposite the fortified island castle which lies a few hundred yards from the coast. It was protected to the south and west by the sea, to the north by marshes and to the east by a rock-cut ditch. It is a large (approximately 150 m across) almost square castle constructed mostly in re-used antique stones which give its fabric a very different texture from the small stones of Byzantine Saone. It consists of an inner and an outer line of walls, the inner, as at Constantinople, totally overlooking and dominating the outer. The inner walls are strengthened by boldly projecting flanking towers especially closed spaced along the vulnerable eastern curtain. If the dating is correct, Korikos is a very important

example of state-of-the-art Byzantine military architecture at the time of the
Crusader settlement. Three features are conspicuous: the regular, almost symmetrical plan, the use of inner and outer walls in what might be described as a
concentric plan and the provision of numerous flanking towers on the inner
circuit. All these can be found to a greater or lesser extent in Crusader work
of the twelfth century but whether we should imagine direct borrowing or
independent solutions to the same problems of defence is open to question.

Alongside the Byzantine tradition there was the Armenian style in military
architecture. Unlike the Byzantine, the local Armenian tradition has been
extremely thoroughly explored by Robert Edwards and his pioneering work
means that we can make some fairly confident generalisations.[15] The Armenians had for centuries inhabited the area of Greater Armenia, on both sides
of the modern Turkish–Armenian border. Here they built both fortifications
and churches, but while the churches have received at least some attention,
the fortifications remain largely unexplored and unpublished: even the great
city walls of the capital at Ani are not adequately analysed or dated.

In the second half of the eleventh century many Armenians migrated south
and west and settled in Cilicia where they established a second homeland
which is sometimes known as Cilician or Lesser Armenia. Originally a collection of independent baronies, it became a kingdom in 1199 and survived,
under ever increasing pressure from the Mamlukes of Egypt, until 1374. The
Armenians brought with them a highly developed architectural and stone-
working tradition. They also had a social structure in which individual
baronial families enjoyed a great degree of independence and in which private
fortification flourished. Most of these fortresses were not city defences as
found in the Byzantine and Muslim traditions but were castles in the western
European sense, constructed, almost without exception, away from the plains
on rocky ridges or outcrops where the natural defences were of major
importance.

As a result of his extensive and meticulous explorations, Edwards has com-
piled a checklist of characteristics of Armenian military architecture. In addition to the use of natural features as a means of defence, with the curtain wall
hugging the cliff edge, often in so dramatic and precarious a position that it
must have required a cool head for heights from the builders, he lists, among
other features, the absence of donjons or keeps and the use of round towers to
flank the curtain walls.

The use of round towers can be seen most clearly in the defences of the
large enclosure site at Anavarza, on an isolated outcrop in the middle of the
Cilician plain.[16] The fortifications of this strategic site date from many different periods but probably the most impressive are to be found on the south
side of the south bailey, overlooking a slope which descends steeply to the
plain. Here, strengthening a wall which was probably built during the Arab

occupation of the eighth and ninth centuries, we find four boldly projecting rounded towers with internal chambers from which flanking fire could be directed through arrow slits along the side of the wall from a position of comparative safety. These towers can be dated to the period c.1111–29. Such towers were to become the characteristic defensive device in both Crusader building and western Europe from the beginning of the thirteenth century but were almost completely unknown at this stage.

A further interesting piece of evidence about Armenian styles can be found in Edessa. Although it lay far to the northeast of the Holy Land and well away from the Mediterranean sea, distant Edessa was the first Middle Eastern city to be occupied by the Crusaders, who were invited to come by the local Armenian ruler. For the half-century that it was in Crusader hands before its fall to Zengi in 1144, the Armenian community played a major role in the life of the city and the county of which it was the capital. In 1122 the administrator of the city for Count Joscelyn I, an Armenian called Vasil, had the fortifications of the city strengthened. Among these works was a round tower projecting from the wall with arrow slits to provide flanking fire. In order to commemorate his work, Vasil had an inscription inserted in the masonry, which is how we know about him and the date of the tower.[17] Once again, the connection of a round tower with the Armenians is noticeable.

While the links between Byzantine and Crusader fortifications are tenuous, the connections with Armenian work are clearer. There can be no doubt that fortifications in the Principality of Antioch owed much to them and it may be that the great round towers which appear in Crusader work at the end of the twelfth century were the result of Armenian inspiration.

We know little of contemporary Muslim fortification.[18] The frequent wars between Muslim powers were usually decided not by sieges but by combat in the open field. Cities were certainly fortified; Jerusalem itself had powerful walls (which have now totally disappeared under sixteenth-century rebuilding) and the walls of Tyre and Ascalon were able to keep the Crusaders out for many years. Aleppo was certainly dominated, then as now, by the citadel on the ancient tell, though the dramatic gate and associated buildings we see today date from the end of the twelfth century. Castles as such were much rarer but it does seem if local lords, among them the Banu Munqidh of Shayzar, had established themselves in castles in the mountains of northern Syria.

Two interesting forts survive on the coast of the Kingdom of Jerusalem to give us some idea of Muslim fortification in the area in the early Middle Ages. The oldest of these is at Cafarlet (modern Habonim) north of Caesarea. It stands on a small hill overlooking the coast road. In shape it is almost square about 58 × 50 m, with small round towers at each corner and semi-circular towers each side of the main gate. Although it is referred to in Crusader documents, the building is clearly a very good example of an Umayyad *qasr* or castle. The Arab geographer Yaqut, who says that Kafar Lab near Caesarea was built by Hisham b. ʿAbd al-Malik (Caliph, 724–43), is probably correct. More problematic is a fort just south of the modern port of Ashdod known as Qalʿat al-Mina. According to the geographer al-Maqdisi, writing in the tenth century, there was a fort there to which Byzantine ships came bringing Muslim prisoners for ransom. The building, whose walls survive to a considerable height, is rectangular, about 60 × 45 m. It is defended by a combination of round and square towers, larger than those at Cafarlet, and all solid. The building might be Byzantine or Umayyad but is more probably a rare example of Fatimid fortification, erected to serve as a base during the extended Fatimid campaigns in Palestine in the late tenth and early eleventh centuries. Both these buildings show that planned fortifications reminiscent of Roman castra continued to be built in this area but there is no evidence that they had any direct influence on Crusader military architecture.[19]

The finest examples of Muslim military architecture from the immediately pre-Crusader period come from Cairo.[20] Between 1087 and 1092 three of the Fatimid gates and a stretch of city wall were rebuilt. Muslim sources state that the architects were three brothers from Edessa, probably Armenians. All three gates are protected by boldly projecting flanking towers. Two of these, the Bab al-Futuh of 1087 and the Bab Zuwayla of 1092, are rounded on the outside; the third, Bab al-Nasr (1087), is rectangular. All are solid for the first two-thirds of their height but have large spacious chambers to survey the gates and the walls in the upper section. All are built in very fine ashlar masonry. The wall-head defences were simple, round-headed crenellations and there is no trace of machicolation in the original structure or of a portcullis in the gate itself. The rebuilt sections of the city wall had a vaulted passage along the top with regularly placed arrow slits, and there are two surviving flanking towers, one a massive bastion on a corner of the wall, the other quite small, and both square in plan. The gates of Cairo seem to reflect northern Syrian or Mesopotamian practice and are very much in the classical Roman tradition of town defences, very impressive but thoroughly traditional: Vitruvius would have been proud of them.

There are some indications that the eleventh century saw an increase in the building of fortifications by the Muslims of Syria, although the evidence is not extensive. Recent research in Muslim Spain[21] has shown how *husun*, hill-top fortifications, were widespread in the southeast of al-Andalus and that many of them, like the castle of Uxo near Valencia which was the subject of archaeological investigation, were constructed or rebuilt in the early part of the eleventh century. These castles are characterised by their positions on isolated rocks or ridges, the comparatively large irregularly shaped areas they enclose and the use of square projecting towers to defend a curtain wall. It is plausibly suggested that many of them were constructed as places of refuge in times of disturbance, though some also became the sites of permanent settlements. It seems, too, that these fortifications were built by the local communities for their own protection rather than by the central government or local lords attempting to use them as bases for exercising power.

There is some evidence that similar fortifications were built in the Nusayri mountains of northern Syria. The first fortress at the ridge-top site of Akkar, later to be rebuilt by the Crusaders, is said by the Arabic sources to have been built by one Muhriz b. Akkar around the year 1000.[22] Further north, Maniqa (Frankish Malaicas) was founded at the same time by a local mountain chief, Nasr b. Musraf al-Rawadifi,[23] and Qal'at Mehelbe (Fr. Balatanos) was begun by the mountain clan of the Banu Ahmar at the beginning of the eleventh century.[24] In addition, Arab accounts say that the plateau of Margat was first fortified by the Muslims in 1062 and that the site of Crac des Chevaliers was first occupied by a settlement of Kurds (hence its original Arabic name of Hisn al-akrad or Castle of the Kurds) in 1030. All these were plateau or ridge sites, and the only one on which eleventh-century Muslim building may survive, Qal'at Mehelbe, shows an oval enclosure about 200 m across surrounded by a curtain wall with projecting square towers. The literary evidence is fragmentary, the archaeological material virtually unexplored, but it may be that the Nusayri mountains in the century before the arrival of the Crusaders were the scene of castle building by local Muslim groups very similar to the much better documented examples from Spain.

The coming of the Saljuks may also have led to the development of urban fortifications. The citadel of Damascus seems to have been founded by the Turkish adventurer Atsiz b. Uvak, who took possession of the city in 1076–7.[25] This seems to have been the first time a fortress was constructed in the city. Similarly the earliest fortification of the Roman theatre at Bosra, a single tower, was constructed by a Turkish commander in the 1080s.

The crusaders could draw on a number of different styles of military architecture but how important these borrowings were is more problematic. There is a model which suggests that, in cultural matters, people only borrow from others what they are on the verge of inventing themselves. If there were borrowings of military technology it was because the Franks could appreciate that such devices were useful and served their immediate purposes. There is no question of slavish imitation but of adaptation of particular designs whose utility was apparent. At the same time, we should never underestimate the pragmatism and inventiveness of castle builders and we shall probably understand more about the architecture of Crusader castles by investigating the needs and purposes of the builders and the threats they faced than by searching for outside influences.

3

CASTLES OF THE TWELFTH-CENTURY KINGDOM OF JERUSALEM

THE Kingdom of Jerusalem was by far the largest and most prosperous of the Crusader states. At its apogee in the half-century before the disastrous defeat at Hattin in 1187, it comprised not only Palestine between the Jordan valley and the Mediterranean but also the lordship of Oultrejourdain to the east of the Dead Sea, which extended as far south as the Gulf of Aqaba, and much of the coast of modern Lebanon as far north as Beirut. The castles in this area are not as spectacular as Margat, Saone or Crac des Chevaliers in Syria, but they are still very interesting. In the Kingdom of Jerusalem in the twelfth century we can see the traces of real attempts at settlement of the land. In the modest towers of knightly families and the first enclosure fortifications of the military orders we see the hopes and aspirations of a generation who believed that the Holy Land would become a part of Latin Christendom as surely as the newly conquered lands of Sicily and Toledo.

ROYAL AND COMMUNITY CASTLE BUILDING

Almost as soon as they set foot in the area which was to form the Crusader States, the Franks began to build fortifications, among the earliest of them being the three towers constructed outside Antioch when the Crusaders were besieging the city in the winter of 1097–8.[1] The siege of Jerusalem in the summer of 1099 was much shorter than the blockade of Antioch and it seems that no substantial fortifications were built to assist it. When the city was captured, most of the army of the Crusade returned home to the west. Godfrey de Bouillon, one of the leaders of the Crusade, was chosen as 'Advocate of the Holy Sepulchre', in effect ruler, and he began the process of establishing a state which would support and protect the newly conquered Holy City. After his death in 1100, his position was taken over by his brother Baldwin, who had himself crowned as King of Jerusalem (1100–18). Baldwin set about securing and expanding his lands in Palestine and east of the Jordan. He faced a hard struggle; according to Fulcher of Chartres, who knew the situation at first hand, only 300 knights remained in the whole kingdom.[2] In these circumstances, Baldwin naturally began to build fortifications to supplement his meagre resources of manpower. He needed to; it was only because he was able to take refuge in a tower he had built the previous year at Ramlah that he (and the kingdom) were able to survive a crushing defeat by the Fatimid army in May 1102.[3]

Before his death, Godfrey had fortified Hebron and Jaffa, the only port then in Crusader hands and a vital link with the west. No trace of the works at Jaffa have survived but there are scanty remains of Crusader fortification attached to the Herodian precinct at Hebron.[4] Baldwin also built some castles: in a continuation of the Gesta Francorum, he is credited with the following fortresses (munitiones): Mons Regalis (Montreal, Shawbak, discussed below), Turris Neapolitana (Nablus), Malue, on the coastal plain of Sharon but not exactly located, Caun Mons (Qaimun), Acre and Scandelion, on the coast between Tyre and Acre.[5] Of these works, only Montreal has left any significant traces.

Godfrey and Baldwin also made use of the citadel at Jerusalem.[6] When the Crusaders captured the city in the summer of 1099, this seems to have consisted mainly of Herod the Great's Phasael tower with a courtyard, strengthened in Fatimid times, attached. It had been surrendered to Raymond of Toulouse but Godfrey had taken it over. On his death the next year, it was seized by a Lotharingian knight, Warner de Gray, who held it until Godfrey's brother Baldwin could arrive from Edessa and take over the crown. It was known as the Tower of David and figures prominently as a symbol of the city on the royal seal. The Russian pilgrim, abbot Daniel, described what he saw in 1106–7:

> It is curiously built in massive stone, is very high, and of square, solid impregnable form; it is like a single stone from its base up. It contains plenty of water, five iron gates and two hundred steps to the summit. An immense quantity of corn is stored in this tower. It is very difficult to take and forms the main defence of the city. It is carefully guarded and no one is allowed to enter except under supervision.[7]

For all its strength it was clearly a single tower at this stage and it seems to have remained like that until about 1170 when it is described as having a newly built solar and palace next to it and being strongly fortified with ditches and barbicans. In the Cambrai plan of the late twelfth century, the tower is

Plate 1   Montreal (Shawbak), founded by King Baldwin I in 1115: general
view from the south, showing its position on a hill isolated from the rest of
the plateau of Edom. All the visible fortifications are Mamluke, enclosing the
surviving Crusader work

shown with a loggia surmounted by battlements on top and a building called
the Curia Regis on one side and the Porta David (Jaffa Gate) on the other. Of
these structures, only the massive stump of Herod's original towers still survives, surrounded at its base by a typical Crusader glacis, and some vaults in
the courtyard. All the rest was rebuilt in the Mamluke period.

King Baldwin I pursued an ambitious expansionist policy, especially in the
area to the east of the Dead Sea which became known to the Crusaders as
Oultrejourdain. The man who had broken away from the Crusader army in
1097 to seize power in distant Edessa was unlikely to be deterred by the
remoteness of these areas from the Mediterranean life-lines of the kingdom.
From the beginning of his reign Baldwin had been attracted by the commercial
possibilities of the area and he particularly wanted to control and tax the
caravan route from Damascus to Egypt and the Muslim Holy Places in the
Hijaz which lay along the old King's Highway to the east of the Dead Sea. In
1115 he led an expedition beyond the Dead Sea to the mountains of Moab and
Edom which formed the core of Oultrejourdain. Here he founded a castle on
an isolated hill dominating a well-watered and settled valley at a place he
called Montreal (modern Shawbak).[8] Albert of Aix specifically says that the
main intention was to control the commerce of the area so that merchants

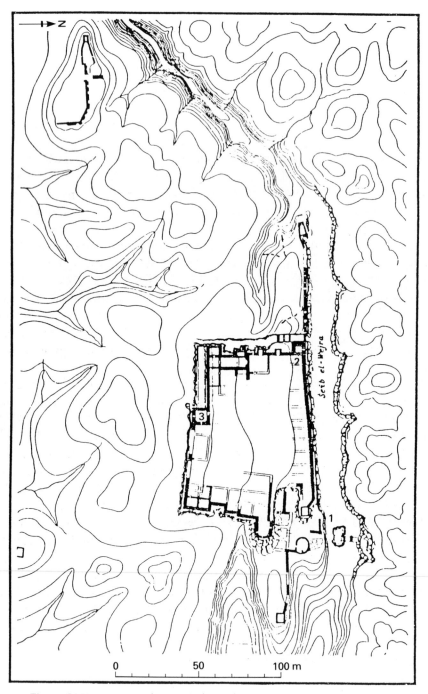

Fig. 1 Li Vaux Moise: plan. Note the wadi running along the north side with the bridge and gatehouse at the eastern end. 1. Bridge and gatehouse; 2. northwest tower; 3. donjon.

could not travel without the 'goodwill and permission of the king' (*regis gratia et licentia*).[9]

The natural strength of the round hill-top site at Montreal, separated from the high plateau of Edom, no doubt attracted the king (plate 1). Below the conical hill on which the castle stands is a well-watered valley and the bleak plateau of Edom around is more fertile than might at first appear. Much of the fortification which now crowns the summit dates from the post-Crusader Mamluke period but it is possible to see traces of a curtain wall running inside the later structure, and two chapels. Thietmar, who saw the castle in 1217 after the Muslim conquest but before their rebuilding, describes it as 'a most excellent fortress, surrounded by triple walls and as strong as any I have ever seen' and he stayed there in the house of a French widow who sent him on his way with supplies for his journey to Sinai.[10] The only weakness of the site was the lack of water but this problem was solved by the construction of a staircase-tunnel which led down inside the hill to two spring-fed cisterns carved in the rock so that water could be brought to the fortress without exposing the defenders to enemy power. (This system was explored by Savignac in 1932, a truly terrifying prospect, and he counted 365 steps in the steep and twisting passage.[11]) In the absence of a thorough survey of the extant remains, it is impossible to make any reliable assessment of the military architecture.

The next year Baldwin led another expedition to the area, which resulted in the foundation of the castle at Li Vaux Moise and probably Aqaba. Li Vaux Moise (The Valleys of Moses)[12] stands by the well-watered valley of Wadi Musa, outside the ancient city of Petra. It was close beside the road which led from the King's Highway, the main north–south route east of the Dead Sea, down into the Wadi Arabah and thence to Egypt. The surviving building is probably all twelfth-century work. The site is remarkable (Fig. 1). In the wilderness of lumpy, wierdly eroded rocks, the Crusaders chose a ridge separated from the surrounding massif by sheer precipices (plate 2). They improved this isolation by smoothing the rocks so that an attacker could not possibly find any hand or foot holds. The only access is across a single narrow bridge, completely overlooked by the walls of the castle. Guarding this bridge stands the most remarkable architectural feature of the defences, a gatehouse carved out of the solid rock (plate 3). The red sandstone of nearby Petra is, of course, famous for its rock-cut buildings. Whether knowingly or not, the Crusaders followed the ancient tradition and hollowed out a gatehouse cave, complete with benches along each side.

The rest of the architecture is less remarkable. The fortifications cling precariously to the edge of the cliffs which surround them on every side. The masonry is of fairly small, squared and coursed stones which comprise a curtain wall. The basic plan is a rectangular enclosure, approximately 100 × 35 m,

Plate 2   Li Vaux Moise (al-Wu'ayrah), founded by King Baldwin I in 1116:
general view from the north. The square western tower with its arrow slit can
be seen to the right and the remains of the donjon on the skyline, centre left.
In the foreground is the partly artificial ravine which separates the castle from
the massif. The hills overlooking the ancient city of Petra can be seen on the
top right.

with traces of chambers on the insides of some of the walls. The few towers
are square but are provided with arrow slits, and one of them, on the centre of
the south wall, could be described as a donjon. Outside the main body of the
fort, there are remains of watchtowers perched on isolated outcrops and connected to the centre by rock-cut paths and stairs. The architecture is not grand
but curiously impressive in this remote landscape. It was militarily very
effective. In 1144 it was taken by a surprise attack by Turks and the young
Baldwin III was only able to retake it for the Crusaders by alternative means.
William of Tyre takes up this story of twelfth-century economic warfare:[13]

> When it became known that the enemy had seized this fortress and had killed
> the Christians dwelling there, the king, although still very young, levied forces
> from all over the land and set out for it ... The inhabitants of the country had
> already had news of our approach and with their wives and children had fled
> into the fortress [*presidium*], the defences of which seemed to render it impreg-
> nable. For several days our forces exerted themselves in vain before the place.
> Volleys of stone missiles, repeated showers of arrows, and other methods of
> assault were tried with no result. Finally the Christians became convinced that,
> because of its fortifications, the place could not be taken. They therefore turned
> to other plans.

Plate 3   Li Vaux Moise, showing the rock-cut gatehouse from the exterior
(north), and to the right the twelfth-century Crusader wall with its
characteristically rough-cut rectangular blocks. The steps have been repaired.

The entire region was covered with luxuriant olive groves which shaded the surface of the land like a dense forest. The inhabitants of the land made their living from these trees as their fathers had done before them. If these failed, then all means of livelihood would be taken away. It was decided, therefore, to root out the trees and burn them. It was thought that the terrified inhabitants, rendered desperate by the destruction of their olive groves, would either give up or drive out the Turks who had taken refuge in the citadel and surrender the fortress to us. The plan was entirely successful. As soon as they saw their beloved trees cut down, the people changed their tactics and adopted others. On condition that the Turks whom they had called in were allowed to depart unharmed and that they themselves with their families should not be punished by death for their wicked conduct, they restored the stronghold [*castrum*] to the king.

The king left a new garrison to defend this lonely spot and they held it against an Egyptian expedition in 1158 but, like all the Crusader fortresses in Oultrejourdain, it fell to the Muslims in 1188 after the defeat at Hattin.

Plate 4 Al-Habis (possibly Crusader Sela), twelfth-century: general view from the east. The castle crowned the top of this isolated rock. The small donjon stands on the right-hand summit with the upper bailey to the left of it and a lower bailey on the side. The main access was by stairs up the cliff to the left. Nabatean and classical tombs can be seen at the foot of the massif.

Plate 5 Al-Habis: Crusader curtain wall on crag at northeast corner of lower bailey. Two courses of squared stones can be seen.

Plate 6   Al-Habis: curtain wall of lower bailey showing coursed, square
blocks and arrow slit. Note how the built wall integrates with the natural
rock to form a single defensive system. There are two casemates, now largely
filled with rubble, behind the wall.

Still more remarkable is the small Crusader fort which crowns the rocky
pinnacle known as al-Habis overlooking the basin of ancient Petra (plates 4
and 5). The only Latin source of the Crusader period to mention the ancient
site of Petra was the pilgrim Thietmar, who visited it in 1217. His short but
very interesting account makes it clear that the site was uninhabited at that
time.[14] Despite this, there are clear traces of fortification on the top of al-
Habis.[15] These were long thought to be the remains of the Nabataean citadel
but G. and A. Horsfeld in 1937 suggested that this work was Crusader and
this opinion was supported by Hamond after a full survey and more recently
by Marino *et al.* Nonetheless, scholarly opinion remains divided on the issue
and Mayer[16] is doubtful that this is Crusader work, on the grounds that there
was no purpose in the Franks building an outpost overlooking this vast,
barren and depopulated archaeological site.

Inspection of the site shows clearly that this is indeed Crusader work, even
if some of the stone is re-used; an arrow slit on the north wall is so clearly
twelfth-century Frankish as to leave no doubt (plate 6). The situation of the
fortress is spectacular. The actual walls and buildings are comparatively
modest. One rough pointed arch survives along with two cisterns to catch
rainwater (there being of course no spring) and the walls which cling precariously to the edge of the rock. The topography absolutely dictates the design.

It is possible to distinguish a lower bailey and an upper bailey but the irregular shapes of these are decided by the lines of the precipices which surround it. The rock is crowned by a small keep. What makes the site so impressive is not the built structure but the position, overhanging a great sheer drop down to the basin of Petra below. In every direction the views are wild and vertiginous and the chasms which open up beyond the walls quite heart-stopping. The identification of this site as containing at least some Crusader work does not, however, solve the difficulties raised by Mayer. The site is chosen for its absolute inaccessibility; it could not act as a customs post or the centre of an agricultural estate and it is not even very well situated as a watchtower. The only explanation which makes any sense is that it was fortified at a time when the Frankish garrison at Li Vaux Moise had been driven out and needed a place of refuge. This could have been after the surprise attack by the Turks in 1144 or perhaps after its final fall in 1188 when a remnant of the garrison could have taken refuge in this lonely outpost hoping desperately that one day help might come.

Also claimed as Crusader work is the ruined castle on the island known today as Jazirat Far'un (Pharaoh's Island), in the Gulf of Aqaba, off the coast of Sinai just south of Eilat. Scholarly opinion has even given these impressive ruins the splendidly Frankish name of Ile de Graye. In fact there is no evidence at all for Frankish building here and the name is never mentioned in Crusader sources. It is most likely that the fortifications were begun by the Muslims in the twelfth century as a protection against Frankish raids from Oultrejourdain; and the name, it turns out, is no more than an imaginative embroidery of the Arabic word *qurayya*, meaning 'little village'.[17]

The works in Oultrejourdain were Baldwin I's most important surviving foundations. His successor Baldwin II (1118–31) does not seem to have been a great castle builder though Fulcher of Chartres credits him with the building of the small, now vanished castle at Mont Glavianus (possibly Dayr al-Qal'ah) near Beirut in 1125: 'In this year, in the month of October, the king built a castle in the mountains of Beirut in a region which was very fertile ... Previously the Saracen peasantry had been unwilling to pay taxes for their lands, but afterwards they were forced to do so'.[18] A clearer statement of the reasons for castle building would be hard to find. The coming of Fulk of Anjou as heir apparent in 1129 and then as king from 1131 to 1143 gave an added impetus to the building of castles in the Kingdom of Jerusalem. He had been Count of Anjou since 1109. The stone donjon so characteristic of twelfth-century military architecture in western France had originated in Anjou; Fulk, like all his family, had already shown himself a castle builder in his homeland and he himself is credited with the construction of the fine keep at Montrichard on the river Cher.

From 1130 a series of castles were built in the south of the kingdom, in the

Ascalon area, which were as much communal initiatives as examples of royal castle building. Ascalon, at the southern end of the coast of Palestine, remained in Muslim hands until 1153. Sea communications with Egypt remained open and the garrison was regularly changed to avoid fatigue. Nor were they content to remain behind their walls but made frequent sorties to ravage the southeastern areas of the Kingdom of Jerusalem. In response to this a series of castles were constructed to serve as refuges and as bases for attacks on the Muslim-held city.

The first of these was at the site known as Castrum Arnaldi on the road from the coastal plain to Jerusalem where a narrow defile had given the Muslims the chance to ambush pilgrims. In 1132–3, while the king was still occupied in sorting out the affairs of the Principality of Antioch far to the north, the patriarch and the citizens (cives) of Jerusalem organised the construction of a castle of solid masonry to guard the road.[19] A few years later, in 1136 another castle was constructed, in rolling countryside some 40 km to the east of Ascalon: 'the people of the whole kingdom' (universi regni populo), the patriarch William and the magnates gathered and built a castle (presidium) with a high wall, outer walls (antemuralibus), towers and a moat on the plains near the city. The castle, known as Bethgibelin, was handed over 'by common consent' to the Knights Hospitallers,[20] a move which seems to have marked the beginning of the Knights' involvement with castle holding in the Kingdom of Jerusalem.

In 1141 King Fulk and all the leading barons (principes) of the kingdom, with the patriarch and the bishops, made the joint decision to build a castle to the north of Ascalon at a place the Crusaders knew as Ibelin. It was built with four towers (presumably one at each corner) and entrusted to one Balian, who was to take his name from the castle and became the founder of the most important of all the baronial families of the Kingdom.[21] Encouraged by this success, the next spring the king and his nobles as well as the church leaders assembled to construct a castle on a site they were to call Blanchegarde. Workmen (artifices) were called and the people were provided with materials. Like Ibelin, the castle had four towers and served as a base for attacking the Ascalonites as well as a place of refuge.[22] In 1150, King Baldwin III and his nobles fortified Gaza, on the Egyptian side of Ascalon, and entrusted it to the Templars[23] and finally, shortly before 1170, founded a castle at Darum with four towers, one larger than the others.[24]

Of these castles, only Castrum Arnaldi, where a length of curtain wall survives, and Bethgibelin have left any traces. At Bethgibelin (modern Bet Govrin) the castle took the form of an enclosure about 50 m square with towers at each corner, in the northwest corner of the Byzantine city walls. The interior arrangements are quite unclear but excavations currently being conducted by the Israel Department of Antiquities may shed light on this.

Despite the lack of surviving buildings to illustrate the written accounts, they are of great interest in understanding the building of castles in the early twelfth century. The purposes are made abundantly clear: above all to prevent raids from Ascalon and provide a refuge for those who are attacked, but there is also the intention that they should serve as a base for launching attacks on the city. The building of castles also brought economic benefits and the description of the effect that the building of Blanchegarde had on the surrounding country is a classic statement of the role of the castle as a bringer of wealth: 'The people of the surrounding region began to place great reliance on this castle as well as on the other strongholds and many suburban places grew up around it with numerous households and tillers of the fields. The whole district became much safer because it was inhabited and a more plentiful supply of food for the surrounding areas was made possible.'[25] In the case of Bethgibelin we also have a charter of Raymond du Puy, Master of the Hospitallers, dated before 1160 in which he granted lands on very favourable terms to thirty-two Frankish families to try to encourage them to settle. As Riley-Smith observes, this was a *charte de peuplement* very similar to contemporary examples from western Europe and it shows clearly the role of the castle as a centre of economic activity. In this context it is also worth noting that the castle is not on a hill-top site, which would have been better for both observation and defence, but in the valley near the springs and the road.[26] From the comments of William of Tyre, it would seem that Ibelin and Blanchegarde were also rectangular structures with towers at the corners. Rey gives a plan of the ruins of Blanchegarde as they existed at the time of his visit which suggests a square enclosure about 50 m across with towers at the corners and possibly a cistern in the centre.[27]

Also interesting is the impression of communal effort in the building of a castle. Sometimes the king was present, as at Ibelin, Blanchegarde and Gaza, but he is always said to have acted in consort with the great men of the kingdom, while at Castrum Arnaldi and Bethgibelin, the king was not present at all. Not only was there communal decision-making, but we also have the impression of voluntary labour, especially at Blanchegarde where there may be an implied distinction between the professional *artifices* who were summoned and the voluntary labour of the *populus*. We can also see the importance of ancient ruins in deciding the position of the castles and providing building materials: Bethgibelin, Ibelin and Gaza were all built on such sites. Ancient wells and cisterns also provided a useful water supply at Ibelin.

Apart from these projects, there is little trace of royal castle building in the Kingdom of Jerusalem, the kings being mostly based in urban centres like Jerusalem and Acre. Contemporary observers noted this: when Thoros of Armenia was travelling through the kingdom in the 1160s, he is said to have remarked to Baldwin III, 'When I came to your land and enquired to whom the castles belonged, I sometimes received the reply, "This belongs to the Temple [the Knights Templars]"; elsewhere I was told, "It is the Hospital's". I found no castle or city or town which was said to be yours except three.'[28]

CASTLES OF THE LAY NOBILITY

One of the most important recent developments in the study of Crusader castles has been the discovery of the extent of Latin settlement in the Kingdom of Jerusalem. In many cases the buildings of these colonists were modest and have either vanished completely or left undistinguished remains which have attracted little attention. A study of Crusader castles which concentrates only on spectacular structures like Crac des Chevaliers and Margat, however, would give a very misleading impression of the nature and variety of Crusader military architecture.

Many of the earliest fortifications in the Kingdom of Jerusalem were built by knights who wished to make them the centres of small estates, men like Amalric of Franclieu at Jaba or Geoffrey of Flujeac at Calansue. These fortifications almost always took the form of stone towers, usually two stories high and roofed by stone groin or barrel vaults. A recent study by Pringle[29] locates seventy-five such towers and there were no doubt more. They ranged in size from a tiny 8.4 × 5.3 m at al-Habis in Petra to over 26 m square at Forbelet in Galilee (rather smaller than those in northern France and England) and do not normally seem to have been more than 15 m tall, though none survives to its full height. Sometimes these towers remained isolated structures; at others they became the strong points of a series of buildings ranged round a courtyard. At Magna Mahumeria (al-Bira) and Rama (al-Ram), north of Jerusalem, the tower was part of a complex of buildings which probably formed the *curia* of the steward who administered the estate for the canons of the Holy Sepulchre. Such towers were also attached to ecclesiastical complexes. At Bethlehem a defensive tower was built on ancient foundations next to the Church of the Nativity.[30] When Queen Melissende came to found a nunnery at Bethany in 1143, even though it was so close to Jerusalem itself, a tower was her first construction: 'Since the place lay on the edge of the desert and thus might be exposed to the attacks of the enemy', explains William of Tyre, 'the Queen at great expense caused to be built a strongly fortified tower of hewn and polished stone. This was devoted to the necessary purpose of defence, that the maidens dedicated to God might have an impregnable fortress as a protection against the enemy.'[31]

As a result of important recent research by Pringle and the British School of Archaeology in Jerusalem, we now have a fairly full picture of the development of Crusader settlement in the plain of Sharon which was then part of the lordship of Caesarea, held throughout the Crusader period by the Garnier

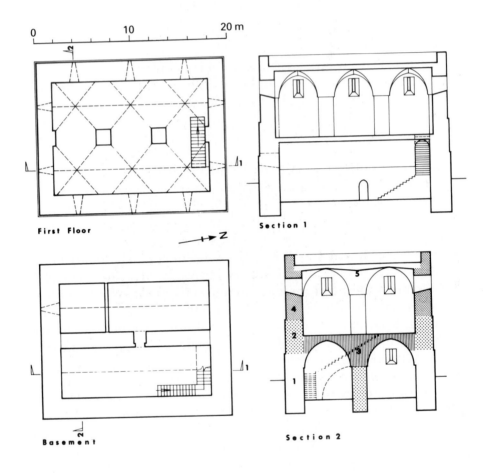

First Floor

Section 1

Basement

Section 2

Fig. 2   Red Tower: plan and section of a typical twelfth-century Crusader
tower.

Plate 7   Red Tower (Castrum Rubrum; Burj al-Ahmar): probably early
twelfth-century; general view from the northwest. The surviving wall is part
of the short southern end of this rectangular donjon. Note the barrel-vaulted
undercroft and the outline of the first-floor arches. From this fragment and
the excavated foundations, Pringle was able to reconstruct the form of this
donjon (see fig. 2). Red Tower is typical of many small Crusader donjons
erected by Frankish laymen in the early twelfth century.

family.[32] In this fairly small area, there are five castles of which significant evidence remains: Calansue (Qalansuwa), Caco (Qaqun), Montdidier (Madd
al-Dair), Castrum Rubrum (Burj al-Ahmar, Red Tower) and the Castle of
Roger the Lombard.

Calansue, Montdidier, the Castle of Roger the Lombard and Red Tower all
seem to have been held originally by knights who were vassals of the lords of
Caesarea and it may have been at this period that the fortifications were constructed. During the twelfth century almost all these castles passed into the
hands of institutions: the Benedictines of St Mary Latin held Montdidier by
1123 and Red Tower by 1158; the Hospitallers had Calansue by 1128. Only
Caco seems to have remained in the hands of a lay lord; in this case the lords

Plate 8   Caco (Qaqun), probably early twelfth-century: southeast corner of
this ruined donjon. Although the design was similar to Red Tower, the
masonry work is finer, using squared blocks and classical fragments.

of Caesarea held it directly, though some of the land which surrounded it was
in institutional hands.

Architecturally these castles are varied. Montdidier (now completely
ruined), Caco and Red Tower (fig. 2, plate 7) are all rectangular donjons in
the Crusader manner, that is fairly low and stone vaulted throughout. They
may have stood within an enclosure but no trace of this now remains. Calansue also has a tower, of which only one, finely built wall survives, but it also
has a hall above an undercroft and traces of other structures. The buildings
are not joined in any planned whole or defensive enclosure, perhaps suggest-
ing more a fortified manorial complex than a serious castle. The castle of
Roger the Lombard was probably a courtyard building of which only one side
survives, with a single vaulted chamber. Crusader towers show a variety of
ground plans: the simplest are those like Burj Arab and Giblet in the County
of Tripoli, with a simple barrel or groin vault over the whole area. More elaborate were Caco (plate 8) in the lordship of Caesarea and Chastel Rouge and
Saone in the County of Tripoli which had central pillars on both floors supporting four groin vaults, one in each corner. Red Tower itself seems to have
had a solid dividing wall on the ground floor and two pillars on the upper.

Pringle's work in the lordship of Caesarea shows us a pattern of castle
building very different from the grander structures usually associated with
Crusader castles. These simple towers show no great ingenuity and military

Plate 9   Chastiau dou Rei (Mi'liya), twelfth-century: general view from
northwest showing corner tower of this enclosure castle and, to the left, part
of the north curtain.

science but they were nonetheless useful fortresses. Caco was finally taken by
the Mamlukes in 1265 and its loss was grievously felt by the Crusaders of
Chastel Pelerin. In 1271 King Hugh of Cyprus and Jerusalem and Prince
Edward of England, then on his Crusade, launched a major attack on Caco
which a contemporary describes as 'Very strongly surrounded by ditches of
water' and Baybars himself felt obliged to mobilise an expedition to relieve it.
It would be wrong to see these castles as primitive or simple designs later to
be replaced by more elaborate structures. They were small and simple because
they were built to accommodate the small and not particularly wealthy households of the knights who settled these areas. If they resemble the smaller stone
castles of western Europe, it is because the society which produced them in
the early decades of the twelfth century attempted to replicate the structures
of its homelands. Others were built more simply as places of refuge from
enemy raids or storage places for valuables.

Towers were the most common form of baronial fortification in the
twelfth-century kingdom but they were not the only one. Substantial remains
of an enclosure castle still exist as Chastiau dou Rei much further north in the
kingdom (plate 9). Its name suggests that it was built by one of the kings of
Jerusalem, possibly by that great castle builder Fulk, though it only appears in
the records when it, and the thirty-six casals (villages) attached to it, were
passed on to baronial families from the 1160s onwards. The castle now stands

Plate 10 Mirabel, probably early twelfth-century with eighteenth-century
rebuilding: general view from northwest. The northwest tower of the
Crusader enclosure can be clearly seen, with the donjon behind largely
enveloped in eighteenth-century buildings.

at the core of the large Christian village of Mi'liya in Galilee and the houses of
the old centre of the village are built into the towers and court. The castle
stood on the summit of a small knoll and was about 40 m square with projecting, square towers at each of the corners. There are some traces of ranges of
buildings along the insides of the walls. Interestingly, it was acquired in 1220
by the Teutonic Order but in 1228 they effectively abandoned it and moved to
the nearby ridge castle at Montfort; perhaps the experiences of 1187–9 when
so many castles fell to Saladin convinced them that the enclosure plan was no
longer strong enough to withstand the seige techniques of the early thirteenth
century. Certainly, while some of the towers of the plain of Sharon, like Caco,
were used in the thirteenth century, none of the simple enclosure castles seems
to have been refortified by the depleted Crusader forces of that time. New
designs were required to combat new threats.

Another baronial courtyard castle can be seen at Mirabel (plate 10), the
centre of a lordship established by King Fulk for Balian of Ibelin between 1134
and 1143, and the castle was probably built at this time. It stands on a small
hill overlooking the road which led from Jerusalem to Caesarea and Acre and
the lush pools and springs which the Crusaders called Sourdes Fontaines (the
Deaf or Silent Springs). The castle itself was much rebuilt in Ottoman times
but enough remains to show that the Crusader building was an enclosure
castle protected by corner towers with a thick-walled central keep (plate 11).[33]

The Principality of Galilee had been independently conquered originally by
Tancred, a Norman from southern Italy who went on to become Prince of

Plate 11   Mirabel: interior of courtyard looking northwest. The south-east corner of the donjon can clearly be distinguished from the later building by the large size of the blocks.

Plate 12   Bet Shean (Beisan), twelfth-century: general view from northwest. This Crusader tower seems to have been surrounded by a bailey. The Crusader work can be distinguished from later work by the large size of the blocks, almost all re-used antique masonry from ancient Scythopolis. The castle is currently being cleared of later accretions.

Antioch. He built no castles in his short tenure but fortified the cities of Tiberias and Bet Shean (Beisan) (plate 12). The Crusader fortress at Tiberias, undoubtedly one of the more important urban castles they built, has completely disappeared, but its position by the Sea of Galilee, on the southern walls of the town, has recently been established and surviving seventeenth-century representations suggest an enclosure fortress with square corner towers.[34] At Bet Shean a rectangular Crusader castle survives and is currently being disengaged from the surrounding later buildings. Tancred was succeeded by an associate of the house of Bouillon, Hugh of St Omer, who determined to build up the fortifications of his domain. Like his king, he looked east across the Jordan to expand his territories. Here he cast covetous eyes on the plains of the Golan Heights and the Hawran, the area the Crusaders called the Terre de Sueth and which Frankish sources describe as rich in wine, corn, oil and good pastures for beasts.[35] In 1105 King Baldwin I had founded a castle to exploit these lands at a site still known as Qasr Bardawil (Baldwin's Castle). Aerial photographs show that it was a promontory fort at the join of two steep wadis.[36] The attempt to establish a permanent Frankish presence in this area was not a success: Tughtagin of Damascus attacked and destroyed the site in the same year, leading the garrison captive to Damascus. Thereafter the Christians were more circumspect and kept a presence in the area only in the remarkable cave-castle at al-Habis Jaldak.

Hugh is credited with a number of castles within Galilee itself. It was probably he who built the first castle at Saphet, a strong position on an isolated hill-top. The foundation is recorded in Arabic sources[37] in 1101–2 but nothing of the original structure now remains. In 1107 he constructed another castle destined to survive until the end of Frankish rule at Toron. William of Tyre explains that Hugh often led his men from his capital at Tiberias to attack Tyre (which remained in Muslim hands until 1124) but that on the 48 km journey they would be harassed by the enemy. He built Toron as a refuge to shelter them before and after attacks and the chronicler goes on to comment how, now its immediate military purpose had disappeared, it was still valuable as the administrative centre of a flourishing district:

> This place, famous for its salubrious air and delightful climate, lies in the tribe of Asher between the sea and Mt Lebanon and is about equally distant from the two cities, Tyre and Banyas. The soil is very fertile and admirably adapted to the cultivation of vines and trees. It also produces abundant crops under the care of the farmer. Consequently this site not only offered its founder advantages well suited to his needs at the time, but even now [c. 1180], because of its rich soil and the excellence of its famous fortifications, it is of the greatest benefit to the city of Tyre and the whole locality.[38]

Here we have the Crusader castle as the centre of a smiling and prosperous country estate and it was here at that time that the Arab traveller Ibn Jubayr

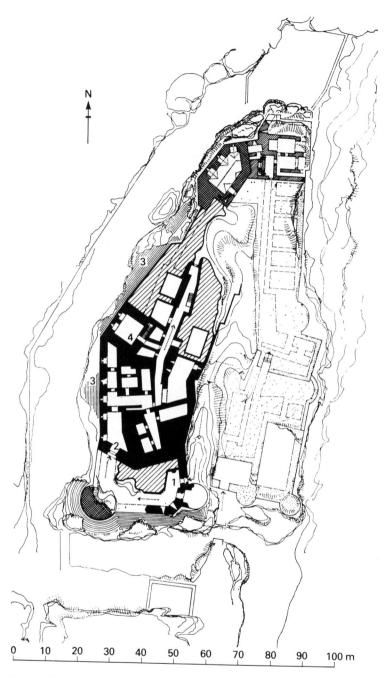

Fig. 3 Beaufort: plan. Crusader work is indicated in black; Arab work of 1190–1240 is cross-hatched. The castle stands on a cliff-top site, overlooking the Litani river to the east. The lower, east bailey is Arab work. 1. Gate to Crusader fortress; 2. gate to inner bailey; 3. glacis; 4. donjon.

Plate 13   Beaufort (Qal'at al-Shaqif), after 1139: from south. On the left-hand side is the Crusader glacis and curtain wall with the top of the donjon projecting above it. Upper right, Crusader wall of upper bailey. The round tower in the foreground is part of the Arab strengthening of the castle after its first fall in 1190. The photograph is taken from the outworks where Muslim siege engines were mounted in 1190 and again in 1268.

and his caravan were obliged to pay their dues on their way from Damascus to Acre. Toron was completely rebuilt by a local Lebanese lord, Zahir al-Umar, in the eighteenth century, and only fragments of Crusader masonry survive.

At about the same time Hugh also built the castle of Chastel Neuf (Hunin). This was in a spectacular position: to the west lie the rugged hills of upper Galilee, to the east the land falls dramatically some 600 m to the fertile and much coveted plains around Banyas and the headwaters of the Jordan while the northeastern skyline is dominated by the snow-covered massif of Mount Hermon. The land was rich and very well watered but it also lay on the exposed frontier between Christian and Muslim territory. At some periods in the twelfth century, the revenues of this area were divided peacefully between

Christians and Muslims. Chastel Neuf provided a centre for this lordship and a staging post on the road to Banyas when this was in Crusader hands. Of the Crusader structure, only the rock-cut ditch and a few fragments of masonry survive, showing that it was a rectangular enclosure, about 86 × 65 m, without any large projecting towers. Nothing of the interior can now be distinguished.[39]

In 1139 King Fulk captured a fortified site known as Qal'at al-Shaqif which the Franks were to know as Beaufort.[40] It stands in a dramatic situation high above the Litani river, now in southern Lebanon. The castle site is protected on the east by a sheer precipice which falls to the Litani 300 m below (fig. 3). On the west side the ground slopes more gently to the village of Arnun and it was here that the original builders concentrated their defences. On the north the castle is protected by a vast rock-cut basin. The site was handed over by Fulk to the lords of Sidon and it seems that building work began very soon after its capture. The castle passed into Muslim hands in 1190, back into Frankish hands in 1240 and then again into Muslim hands in 1268. At each stage the defences and accommodation were altered so it is not easy to reconstruct the twelfth-century work.

The fortress was on two main levels. A lower court lay to the east overlooking the Litani valley but nothing of the earliest phase remains in this part. Twelfth-century Frankish work does, however, survive in the upper bailey (plate 13). The main feature was a donjon, a solid two-storey structure of typical Crusader design, placed in the middle of the west wall where the castle was most vulnerable, like the almost contemporary donjon at Saone in the Principality of Antioch. A considerable length of the west wall of the inner bailey still survives, protected at the foot by a small glacis of dressed stone but without projecting towers. The south wall of this inner bailey is extant with a fine pointed entrance arch protected by a slot machicolation (plate 14). Also surviving is the entrance from the lower bailey to the inner fortification, but both the southern and northern ends of the castle seem to have been badly damaged by siege engines in the 1190 campaign and were rebuilt by the Muslims. Immediately before Saladin's assault the inner castle was modified, probably with the intention of providing more covered space and protection from missiles; as at Saone, much of the courtyard around the donjon was built over. Both the donjon and the entrance gate show well-cut bossed stonework which is characteristic of much Crusader building, the stones around doors and windows having almost flat, smooth centres while those in the rest of the donjon are more grossly rusticated.

The castle was the scene of Reynald of Sidon's devious resistance to Saladin, recounted at some length in the Arab sources. Reynald was one of the survivors of the battle of Hattin (July 1187) in which Saladin had destroyed the Crusader army. He was also, by the testimony of the Muslim authors, a

Plate 14 Beaufort: gateway to upper bailey from south. Note the finely cut
masonry with lowered margins, typical of Crusader work.

cultivated and charming man who spoke good Arabic. At the end of April
1189 Saladin had encamped at Marjayun, near the castle, and was preparing
to lay siege to it. Reynald presented himself at the Muslim camp and soon
made friends with Saladin. He told him that he wished to surrender the castle,
for he was really a Muslim sympathiser, and go to live in Damascus but
unhappily his family were in Tyre, then held for the Christians by Conrad of
Montferrat, and he would have to wait until he could get them out. Accordingly he was given three months grace during which he quietly repaired
damage to the castle and brought in supplies. When his time was up the
engaging Reynald again presented himself and explained how some of his
family were still in Tyre and he needed some more time. Now Saladin began
to be impatient, especially as the delay was allowing Guy of Lusignan to begin
the siege of Acre. Reynald was obliged to order his men to surrender but,
perhaps by prior arrangement, they refused. Reynald was confined first in
Banyas and then in Damascus but when the garrison did finally capitulate in

April 1190, one of the conditions they made was that Reynald should be released. He was, and in fact later met Saladin again on friendly terms when acting as an ambassador for Conrad of Montferrat. Even in the disastrous situation which followed Hattin, a strong castle and a shrewd leader could prove a major obstacle to the enemy.[41]

The most impressive castle of the mid-twelfth century was constructed beyond the Dead Sea in the lordship of Oultrejourdain. When Baldwin I had caused the castles at Montreal and Li Vaux Moise to be built, he seems to have kept them in royal hands. Fulk, however, decided to grant out Oultre-jourdain and establish it as a lordship in its own right. In 1142 the lord of Oul-trejourdain, Paganus Pincerna, or Pagan the Butler, transferred the centre of his power from Montreal to Kerak, further to the north (not to be confused with Crac des Chevaliers, though the Crusader sources spell them both in the same way).[42] Here

> [writes William of Tyre] upon a very high mountain surrounded by deep valleys the city of Petra had once been located [a misidentification of the ancient site, of course]. For a long time it had lain in ruins, utterly desolate. Eventually, during the reign of Fulk, the third King of the Latins in the Orient, one Paganus, called the Butler, Lord of Oultrejourdain, built a castle [*presidium*] on this site . . . The successors of Paganus, namely Maurice, his nephew, and Philip of Nablus, had added a moat [*vallum*] and towers to make the place more secure. Outside the fortress, on the site of the earlier city, was now a settlement [*suburbium*] whose inhabitants had put their homes there as a fairly safe position: east [actually south] of them lay the castle, the best of protection, while on the other sides the mountain was surrounded by deep valleys.[43]

Why Pagan made the move is not stated but it may have been because it is closer to Jerusalem; indeed on a very clear day you can actually see the Mount of Olives from the castle, and it had good access to the Dead Sea and thence by boat to the west bank.[44] Here he and his successors constructed a vast but rather crude fortification. The position had many natural advantages (plate 15). The site of Kerak town is a triangular plateau which extends northwards from the main massif and it is bordered on all three sides by steep slopes leading down to the ravine of the Wadi Kerak. Only at the southern apex did the site join onto the main plateau of Moab where it was overlooked from the adjoining hill. The castle was built to secure this narrow neck of land (fig. 4). The natural defences were augmented at the south end by a rock-cut ditch in which a reservoir was constructed, wide enough to keep siege engines at a dis-tance (a technique also used at Beaufort). At the north end, where the town is situated, there is another ditch, narrower than the southern one but much deeper: Ibn al-Athir says it was originally 60 cubits (30 m) deep, which would make it about the same as the ditch at Saone, but it has subsequently been filled up almost completely

Plate 15 Kerak (Crac), twelfth-century and later: general view from east.
The length of the castle ridge can be seen, with the town to the right (north).
The Crusader curtain wall, with its square towers, runs along the crest of the
ridge; beneath it is the glacis. The great ruined tower at the right-hand end
overlooks the trench which separated castle from town. The great tower at
the left (south) end is later Mamluke work, possibly replacing a Crusader
donjon demolished in one of the sieges of the 1180s. At the extreme left is
another rock-cut ditch and open cistern which cut the castle off from the
mountains of Moab to the south.

The Crusader work is built of the hard volcanic stone, roughly shaped into
rectangular blocks but without any of the fine stonecraft we see in twelfth-
century work at Beaufort or Saone, either because the masons were not available in this remote area or because the stone did not lend itself to fine shaping.
The later Arab work, by contrast, uses a finely drafted limestone from a
nearby quarry and is easily distinguishable.

The walls of the castle run along the upper contours of the ridge. On the
west side there is a lower bailey, as at Beaufort, but the surviving fortifications
are later Muslim work, although Deschamps has pointed out that fragments
of twelfth-century masonry show that there was a lower bailey on the site in
Crusader times. The western flank of the inner bailey still shows the rough
Crusader stonework but it is on the long eastern flank that the twelfth-century
defences can best be seen (plate 16). The structures on this side are quite
complex and Deschamps suggests that there are two phases, an inner curtain
wall to which was later added an outer curtain separated from the earlier

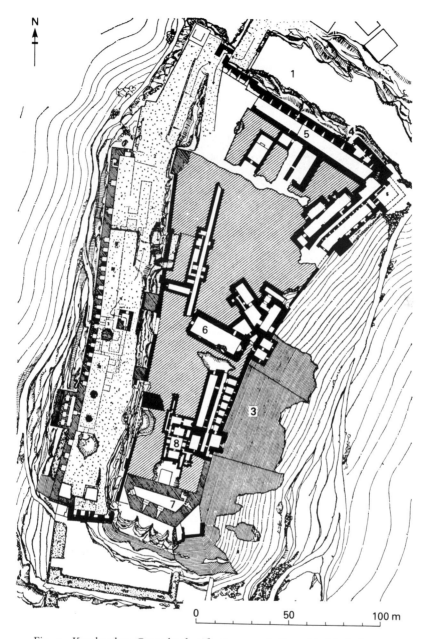

Fig. 4   Kerak: plan. Crusader fortifications are indicated in black; later Muslim work is hatched. 1. Ditch separating castle from town; 2. lower bailey; 3. glacis; 4. original entrance; 5. vaulted halls; 6. chapel; 7. Muslim donjon; 8. palace, now known to be Muslim work.

Plate 16 Kerak: east wall looking south. The square Crusader towers with
their crude, rough-hewn masonry surmount the glacis; note the arrow slits to
provide flanking fire. The high block with the arches near the far end is
Mamluke work.

structure by a vaulted passage. This new wall was strengthened by three surviving rectangular towers projecting boldly from the line of the curtain wall
and providing covering fire with the sites of two more, one at each end, still
visible. Below this curtain wall, sloping dramatically down the sides of the
Wadi, is a great glacis which is one of the most impressive features of the castle,
presenting a steeply inclined and entirely smooth surface to any assailant from
that direction.

The wall which faces the town is a massive, chunky curtain with arrow slits
pointing directly out from the wall (plate 17). It was on this side that the
entrance lay, not where the present arch, which dates from the Muslim
period, leads into the lower court, but further east where a bend in the wall, at
first sight inexplicable, sheltered in its re-entrant angle a small gate no bigger
than a postern which led directly to a chamber and then to a great vaulted hall
which probably served, amongst other things, as a stable.

Plate 17   Kerak: north wall on the town side, looking east. The rock-cut
ditch to the left was originally much deeper and could be compared with the
one at Saone. Flanking fire was provided by the salient at the end which had a
postern gate at ground level in the re-entrant angle.

We would expect to find the strongest defences at the south end where the site was most vulnerable, but the fortifications here were largely destroyed at the time of the castle's conquest by the Muslims and rebuilt in Ayyubid and Mamluke times. The outer line of defence was a rock-cut reservoir running across the neck of the land and about 20 m wide. As in other castles (Beaufort, Akkar) this served as a water store in peacetime and a moat in time of war. Some fragments of the Crusader curtain wall at this end of the castle survive but the mighty oblong bastion there dates from the Muslim period. It may well be that there was a Crusader donjon on this site in the twelfth century; certainly by analogy with the contemporary castles at Saone and Beaufort, we would expect to find it here at the most vulnerable point, but if so, no trace of it survives.

Plate 18   Kerak: vaulted halls along inside of north wall. These cavernous
halls, on the scale of Victorian railway tunnels, provided accommodation,
stabling, access to arrow slits in the wall itself and shelter from in-coming
missiles.

Apart from great long vaults along the inside of the north wall, with
roughly built pointed barrel vaults, it is difficult to distinguish very much in
the chaos of the interior which was, in any case, much remodelled in the
Mamluke period. The maze of vaults, subterranean passages and mysterious
holes which lie under the surface of the inner bailey remain to be explored,
though a chapel and a small Mamluke palace have been distinguished.

In 1177 the lordship of Oultrejourdain had been granted to Reynald of
Chatillon who had married the heiress Etiennette de Milly, 'la dame dou
Crac'. His notorious exploits, including launching ships on the Red Sea to
attack Mecca and the looting of Muslim caravans, meant that his exposed
lands were a prime target for Muslim armies, and the castle at Kerak was
besieged no less than three times in the 1180s. In October 1183 Saladin's army

Plate 19   Kerak: embrasure and arrow slit in north wall, showing the massive
and vigorous masonry typical of the castle.

was able to take the town by assault which caused a mass of refugees to flood
into the castle. The Muslims would have forced the gate there and then but
for the firmness of one knight called Iven who held the gate until the bridge
across the ditch had been destroyed. Saladin then began a regular siege, setting
up six engines in the town and two on the mountain at the opposite end of the
castle. Attempts by the garrison to set up siege engines of their own were
abandoned because of the danger from incoming missiles and William of Tyre
gives a vivid word-picture of the besieged cowering in the castles:

> These dangers, which caused men to shake with fear, affected not only those who
> crept out of their hiding places to the battlements [*propugnacula*] to hurl weapons
> or stones or to spy on the enemy forces but also those who had fled to the innermost
> chambers and most secret places. They were terrified by the crash and roar of the
> incoming missiles, which seemed like thunder, and they awaited the bolt fearing all
> the time that the building would be destroyed and collapse on top of them.[45]

This account illustrates the power of siege engines, not least in psychological warfare, and the importance of having, or not having, engines for defensive purposes. But it was also from this siege that we have one of the most famous accounts of chivalry in action. When the enemy approached, a wedding was being celebrated between the King of Jerusalem's sister Isabel and Humphrey IV of Toron, son of Etiennette de Milly. Indeed, along with the garrison and the other refugees, there were many musicians and entertainers who had come for the party in the castle. Etiennette sent messengers to Saladin, reminding him how, when he was a prisoner in the castle, he had held her as a child in his arms. Touched by this, he enquired which tower the wedding party was in and ordered his men not to bombard it.

By December, Saladin had made very little progress and the threatened arrival of the army of the Kingdom of Jerusalem persuaded him to give up. He was back again at the end of July the next year (1184) and began another siege. The first assault failed, not least because the defenders had built their own engines over the winter. Then Saladin concentrated on filling up the ditch between the castle and the town and built elaborate shelters for his men. Once again, however, the impending arrival of a relieving army forced him to abandon the siege after four weeks. The third siege was begun in March 1188 by Saladin's nephew, Sa'd al-Din. Once again the garrison defended themselves with determination but this time the situation was very different. After the defeat of the army of the Kingdom at Hattin the year before, there was no prospect of relief, and in the end hunger forced the defenders to give in. It is said that when they surrendered in October/November, the Muslims were so impressed by their courage that they allowed them to go free.

Among the strangest of the Frankish fortifications of the twelfth-century Kingdom of Jerusalem are the two cave-castles, al-Habis Jaldak and the Cave of Tyron.

We do not know the Frankish name for the cave which the Arab sources call al-Habis Jaldak but it has been clearly identified with the cave-fortress described by William of Tyre.[46] It was 'built' on the far side of the Jordan in the side of a cliff overlooking the Yarmuk river valley. The failure to hold the castle of Qasr Bardawil convinced the Franks that they could not build a conventional fortress in the Terre de Suete: on the other hand they made a series of agreements with the rulers of Damascus to share the crops and revenues of this fertile land and they needed a base from which to enforce their rights. Both the Princes of Galilee and the Abbey of St Mary of Josaphat had extensive properties in this area. The Franks established a presence in this inaccessible cavern some time before 1112 when it was first taken by the Muslims. The cave overlooks a deep wadi and the main Yarmuk river valley, commanding an extensive view over the plains to the north: a superb observation point but hardly a congenial residence. The natural cave had been extended to form chambers on three floors connected by ladders and stairs cut in the rocks. Water was collected in cisterns and the only approach was by a narrow track along the cliff face. It was secure enough but, as its Muslim garrison found in 1182 (it had been taken from the Franks a few months before), passive defence, sitting in the cave while the enemy methodically set about digging you out, hearing his picks at work night and day, could lead to despair and surrender.

Once again, William of Tyre gives a vivid account of the warfare:[47]

On arriving here the Christians judged that it would be desirable to besiege the stronghold . . . Accordingly a camp was established before the castle just named, and vigorous efforts were made to force those inside to surrender. The fortress was extremely well defended. Its situation was such that it was assailable only through the upper part and not even there unless the rocks were cut through to the dwelling place itself. It was decided therefore to put stone cutters to work on the upper portion. All the helpers needed were provided as well as guards so that they could work in safety and without danger of attack.

The cave was located on the side of the very high mountain. Approach to it was very difficult along a path hard even for a single footsoldier free from all encumbrance. The path approaching from the side was scarcely a foot wide, and below yawned a deep and dreadful precipice which extended to the bottom of the valley. This cave had three stories, one above the other. A wooden staircase with narrow openings connected the different levels.

Since this was the only method by which it could be attacked, the Christians tried to cut into the cave from above, as we have said, in the hope that in this way they might be able to penetrate into the first and upper level of the citadel. This was their aim and intention and every effort was made to attain it. All the workmen needed were placed in position and helpers provided who, as fast as the bits of rock and stone were cut away, threw the refuse down into the valley below. In order that the work might proceed without interruption, shifts were arranged during both night and day so that when those on the first crew were weary, their places were taken by fresh workers who had the necessary skill and ability. The labour progressed quickly because of the number and enthusiasm of the workers and also because the rock itself was easily cut, for it was of a cretaceous nature and readily penetrated except where veins of very hard flint obtruded which often damaged the iron tools and hindered the eager workers. The bits were rolled down into the valley below to clear the place, as has been explained. All these passed in full view of those shut up inside the cave and greatly increased their fear for all the time they could anticipate the moment when the work would be finished and an entrance achieved by force.

Our army was divided into two sections: one part, as has been said, set up camp on the top of the hill occupied by the cave where they could more easily protect those engaged on the work from the wiles of the enemy. The other part stayed in the plain below to prevent anyone going from or coming to the besieged. Occasionally some of the latter force approached the lower level of the cave along the narrow path described above and attempted to attack those inside. However, these efforts were futile for within, well supplied with food and weapons, was a force of about seventy strong and valiant men. These experienced men had been chosen by Saladin as he was about to depart and he had entrusted the stronghold to their vigilant care and to those on whose fidelity and steadfastness he had special reason to rely.

The work had now reached the point where the almost incessant blows of the hammers allowed the garrison in the cave no rest. As the strokes redoubled, the whole mass seemed to shake and tremble so that fear that a forcible entrance would be made gave way to apprehension that the whole cave, shattered by repeated blows, might suddenly collapse and crush all those inside. It was useless to hope that any aid would arrive, for Saladin had departed with all his troops to far distant parts from where he could not easily return. Finally after the siege had lasted three weeks or a little longer, they sent an embassy to the King and, through the intervention of the count of Tripoli [Raymond III, also prince of Galilee] obtained permission to depart freely to Bosra. The condition was made that they should surrender the citadel and give up the arms they had borne and all their equipment.

The cave at Tyron[48] was fortified by the Franks at some time between 1134 and 1165 and it remained intermittently in Latin hands, an outpost of the lordship of Sidon, until Julien handed it over to the Teutonic Knights in 1257. It fell to the Muslims just three years later in 1260. Like al-Habis Jaldak the fortress is half way up a sheer cliff commanding dramatic views over the main route from the Beqa' valley to Tyre and Sidon and we should probably think of it as an observation point manned in times of war. An ingenious system of canalisation brings water from a spring about a kilometre away. Access for people is by a narrow path along the face of the cliff and at one point it is necessary to go on hands and knees along a low, narrow ledge above a sheer drop of 300 m. The chambers in the rock which form the accommodation front on to a small paved terrace and the complex is provided with rock-cut grain stores and cisterns. The garrison can never have been large but the site was obviously considered to be of considerable importance: in 1182 Saladin wrote to the Caliph claiming that the Mosulis, with whom he was in dispute, were prepared to hand over al-Habis Jaldak and the Cave de Tyron to the Franks and in 1250 it is mentioned along with such important sites as Tyre, Sidon, Beaufort and Saphet in the treaty St Louis made with the Sultan as one of the strong points the Franks were able to retain.

THE CASTLES OF THE MILITARY ORDERS

As well as these royal and baronial castles, the twelfth century saw the building of the first castles of the Military Orders, the Hospitallers and the Templars. As far as we can tell from the often fragmentary remains, the twelfth-century castles of the Military Orders in the Kingdom of Jerusalem were mostly enclosure castles rather than simple towers, the use of the donjon by itself being, in the main, confined to the castles of secular lords. The exceptions to this general rule were isolated posts providing a refuge on exposed and dangerous highways, like Le Destroit by Chastel Pelerin on the coast road from Acre to Caesarea and Bait Jubr al-Tahtani on the pilgrim road from Jerusalem to Jericho. Recent archaeological work has added substantially to our understanding of the design of these castles.

It was in about 1120 that Hugh of Payens founded an Order of knights to protect pilgrims on their way to the Holy Sepulchre and the Order took the name of Templars from the position of their headquarters in Jerusalem near the Dome of the Rock which the Crusaders knew as the Templum Domini or Temple of the Lord. They soon began to construct fortifications.[49] The archives of the Order were lost after its dramatic and brutal suppression in the early fourteenth century so we have no clear dates for the foundation of most Templar castles but it was probably soon after the beginnings of the Order that they began to build enclosure fortifications to serve as local bases to defend pilgrim roads at dangerous places.

Two of these guarded approaches to Jerusalem from the coastal port of Jaffa, the usual route for pilgrims visiting the Holy City. Castrum Arnaldi, already mentioned above, was originally built in 1132–3 by the patriarch and citizens of Jerusalem, but it was later entrusted to the Templars. It lay on a spur between two valleys in fertile land where the road from Jaffa begins the ascent to Jerusalem. The ruins have never been excavated but it seems to have been a simple oblong shape, about 40 m from east to west, with one rectangular tower projecting from the west wall and, possibly, vaulted chambers in the interior.[50]

Some 8 km to the southeast, guarding the entrance to the southern route through the hills to Jerusalem (now the course of the main road) lay the Templar castle of Le Toron des Chevaliers (so called to distinguish it from the Toron in Galilee). The unimpressive ruins of the castle stand in a fine position on a low, isolated hill with a commanding view over the entrance to the valley and the well-tended orchards and gardens of the monastery of Latrun immediately to the west. It is not known who built it originally but it was in the hands of the Templars before 1187. The oldest part was a tower which was later surrounded by a rectangular enclosure, 72 × 55 m, with vaulted chambers along the insides of the walls. Outside this there was a polygonal outer court whose walls followed the line of the hills; one rectangular defensive tower survives from this.[51]

Further north, in Galilee, the Templars built the castle of La Fève near a water source on the road which led through the vale of Jezreel from Acre to Bet Shean.[52] The site of La Fève, on an ancient tell, is almost completely obscured by later building but it has been possible to reconstruct something of the plan from existing remains, old descriptions and aerial photographs. The castle, which was certainly in existence by 1172 and may have been built some time before, probably consisted of a more or less rectangular enclosure about 90 × 120 m, with vaulted chambers running along the insides of the walls. There may have been both projecting towers and an outer wall. Certainly it impressed 'Imad al-Din when his master, Saladin, conquered it in 1187.

> Al-Fula [he writes] was the best castle and the most fortified, the fullest of men and munitions and the best provided. It was for the Templars a very powerful fortress, a strong place and a reliable pillar. They had there an inaccessible fountain, an excellent pasture place, a firm base; and there they spent winter and summer. It was a place where they met and received people, a place where they guarded their horses, a place where the torrents of their men flowed, a meeting place of their brethren, the residence of their devil and the place of their crosses, where their masses assembled and their fire was kindled

and he goes on to explain how the knights had all perished and the place was surrendered by the squires and servants who abandoned all its treasures in exchange for a safe conduct. The importance of the castle to the Templars is demonstrated by events earlier in the 1180s. In 1183 more than 100 Templars gathered there to discuss a disciplinary case against one of the brothers. It served as a base for the Frankish army which headed off Saladin in September 1183. In May 1187 it served as a base for Gerard de Ridefort who led 100 Templars from La Fève and elsewhere to a disastrous defeat at the spring of Cresson, near Nazareth, a calamity which presaged the complete destruction of the Frankish army two months later at Hattin. The history of La Fève is a good example of a castle in open country at a centre of communications being used as a base for military activity.

Another Templar castle of the same period guarding a road was to be found at Maldoim on the parched and barren hills overlooking the route from Jerusalem to Jericho and the Jordan valley, a route much frequented by pilgrims. Again it is a square enclosure, about 60 × 50 m. It has a deep moat and the traces of vaults and towers in the interior but no obvious flanking towers.[53]

The Templars also built some isolated towers. The best documented of these is Le Destroit near the later castle at Chastel Pelerin which was built to protect the coastal road where it ran through a narrow defile. No less a person than King Baldwin I had been attacked and wounded there in 1103. 'A tower was formerly placed there', writes Oliver of Cologne in his account of the thirteenth-century building of the castle, 'on account of the robbers who used to lie in ambush in the narrow way for pilgrims going up to Jerusalem and coming down from it, not far from the sea. This tower was called Districtum because of the narrow road.' The rock-cut foundations of this fairly small tower still survive in a small nature reserve on the low hills overlooking the sands of Athlit and the later Templar castle.[54]

In 1178 the Templars built a large enclosure castle at Le Chastellet in an idyllic situation overlooking the upper Jordan, little more than a stream at this point, at the Ford of Jacob's Daughters. It was built on a massive scale; a Muslim commentator noted: 'The width of the wall exceeded ten cubits [about 6.5 m]; it was built of enormous slabs of stone, each of which measured seven cubits across, more or less. The number of slabs was more than 20,000, and each slab which was put in place and fixed in the structure cost not less than four dinars and perhaps more.' It is interesting to note the emphasis put on the expense of castle building here. The investment proved to be in vain. Saladin offered Baldwin IV 100,000 dinars (probably about the total cost of the work) if he would demolish it but he refused. The Muslims invested the castle in August; their sappers brought one of the towers crashing down in smoke and flames. The commander and many of the garrison perished and 700 survivors were made prisoner. It was the first time Muslim sappers had shown their effectiveness against a major Crusader fortification and it was a sign of things to come. The outlines of the walls, on a knoll by the river, can still be distinguished and the site is shortly to be excavated, which should shed interesting light on this very precisely dated structure.[55]

Despite the fragmentary nature of the evidence, it is possible to make some generalisations about the castles built by the Templars in the twelfth-century Kingdom of Jerusalem. The clearest of these is that they tended to be on roads, especially those frequented by pilgrims, rather than being centres of estates. They also seem to have favoured rectangular, enclosure-type castles, probably defended by projecting square towers and having vaulted chambers around the insides of the walls. Both Templars and Hospitallers probably used the enclosure plan because their castles were fortified cloisters and they required space for chapel, refectory and other conventual buildings which usually seem to have been constructed on the upper floors of the vaulted chambers which ran round the walls. It is these functional considerations, rather than any following of Roman or Islamic examples, which led the Orders to adopt the rectangular 'castrum' plan.

The Order of the Knights of St John, or Hospitallers, had been founded as a charitable order to look after the welfare of pilgrims in Jerusalem before the coming of the Crusaders and seems to have acquired a military role only in imitation of the Templars.[56] Nonetheless they rapidly began to acquire existing castles and construct new ones of their own. Accidents of survival and excavation have meant that we are better informed about Hospitaller castles than Templar ones. This may be in part because the Hospitallers seem to have chosen more out-of-the-way sites. The positioning of Templar castles on important roads meant that they were very vulnerable to stone robbing. The

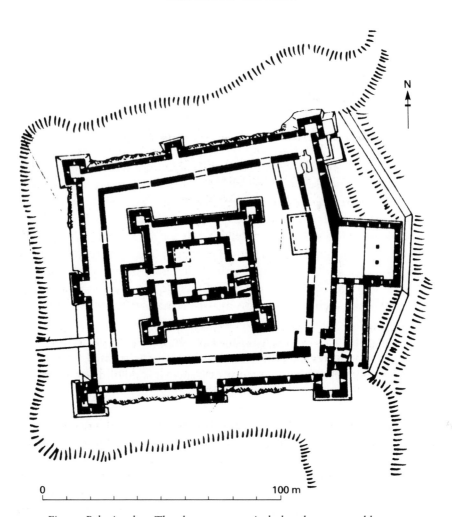

Fig. 5   Belvoir: plan. The almost symmetrical plan shows a roughly square
inner court with towers at each corner and the middle of the east side. This
stands in an outer enclosure, again with corner and half-way towers. Both
courts are surrounded by ranges of vaulted chambers, all now unroofed. Note
the postern gates, leading to the moat, in the towers of the outer walls.

Hospitallers, by contrast, seem to have built castles on their estates or in more
remote positions, which has to a limited extent protected them.

   Their first castle seems to have been Calansue, which they took over in 1128
and where they may have added a hall and other structures to the tower originally constructed by Geoffrey de Flugeac.[57] Their next fortification was the
enclosure castle at Bethgibelin granted to them in 1136 and already discussed
above. Their works soon became more elaborate. Before 1169 the Hospitallers
constructed the castle at Belmont, recently excavated by the British School of

Plate 20   Belvoir, 1168 onwards: south moat and wall of outer enclosure
looking east. Note the massive bastions at each corner with their sloping
walls. The staircase in the left tower led from the interior, through the
thickness of the tower wall, to a postern gate at the level of the bottom of the
moat. The walls of the inner bailey can be seen top left.

Archaeology in Jerusalem.[58] This castle crowned the top of a gentle hill. The
outer curtain, which apparently had no flanking towers, enclosed an area of
about 100 × 115 m. This outer wall had a gatehouse and, like some other
castles of the Military Orders, a vaulted passage running round the inside.
Inside the courtyard there was a rectangular inner bailey, again with no projecting towers. There was no donjon. It is surrounded by vaulted undercrofts
supporting the chapel and living accommodation of the knights, which no
longer survives. The castle fell to the Muslims in August 1187 and was subsequently demolished to provide materials for the Arab village which grew up
on the site.

Belmont was constructed in a haphazard and piecemeal way. Slightly later
the Hospitallers built a much more systematic and developed version of the
two enclosure castles. In 1168 they bought the castle at Belvoir in a magnificent position on a flat summit overlooking the Jordan valley, 'set amidst the
stars like an eagle's nest and abode of the moon' as Abu Shama describes it.
The site commands magnificent views north of the Lake of Tiberias and west
over the rolling hills of Galilee. The stonework, black basalt and white limestone, has been revealed, crisp and clean, by the excavators. Belvoir provides a
good example of the importance of archaeological excavation of Crusader

Plate 21   Belvoir: west gate of inner bailey looking east. Note the high quality
of the stonework and the contrast between the black basalt and the white
limestone.

castles (fig. 5).[59] Plans made before the excavations show a simple enclosure
with something that might be a keep in the centre. Like many excavated
mottes in Britain, what seemed from preliminary surveys to be a basic and
straightforward structure turned out to be much more complex and interesting. The layout is symmetrical and logical, and is clearly the product of a carefully thought-out master-plan. The outer wall, protected by a deep dry moat,
encloses a rectangle 130 × 100 m, making this one of the largest enclosure
castles (plate 20). Massive square towers rising from heavily splayed bases
protect the corners and the centres of each side. Strong stone vaults to protect
the garrison are attached to the inner side of the walls. Within this outer
enclosure, like a sort of castellar Russian doll, is an almost identical inner one,
though here intermediate towers were only considered necessary on one side.

Once again we see the vaulted chambers surrounding a small centre court (plate 21). The whole is well equipped with defensive devices, arrow slits and postern gates allowing the garrison secret access from the corner towers to the bottom of the moat, which the defenders made good use of to launch sallies during the final siege in 1188. Living accommodation must have been limited for a garrison which cannot have been much less than 500 men and may well have been more, but at least they had an Arab-style bath in the outer court in which to relax. A hall, refectory, kitchen, workshop and stables were identified by the excavators as well as a chapel over the entrance to the inner court. The water supply was contained in two rain-fed cisterns. At Belvoir we can see clearly how the inner court functioned as a monastic cloister for the knights. Belvoir is important because it shows how developed and sophisticated the enclosure castle idea had become in the hands of the Military Orders by the end of the twelfth century. At Belvoir, as at Belmont and probably La Fève and Le Toron des Chevaliers, we can see the development of the 'concentric' castle well advanced by the middle of the twelfth century.

CONCLUSION

The castles of the twelfth-century Kingdom of Jerusalem have not, in the main, left grand or imposing remains. Only Kerak and Belvoir can rank among the finest surviving Crusader castles. Of the town castles at Acre, Tyre, Sidon, Caesarea and Tiberias, where the greatest lords lived, nothing is to be found. But these humbler remains provide a fascinating example of the use of castles as instruments of settlement, colonists' castles, even homesteaders' castles, which provide interesting comparisons with the castles of Anglo-Norman England. This colonisation process was ultimately unsuccessful. Even before the cataclysmic defeat of 1187, the smaller castle owners were selling up to the institutions, the Church and above all the Military Orders. As in much of western Europe, the second half of the twelfth century saw the demise of the independent castle holder as a political force in his own right. The events of 1187 merely confirmed that these simple castles were no match for the large-scale warfare of the late twelfth and thirteenth centuries.[60]

4

TWELFTH-CENTURY CASTLES IN
THE NORTHERN STATES (COUNTY
OF TRIPOLI, PRINCIPALITY OF
ANTIOCH AND COUNTY OF EDESSA)

IN BOTH the County of Tripoli and the Principality of Antioch, there are
Crusader castles whose ruins clearly show that they were built in the
twelfth century, although the evidence for dating them is less full than in
the Kingdom of Jerusalem. The great tradition of narrative history
which begins with Fulcher of Chartres and is carried on by William of
Tyre and his continuators is firmly based in the Kingdom of Jerusalem; it does
of course deal with major events in the north but has little to say about less
dramatic matters like the foundation of castles.

A different landscape also produced different styles of castle building. Apart
from the area around the city of Tripoli itself, the northern Crusader states
had fewer areas of flat fertile land than the Kingdom of Jerusalem. Chronicles
mention Crusader castles built, mostly in the first half of the twelfth century,
in the rolling hills and steppe lands beyond the Orontes river but none of these
has left enough remains for us to form a clear idea of their plans.[1] Few pilgrims visited this part of the Crusader lands so there was less need for castles
to protect the roads. As a result, neither isolated donjons nor rectangular
enclosure plans were widely used in the northern states, except in the fertile
and well-settled areas of the County of Tripoli. On the other hand the rugged
limestone hills of the area lent themselves ideally to the construction of ridge
castles. This development was aided because, unlike the Kingdom of Jerusalem, this was already a land of castles. The Byzantines had built a number
of fortresses in the late tenth and early eleventh centuries to protect their
province of Syria, with its capital at Antioch, which they took from the
Muslims from 969 onwards. At Saone and Bourzey these Byzantine fortifications formed the nucleus of the later Crusader work. During the confused
struggles of the eleventh century, Muslim groups had also established castles

in these rugged hills (Akkar, Margat and Crac des Chevaliers were first fortified by Muslims at this time). Both the Byzantines and the Muslims tended to
build their castles on inaccessible mountain sites. Many of the Crusader
castles in Tripoli and Antioch were redevelopments of existing structures,
whereas, with very few exceptions, the castles of the Kingdom of Jerusalem
were new foundations.

The County of Tripoli was founded by Raymond of St Gilles, Count of
Toulouse. The city of Tripoli itself lay on the coast and was able to put up a
vigorous resistance to his assaults, and Raymond decided to set up a base of
operations on a ridge some 3 km from the old town and separated from it by a
belt of gardens. Here he constructed a castle[2] along the ridge, sections of
which are extant today, and the site is still called Qal'at (castle of) Sanjil (St
Gilles, the name by which Raymond was known to the Arab chroniclers). The
castle remained continuously in Frankish hands longer than any other in the
Levant, surviving the disaster which enveloped so many after the battle of
Hattin in 1187 and finally falling to the Muslims in 1289.

Tripoli is a classic example of the building of a castle for aggressive purposes, for putting both military and economic pressure on a city until it sur-
renders. William of Tyre, with his shrewd eye for practicalities, explains:

> Anxious to make use of every means to drive the adversaries of the Christian
> name out of these lands, he had built a fortress on a hill facing the city of
> Tripoli, about two miles away. Since the place was founded by pilgrims, he gave
> it a name reminiscent of that circumstance, that it might be known forever as
> the Mount of the Pilgrims. The name survives even to the present day. [The
> Latin form was Mons Peregrinus, the French Mont Pelerin, not to be confused
> with Chastel Pelerin or Athlit to the south of Haifa.] The Mount of the Pilgrims
> is well fortified both by its natural site and by the skill of those who built it.
> From it as a base, almost daily Raymond caused new trouble to the people of
> Tripoli. As the result of this constant harrying, the natives of the entire district
> and even those who dwelt in the city itself were forced to pay him an annual
> tribute and in all matters obeyed him as if he owned the city without dispute.[3]

The castle seems to have been used as a seat of government and/or prison
ever since its construction and so has been much rebuilt and repaired, but it is
possible that some of the fabric dates back to the time of Raymond himself,
who died of wounds in 1105, in the castle he had founded. The original building seems to have consisted of a rectangular donjon about 17 × 11 m, with a
single chamber on each of the two floors. There was also a bailey, and the
foundations of the curtain wall, with small buttresses but no flanking towers,
have been unearthed a few metres inside the present eastern curtain which
replaced it later in the century (plate 22). In the bailey there was a twelfth-
century church which incorporated the remains of a Fatimid shrine in its
chancel.

Plate 22   Tripoli, twelfth-century: east wall looking north. The wall along the
crest of the ridge enclosed a court and the donjon. Note the rectangular
towers, hardly projecting from the wall.

At the southern end of the County of Tripoli lay the small and very ancient
port known in antiquity as Byblos and to the Crusaders as Giblet. The
harbour and the little, stone-built town which surrounds it, with its Crusader
church still in use, remains one of the most attractive on the Levantine coast.[4]
It also boasts the best surviving example of an urban castle of the twelfth
century. It must not be forgotten that the greatest lords of the Crusader states
lived in towns, Jerusalem, Tiberias, Caesarea, Tyre, Sidon, Beirut, Tripoli and
Antioch, but that, almost without exception, the castles they resided in have
disappeared. Giblet must have been one of the most modest of these seigneurial residences but it is the only one to survive more or less intact (plate 23).

Giblet surrendered to Raymond of St Gilles on 18 February 1102 and in
1109 his son Bertrand handed the city over to the cathedral of Genoa at the
hands of (*in manibus*) William Embriaco. The Embriacos, a Genoese family,

Plate 23   Giblet (Jubayl, Byblos), twelfth-century: general view from the
west. A classic seigneurial castle of the period, with a square central donjon
surrounded by an almost square bailey with towers at each corner. Much of
the stone was taken from the ruins of ancient Byblos.

made themselves the effective lords of the city and joined the ranks of the aristocracy of Outremer. The lord was taken prisoner at the battle of Hattin in
1187 and the town surrendered to Saladin. In 1190, on the approach of the
Third Crusade, he ordered its demolition but the donjon proved too strong
and survived. The castle was returned to the Embriacos in 1197 and remained
in their hands until, poverty striken and desolate, it was taken by Bohemond
VII of Tripoli in 1282 after he had walled up the last Embriaco lords and left
them to die of starvation. It returned to Muslim hands shortly after Tripoli
itself fell in 1289.

The castle was probably constructed soon after the beginning of the
Frankish occupation (fig. 6). It was built at the most exposed angle of the city
wall, on the site of the acropolis. Antique masonry was extensively re-used,
not just shaped ashlar blocks but the columns of temples, laid transversely
through the walls to give added strength and make undermining more difficult. The stonework is one of the earliest examples of the characteristic Crusader masonry with drafted margins and bossed centres and it may be that
ancient masonry provided the inspiration for this style.

The centre piece of the castle is the great rectangular donjon (22 × 18 m),

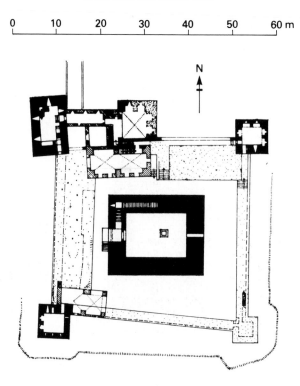

Fig. 6   Giblet: plan of ground floor. Crusader work is indicated in black. The simple rectangular donjon is surrounded by a curtain wall with corner towers. The entrance complex on the northwest incorporated a tower of the Fatimid period, itself built on classical foundations.

two stories in height, with a cistern under the floor of the lower chamber (Fig. 7).[5] Access to the donjon was by ladder to a first-floor entrance door and upwards from there by straight staircases cut in the 4 m thickness of the wall. Inside, there is a single chamber on each level, each storey being roofed with a slightly pointed stone vault. When Rey visited, enough of the wall-head defences survived to show that they were on two levels and similar to the much better preserved ones at Saone. The donjon is surrounded by a narrow court. This is defended by five projecting towers. Three of these are typical square twelfth-century work with arrow slits to provide flanking fire along the curtain (plate 24). The entrance from the town is defended by two larger oblong towers well provided with arrow slits as is the curtain wall which connects them. It is likely that this work incorporates the remains of a Fatimid tower, itself built on a Roman colonnade, which accounts for the fact that it is out of alignment with the rest of the enclosure wall.

The other baronial castles of the county of Tripoli are less impressive. At Nephin,[6] between Giblet and Tripoli, only a barren finger of land pointing

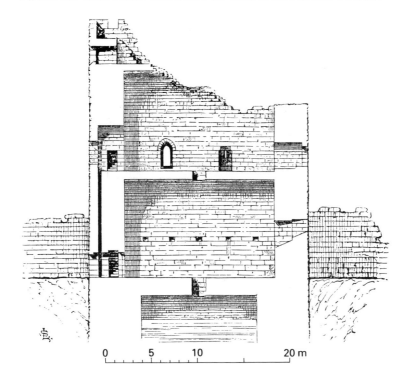

0   5   10   20 m

Fig. 7 Giblet: section of donjon. Note the single barrel-vaulted chamber at each level and the underfloor cistern. The section, drawn in 1859, shows the wall-head defences, which have now entirely disappeared: these were evidently similar to the surviving examples at Saone.

into the Mediterranean survives of the castle of the robber barons who held it in the twelfth and thirteenth centuries: Reynouard of Nephin was infamous for pillaging the refugees fleeing from Jerusalem after Saladin's conquest in 1187. Of the twelve strong towers seen by Burchard of Mount Sion when he passed in 1282 no trace now remains, and no one has found the grisly cavern where the last Embriaco lords of Giblet were walled up by their fellow Christians and left to die.

A more cheerful site is Gibelacar (Akkar),[7] set among the ravines at the northern end of the Lebanese mountains, the other side of the Homs–Tripoli gap from Crac des Chevaliers. In the first half of the twelfth century it was the seat of a baronial family, the Puylaurens. Around 1167 it was taken by Nur al-Din and held for a couple of years before being retaken by the Franks. It eventually passed by inheritance, after a short spell in Hospitaller hands, to the lord of Nephin, who was forced to surrender it to his suzerain Bohemond IV of Antioch-Tripoli. It seems to have remained in the hands of the ruling dynasty until 1271. After his successful attack on the more formidable target

Plate 24   Giblet: north wall of the bailey, looking east. Note the round ends
of antique columns laid horizontally through the walls to provide stability
against earthquakes and mining.

of Crac des Chevaliers, only 27 km away to the north, Baybars launched an
attack on Gibelacar. He had great difficulty hauling siege engines up the
wooded hills but the bombardment finally began on 2 May. Resistance was
fierce and one of the Muslim Amirs was killed while praying outside his tent,
but the outcome was inevitable, and on 11 May the garrison was allowed to
surrender and retire to Tripoli.

The castle itself runs the length of a 200 m ridge. The strongest point of the
defences is a tower 13 m square, smaller than the great donjons of Giblet or
Saone but still formidable, at the south end of the ridge, supported by a glacis
above the man-made cistern which separates the ridge from the rest of the
mountain. The rest of the fortifications hug the edge of the ridge, but in the
absence of a plan or full archaeological investigation it is difficult to date the
work precisely.

There is another twelfth-century ridge-based castle at Arima (fig. 8).[8] It lies

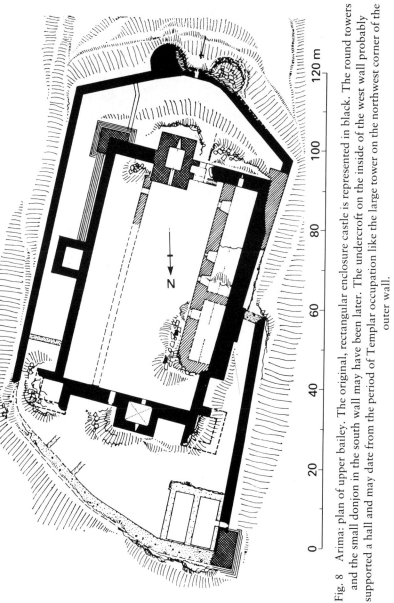

Fig. 8   Arima: plan of upper bailey. The original, rectangular enclosure castle is represented in black. The round towers and the small donjon in the south wall may have been later. The undercroft on the inside of the west wall probably supported a hall and may date from the period of Templar occupation like the large tower on the northwest corner of the outer wall.

Plate 25   Arima, twelfth-century: general view from east. The castle consisted
of three rectangular baileys, end to end along the ridge. The inner bailey, at
the right (north) end stretched as far as the rectangular tower. The southern
bailey, now much overgrown, finished at the left where the white dome of the
modern Muslim shrine can be seen.

on a steep, isolated ridge, commanding wide views on the plains of Tripoli to
the south and east and the sea beyond (plate 25). The site is now much overgrown with rough scrub and some of the walls, especially in the first bailey,
are difficult to distinguish. The castle runs the whole length of the ridge and
consists of three rectangular baileys, end to end, separated by ditches. Of
these the third, most easterly one is the strongest and best defended. There are
at least two phases of building. The first uses roughly coursed black basalt
stones which were employed to construct most of the curtain walls and some
ruinous towers, including two small round ones outside the gate of the eastern
bailey. Along the east and part of the west side of the third bailey there were
outer walls like giant hillside terraces, in the same fabric. To this fairly crude
enclosure were later added a number of strongly built, square towers in a
finely drafted limestone (plate 26). These included a new entrance tower and
gate to the second bailey and a small donjon and two corner towers in the
third. The third bailey also contains a vaulted undercroft, which presumably
carried a hall on top, in the same masonry. The defences are well constructed
though modest in scale beside twelfth-century work at Saone and Margat,
deriving much of their effectiveness from the steeply sloping ground around
the perimeter.

The castle belonged to the Counts of Tripoli and was clearly a fortress of
some importance by 1148 when it was used by Bertrand, an illegitimate
member of a rival branch of the house of St Gilles who had come out with the
Second Crusade and intended to oust Raymond II from his position as Count

Plate 26   Arima, southwest tower of inner bailey, looking west. This finely
built tower, which may date from the Templar occupation of the late twelfth
and thirteenth centuries, contrasts with the rough basalt stonework of the
original enclosure.

of Tripoli. Unhappily for him, Raymond was much more experienced in the
ways of the east and made contact with the Muslim leader Nur al-Din who
took the fortress, leading Bertrand into captivity, where he remained for the
next eleven years while his sister was taken into Nur al-Din's harem (Ibn
al-Athir unkindly remarks of him that he was like the ostrich of which it is
said 'It went into the country to look for horns and came back without its
ears').

The Muslims could not hold the castle itself, which was dismantled. It was
presumably rebuilt by 1167 when it was again taken by Nur al-Din and dismantled. Further damage was done by an earthquake in 1170 but it was
sacked again in 1171. It does not seem to have been taken by Saladin in 1188

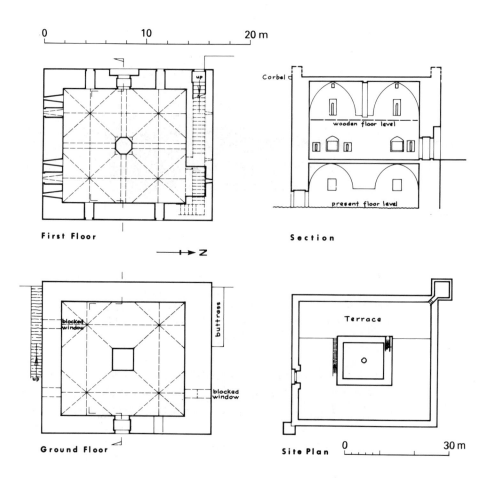

Fig. 9 Chastel Rouge (Qal'at Yahmur): plan and section. The almost square donjon is divided into two storeys, each roofed with groin vaults supported on a single, central pillar. The upper storey was divided by a wooden floor, which has now disappeared. The straight staircase between the first and second floors was contained in the thickness of the wall but there seems to have been no internal access between the ground and first floors. Compare with the donjons of figs. 2 (Red Tower), 7 (Giblet) and 14 (Saone).

Plate 27   Chastel Rouge (Qal'at Yahmur), twelfth-century: general view from southeast. The outer curtain can be seen enclosing a narrow bailey with the square donjon rising behind. The entrance arch can be seen behind the white house centre right. (Photo 1965; the castle is now surrounded by new building.)

when he contemplated attacking Crac des Chevaliers. It probably passed to the Templars in the thirteenth century and it is mentioned in a treaty between the Templars and the Muslims in 1285. It is likely that the first black basalt work dates from the early twelfth century when the castle belonged to the Counts of Tripoli. The second phase may represent strengthening by the Templars at the end of the century and it is most likely that they also built the undercroft and hall typical of the work of the Military Orders.

The County of Tripoli was small, rich and extremely exposed to attack from the east. It was originally settled by Crusader knights and their families, many of them Provençal vassals of Raymond of St Gilles. In the plains around Tripoli itself and in the low hills, which the Crusaders called the Terre de Calife, immediately to the north of the Homs–Tripoli gap, we find a pattern of settlement which seems to be similar to that in the plain of Sharon described by Pringle,[9] a number of simple castles built by knightly families in the first half of the twelfth century. In this area, however, the documentary record is much thinner and it is more difficult to identify them. These castles consisted of square donjons, sometimes surrounded by courts or ancillary buildings.

Chastel Rouge (Qal'at Yahmur)[10] is the best preserved of these (fig. 9). It stands now in the centre of a village in the plains to the northeast of Tripoli. It

Plate 28   Chastel Rouge: interior vault of keep, showing centre pier (bottom)
with groin vaults and transverse rib. Note the high quality of the building
work in this fairly modest castle.

has no natural defences. A substantial keep (16 × 14 m), low and massive in
the Crusader manner, is surrounded by a square enclosure (plate 27). There
are low stone buildings along three sides of this small bailey and access to the
donjon is gained by an outside stair to the roof of one of these buildings and
thence to the first-floor entrance. The interior at this level is impressively spacious, with groin vaults in each of the four quarters supported on a central
octagonal column (plate 28). The space was not always so grand, however,
and corbels and fenestration show that there was a wooden floor just below
the springing of the vaults. Spiral staircases were virtually unknown in
Crusader military architecture and here, as elsewhere, the floors were linked
by straight external and internal staircases. The masonry is in smooth finely
jointed ashlar and the vaults are especially impressive: the whole structure
gives an impression of prosperity and quiet determination.

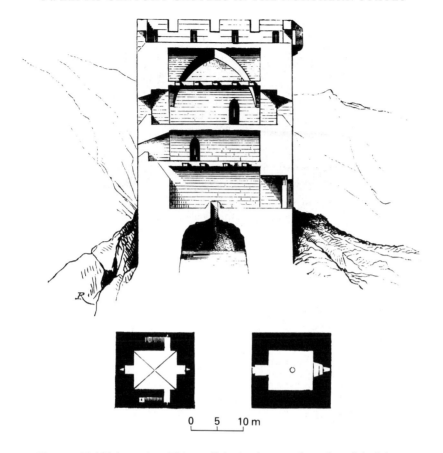

0   5   10 m

Fig. 10   Tukhlah: section. This small donjon has now been demolished down
to the foundations but it seems to have been one of a number of small
tower-houses in the County of Tripoli of which Burj al-Arab is the best
surviving example. Note the barrel vault in the lower half and the groin vault
above, each vaulted storey being divided by a wooden floor. There was a
box-machicolation over the door and a cistern beneath the ground floor.

Chastel Rouge seems to have been built early in the twelfth century and
belonged to the Montolieu family until 1177–8 when Raymond III handed it
over to the Hospitallers and the family received 400 bezants as compensation.
It has obvious similarities with the donjons built on the plains around Caesarea in the Kingdom of Jerusalem and in both cases they reflect the pattern of
settlement by small, lay fief holders in the first half-century of the Latin occupation.

There were a number of smaller keeps in the hills of the Terre de Calife
which probably also belonged to Provençal knights, though their Frankish
names and identities are lost. Rey, followed by Deschamps,[11] has described
them as isolated watchtowers, to keep an eye on the Assassins to the north

Plate 29 Burj al-Arab, twelfth-century: general view from southwest. The
tower was surrounded by a bailey (from whose wall the photograph is taken).
Note one surviving corbel for a machicolation above the window. The black
basalt masonry may represent repairs after earthquake damage.

and other marauders, but this seems unlikely. The landscape in this area is
typically Mediterranean: olive trees cover the limestone hills and vines shade
the courtyards of the village houses. This prosperous and benign landscape
would certainly have encouraged settlers and these towers are the simple
castles in which the newly arrived lords established themselves. Rey published
a drawing of the tower at Tukhlah (which he and Deschamps call Toklé
fig. 10). It is a trim, square tower, 14 × 13.5 m (only slightly smaller than
Chastel Rouge). There was a cistern under the floor of the cellar and access to
the other floors was gained by a ladder to a first-floor door. There were two
vaulted stories divided by wooden floors and the roof terrace was surrounded
by battlements. Tukhlah stood in the middle of a village on a small hill but

Plate 30 Burj al-Arab from east. The two-storey tower had a barrel vault on the ground floor and a groin vault above. Note the massive thickness of the vaults and the typical Crusader walls with cut stone on internal and external faces and a rubble filling. Compare with the surviving wall at Red Tower in the Kingdom of Jerusalem (plate 7).

would have been very badly placed as a watchtower since it is overlooked by a much higher hill about half a kilometre to the east. Unfortunately, on a recent visit I found the tower had been demolished down to a few feet in height, but enough remained to show that is had been a substantial structure and was surrounded by outbuildings, including a vaulted chamber containing a large and ancient stone olive press.

More remains of the small castle at Burj al-Arab, about 16 km away to the south of Safita, where one side of the tower still stands to its full height (plate 29). The lower sections are constructed in a squared limestone but the upper part seems to have been rebuilt in a less well-cut basalt. In the interior there was a ground floor covered by a thick and heavy barrel vault (plate 30). Above this there was a chamber with a groin vault and in this again there is evidence that the original fine limestone structure was either completed or rebuilt in much poorer quality basalt. There is a single, large south-facing window and over it, at the wall head, a projecting corbel which must have carried a simple machicolation, and the interior vaulting can be easily seen. It is most probable that the original limestone keep, which is certainly Crusader, was rebuilt possibly after earthquake damage, along the original plan but with a cruder technique. The tower is surrounded by a square bailey, like the one at Chastel Rouge but smaller, with the remains of single-storey structures around it. Similar towers have been noted in the foothills of northern Lebanon and no doubt there were more which have disappeared without trace.

Quite different in design is the castle of Coliath in the fertile plain north of Tripoli town, given by Count Pons of Tripoli to the Hospitallers in 1127.[12] This is a typical enclosure-plan castle of the sort favoured by the Military Orders: indeed until the excavations at Belvoir, it was the classic example (fig. 11). It is much smaller than Belvoir (63 × 56 m). There is no donjon but it is defended by towers at each corner, one substantially taller than the others, and bastions in the middle of each side except the main entrance which lies between the two small turrets. We know little of its history, save that it was sacked by Al-Malik al-Adil in 1207–8 when he was campaigning against Tripoli and was still in ruins when Wilbrand of Oldenburg passed in 1212. It was finally taken by Baybars in 1266. It looks as if this modest fortification was developed when the Hospitallers first acquired it but was subsequently neglected in favour of Crac des Chevaliers. As such it is a good example of the earliest phase of the castle building of the Military Orders.

The Principality of Antioch also boasted important baronial castles of the twelfth century but we know even less of the residence of the princes of Antioch than of the Counts of Tripoli and there are no surviving buildings which can be attributed to the ruling family who seem not to have possessed any fortifications outside their capital. The citadel at Antioch itself always seems to have been a surprisingly modest affair.[13] Built on the precipitous crest of Mount Silpius, overlooking the city far below, it stood at the apex of the town walls. It had originally been constructed by the Byzantines after their conquest in 969, but some of the walls, which only survive to a few feet above ground level, can be attributed to the Crusaders.

The most powerful baronial family in the principality were the Mazoirs.[14] Renaud I Mazoir was constable of Antioch and effectively governed the principality from 1131 to 1134 after the premature death of Bohemond II. His son Renaud II (d. 1185–6) married Agnes, daughter of Count Pons of Tripoli whose mother Cecily was the sister of Louis VI of France: the Mazoirs were connected with the highest ranks of the Frankish aristocracy. From 1117–18 onwards they began to build up an extensive domain in the mountains between the coast and the Orontes in the south of the principality, including some castles like Qadmus and Bikisrail later occupied by the Ismailis. By

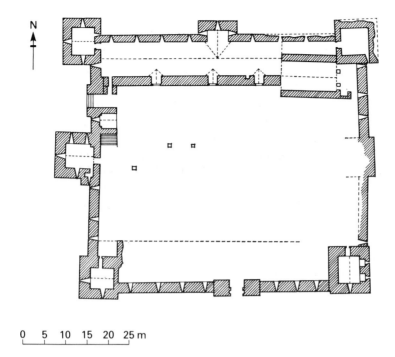

0 5 10 15 20 25 m

Fig. 11   Coliath: plan. A small enclosure castle with square towers at each corner and in the middle of two sides. A vaulted undercroft survives along the north wall.

1140 they had made their centre at the castle of Margat, on the summit of a steep hill commanding wide views over the coast and the Mediterranean sea. Of their work only a few rectangular towers and a length of curtain wall seem to have survived the great Hospitaller rebuilding of the early thirteenth century but they probably fortified the whole of the triangular plateau on which the castle and its dependent town stood. Despite their extensive landed properties, the Mazoirs came under increasing financial pressure. On 1 February 1186, after his father's death, Bertrand Mazoir sold his vast possessions to the Knights Hospitaller: like some great twentieth-century country house sale, everything was disposed of except for a small castle on the coast, the Mazoirs to receive an annual pension of 2,200 bezants to be paid in Tripoli where they were presumably now living. The whole affair shows clearly how even the greatest baronial family in one of the securest areas was unable to sustain the burdens of managing its great estates and was obliged to sell out to institutional buyers.

The most remote of the surviving castles of the principality is Bourzey, which Cahen has plausibly identified with the Frankish Rochefort.[15] The normally sober Deschamps describes it as 'built very high on a rocky spur, it

Plate 31 Bourzey (probably Rochefort), twelfth-century: general view from southwest. The bold square towers on the right enclose the lower bailey. The large tower, centre left, stands at the end of the dividing wall between lower and upper baileys. At the extreme left is the donjon/entrance tower. It was up this rugged slope, the easiest access to the castle, that Saladin launched his attack in August 1188.

Plate 32 Bourzey: southern wall looking east. In the centre middle distance is the east tower, overlooking the Orontes valley. The valley, now cultivated, was mostly swampy in the Middle Ages.

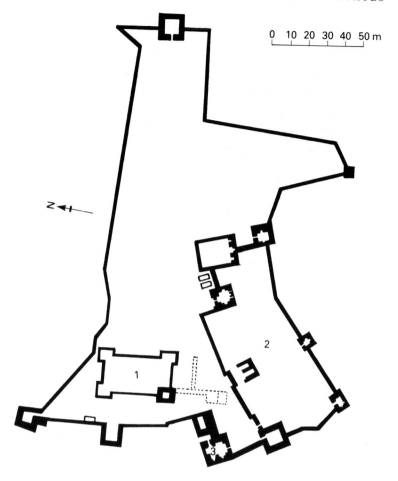

Fig. 12 Bourzey: plan. The original rectangular Byzantine citadel was surrounded by a Crusader curtain wall, following the contours of the top of the cliff and fortified by square towers. Unfortunately the plan does not show the contours and the site is in need of a full survey. 1. Byzantine citadel; 2. lower bailey; 3. entrance donjon.

looks like the prow of a fantastic ship poised to attack the clouds'. It stands on an isolated crag on the inland edge of the mountains where they border on the rift valley of the Orontes (plate 31). To the east of the castle lies the flat river plain, now intensively cultivated, but until recently an unhealthy marsh (plate 32). To the west the steep, forested slopes of the mountains tower above it, making direct communication with the west almost impossible. The only nearby Frankish outpost was the now vanished castle above Jisr al-Shughur to the north and it must have seemed a very cut-off and lonely outpost.

To north and south, the hill on which the castle stands is separated from

Plate 33   Bourzey: north side of tower 3 looking west. Note the arrow slit
and the roughly squared and coursed masonry.

the mountains by rocky gorges, while to the west there is a small enclosed
plain, now occupied only by a deserted village of unknown date and the traces
of fields and orchards, a totally silent, secluded, numinous spot on a hot
Syrian afternoon. The isolated outcrop had been taken by the Byzantines in
975 when the Emperor John Tsimisces referred to it as the 'celebrated
Bourzo'. Ibn Shaddad, describing Saladin's assault, calls it 'Burzayh, an
extremely strong and almost inaccessible castle. It was constructed on the
summit of a mountain and in all the lands occupied by the Franks one said
proverbially "as strong as Burzayh".'

   On the flattened summit was the Byzantine redoubt, not dissimilar from the
one at Saone but now almost completely ruined (fig. 12). Around this the
Franks constructed an enceinte following the edge of the summit plateau, with
a small lower bailey on the south. The walls are strengthened with rectangular

Plate 34   Bourzey: interior of upper floor of donjon/entrance tower showing
crudely built arches and springings for groin vault.

towers in a typically twelfth-century style, especially on the western side
which offered the only possible access. The building is crude and vigorous
(plate 33), a sort of poor man's Saone, with roughly squared limestone blocks
and little attempt at architectural finesse apart from the simple relieving
arches over the massive stone lintels of the doors. The towers were roofed
with simple groin vaults (plate 34). The main and only way in lay in the re-
entrant angle behind the largest of the towers. We do not know who built the
castle but the Arab sources provide some details about its conquest by Saladin
in 1188. Deschamps has used these sources to produce an account which is
worth quoting in full,

> Saladin, who had sent his son on the 17 August to take Sarmaniya, 7 km to the
> north of Bourzey, arrived there on 20 August. On the 21st he went round it to
> find the best place to attack. He discovered that assault was impossible on the
> north and south and difficult on the east. On the west it was possible to shoot
> arrows and set the siege engines to work. This was done but it was realised that
> the missiles hardly reached their target and were ineffective; 'I saw from the top
> of the mountain', wrote Ibn al-Athir, 'a woman who was hurling missiles from
> the citadel with the aid of a *manjaniq* [trebuchet]. It was she who made all our
> efforts useless'. The bombardment lasted all the Sunday and the following night.
> On Monday it continued without achieving any results. When Saladin saw that
> his machines were useless, he ordered an assault. He divided his army into three

sections which were to advance in successive waves. He took command of one of these with his son Taqi'al-Din. However the Muslims only advanced with great difficulty as the ascent was full of obstacles and the Franks attacked them with boulders which they rolled down the slopes. The garrison were few in number and, despite a heroic resistance, they were obliged to surrender. The lord of the place was there with his wife who was the sister of Sybille, third wife of the Prince of Antioch, Bohemond III. Sybille used to betray the Franks to Saladin to whom she passed on their secrets. The Sultan sent this sister of hers, her husband and all her family, seventeen people in all, to Antioch.

In western Europe, bishops often had castles at some distance from their cathedrals (the bishop of Winchester's castle at Farnham and the bishop of Salisbury's at Sherborne are typical twelfth-century English examples). The impoverished bishops of the Crusader states were seldom able to enjoy such an expansive life-style but an exception were the patriarchs of Antioch. The patriarchs were very important figures in the life of the principality, especially Aimery of Limoges (1135–93); twice he was responsible for saving the city from the Muslims, once in 1149 after the death of Raymond of Poitiers and again in 1164 when Bohemond III was captured after the defeat at Harim. After 1155 he acquired the castle at Cursat[16] about 10 km to the south of the city as a refuge and a place to store his treasures. He was soon to need it. In 1165 Bohemond, seeking Byzantine support for his endangered principality, allowed a Greek patriarch into the city and Aimery retreated to his fortress. The Greek was killed in an earthquake in 1170 and Bohemond came to Cursat to lead Aimery back in triumph to the city. Conflict flared up again when the redoubtable patriarch excommunicated the prince for his sexual immorality and it was possession of his castle which enabled the patriarch to maintain his stand. Cursat remained the residence of the patriarchs throughout the Frankish period and it only fell to the Muslims in 1275, seven years after Antioch itself.

Like so many castles in the area, Cursat was built on a natural plateau surrounded by steep valleys, except in the southwest where it joined the neighbouring hill. In true Crusader fashion this flank was protected by a deep artificial ditch and it was here that the defence was concentrated. The most striking feature of the defences are the two great round towers built in 1256 when the Pope ordered that all the ecclesiastical tithes of the patriarchate of Antioch for three years should be devoted to the strengthening of the fortifications. Twelfth-century work can still be found in the rest of the fortress, notably in the curtain wall and the rectangular tower to the north with its bossed and margined stone.

The greatest of all the twelfth-century castles in the principality, and one of the most impressive in the entire corpus of Crusader building in this period, is the castle at Saone (the traditional Arabic name is Sahyun but since this is the Arabic equivalent of Zion, it has now been given the more politically correct title of Qal'at Salah al-Din/Saladin's Castle).[17] The site was not a new one and seems to have been fortified from Hamdanid times (mid-tenth century), if not before. In 975 it was taken by the Byzantine Emperor John Tsimisces at the same time as Bourzey, over the mountains to the east. The Byzantines seem to have held it until it was taken by the Franks, perhaps in 1108 when they took nearby Lattakia from the Greeks. The Frankish lords of Saone were among the greatest barons of the principality of Antioch, second only to the Mazoirs of Margat holding Balatanos to the south and, until its final fall to the Muslims in 1134, Sardana beyond the Orontes. The first of the lords appears in 1108 as Robert son of Fulk. Also known as Robert the Leprous he was an important military commander and maintained good personal relations with the Atabeg Tughtagin of Damascus. This did not save him, however, when in 1119 he was captured trying to relieve his town of Sardana. When he was brought before Tughtagin, he refused to renounce his faith and was executed, his erstwhile friend using his skull, inlaid with jewels, as a drinking cup. His successors are much less well known but the castle remained in the family until it was captured by Saladin from Matthew de Saone in 1188.

It was probably Robert or his son William (d. 1132) who built the castle at Saone around the Byzantine redoubt. It lies on a spur site no less than 700 m long. Unlike other great castles such as Crac des Chevaliers and Margat, Saone does not command the surrounding country; indeed it is hidden away and the traveller is almost surprised in turning the last corner to see it stretched out along its ridge between two steep gorges, both now heavily wooded with aromatic pines (plate 35). The Byzantines had fortified the spur by building walls across the ridge to defend it from the east where it joined the surrounding plateau and by building a castle, an irregular court enclosed by strong walls and flanking towers, all distinguished by their masonry work, small irregular blocks 'drowned', as Deschamps says, in plentiful mortar. On the western end of the spur lay a castletown. This village had at least two small churches and was surrounded by a modest wall.

The Crusader lords set about strengthening the already considerable defences (fig. 13). Where the spur connects with the mass of the mountain the Crusaders dug a great ditch. Robin Fedden describes it thus:

a vast rock hewn channel, like a deep wound, isolates the castle from the body of the mountain ridge. This immense channel, nearly 450 feet long and over 60 wide, is one of the most impressive memorials the Latins left in the Holy Land. Its walls, the haunt of black and scarlet rock-creeper, rise sheer for 90 feet and the battlements tower above. No drawbridge could span such a channel in a single sweep, and the Crusaders therefore left a needle of solid stone to carry their bridge across. It stands like an obelisk and recalls those works of the Nile with which this labour of carving some hundred and seventy thousand tons of solid rock alone seems comparable.

Plate 35   Saone (Sahyun Qal'at Salah al-Din), twelfth-century and earlier:
general view from east. The great rock-cut ditch lies between the hill in the
foreground and the curtain wall. The donjon can be seen centre right, with
the two round towers to the left. The Byzantine citadel is at the high point of
the ridge.

The Crusaders left the Byzantine redoubt but strengthened and extended the walls along the edges of the spur, building great square towers to guard the flanks and the gateways. They also strengthened the walls of the lower, castletown end of the spur with rectangular towers at the entrances. This lower enclosure is separated from the castle proper by a steep slope leading up to a wall, strengthened by square towers and a rock-cut ditch. This ditch, which was never completed, was on a much smaller scale than the mighty trench at the east end and proved to be the Achilles heel of the whole defensive system when it was put to the test in 1188.

The main defensive work was reserved for the eastern end overlooking the great fosse, which presumably also served as a quarry. Here they built the finest of the donjons constructed in the twelfth century (24.5 m square), perched on the very edge of the sheer drop down into the ditch so that the masonry of the tower seems like a direct continuation upwards of the natural rock (fig. 14). The donjon is flanked by a curtain wall, clinging to the edge with, at its southern end, two round towers which grow from semi-circular projections in the walls of the cliff (plate 36). These towers are hollow and provided with arrow slits from which to cover the ditch and the plateau on the other side. To the north of the donjon there is a simple postern gate, flanked by a pair of rounded towers which are little more than bumps in the wall. This led onto a vertiginous wooden bridge across the ditch. On all this front the Crusader work is distinguished by the use of large rectangular

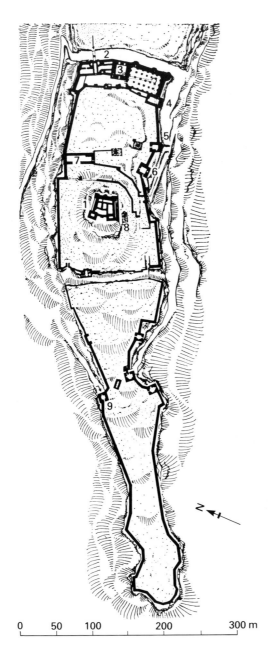

Fig. 13 Saone: plan. The narrow castle runs along the summit of the ridge. Three main sections can be seen, the Byzantine keep, the main Crusader fortifications to the east with the great ditch and the lower castletown to the west, separated from the rest of the fortress by a shallower ditch. 1. Byzantine citadel; 2. great trench; 3. donjon; 4,5,6 large Crusader towers; 7. Cistern; 8. Crusader chapel; 9 gate-tower of lower enclosure.

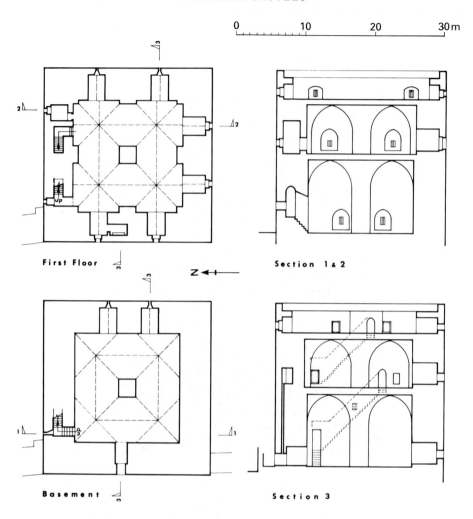

Fig. 14 Saone, section and plan of donjon.

Plate 36 Saone: round tower on eastern curtain. The tower is an extension
of the artificial cliff at the edge of the ditch. As the arrow slit shows, the
tower has an interior chamber. It is one of very few round towers built by the
Crusaders in the twelfth century.

blocks, laid in regular courses with bossed centres and drafted margins (plate
37). At various places, notably in the wall to the north of the donjon, we can
see where repairs were made by the Muslim occupants after the bombardment of 1188.

The donjon at Saone has two vaulted stories with one main chamber on
each level and a central pillar to sustain the stone vaults (plates 38 and 39).
The lower storey is high and dark and the top of the central pillar, made of
large, roughly hewn blocks, is almost lost in the gloom, like a column in some
Piranesi etching. There are straight stairs in the thickness of the wall leading
to the lighter upper chamber and thence to a roof terrace which still survives
almost intact with battlements on the wall head. The donjon was built as a

Plate 37   Saone: tower on south wall from southeast. Note the superb quality
of the stonework with fine rectangular blocks with lowered margins, and the
crenellations, one of the few surviving examples of twelfth-century Crusader
wall-head defences.

self-contained fortress and there is no link between it and the top of the
curtain wall. We know it was used as a place of last resort: in the siege of 1188
when the lower bailey and then the inner bailey had fallen the surviving
defenders, almost all wounded, retreated to the donjon and bargained for
terms. These were granted and, on paying 10 dinars per man, 6 per woman
and 2 per child, they were allowed to leave for Antioch.

Along the north side of the main fortress, the cliffs are so precipitous that
no major fortifications were necessary. The southern flank, however, slopes
more gently and was more vulnerable. The Crusaders strengthened the
defences here by the addition of three large square towers (plate 40), projecting slightly from the curtain, built with the same fine masonry work as the

Plate 38   Saone: donjon from southwest, with tower 4 on right hand. Note
the windows on the walls of the donjon overlooking the court and the
contrast between the massive Crusader masonry and the much smaller blocks
of the superseded Byzantine curtain wall in the foreground.

east front. At their bases the slope was carefully cut away to make a sheer
cliff. The towers do not communicate with the curtain wall walk and seem
designed as individual units. In one of these towers (4) there was a small
postern gate from which one could descend by ladder or rope, while tower 6
contained the main entrance to the fortress, a small door in the flank of the
tower leading into a closed chamber with no access to the upper storeys. It
was necessary to make a 90 degree turn to the left to end the main court. The
outer door is small (it seems likely that horses were normally stabled in the
great trench where there are traces of mangers and troughs, though no doubt
they could be brought into the castle in times of war) and defended by a
simple slot machicolation.

These three secondary towers have some interesting features. They are not
much smaller than the donjon and no less well built. They project much

Plate 39   Saone: interior of first-floor chamber of donjon. The massive groin
vaults are supported by a square central pillar.

further into the interior of the castle than they do outside the walls, and on the
upper floors they have large rectangular windows to light gracious vaulted
apartments within. Possibly connected with this is the apparent absence of
any hall or communal living space. It seems that we should think of these
towers as being residential as well as defensive, providing spacious apartments
for a number of different households, somewhat like some late medieval
English castles (Bolton is perhaps the classic example) and we have already
seen that there were women and children among the defenders who were
allowed to ransom themselves in 1188. In this way the secular castle, with its
individual residential towers, was very different from the castles of the military orders with their halls, chapels and chapter-houses.

There are only three important pieces of Frankish work surviving in the
interior of the court. One of these is a great cistern built into the ground with
fine masonry walls and roofed in a graceful pointed barrel vault which makes
it look more like an early Cistercian church than a water storage facility: very
striking. Another feature is a large stone hall, inserted between the donjon and
the west wall. Apparently a later addition, this has a low stone vault supported by numerous, massive, squat pillars and is almost unlit (plate 41); it
was certainly not designed as the great hall of the castle. It may have been
used for both residential purposes and stabling but its main function was
undoubtedly to provide shelter from incoming missiles for those resting or

Plate 40   Saone: south curtain looking west from tower 4. Note that the
tower projects further into the bailey than it does beyond the curtain wall,
that it has a large window on the upper floor and that there is no direct
communication between the tower and the curtain. The Frankish work at
Soane is almost a group of independent tower houses sharing a common court.

non-combatant and it has direct parallels at Crac des Chevaliers and Beaufort.
Finally the Crusaders built a simple chapel, with a single nave and a rounded
apse, beside the Byzantine citadel.

They also made additions to the defences of the castletown enclosure. Here
there were entrances on the north and the south, where access can be gained
up a narrow path. The Franks fortified both these entrances, on the north
with a single square tower (9) with a slot machicolation over the door, on the
south with three square towers, the central one defending a bent entrance
somewhat similar to the one into the castle.

Saone gives a clear indication of the appearance of wall-head defences as
they existed in the twelfth century (plate 42). These are on two levels. On the
roof-terrace level there are arrow slits in the walls while above that, reached
by a short stair, there is a wall walk which gives access to crenellations with

Plate 41   Saone: vaulted shelter at southeast corner looking east. The shelter was constructed later than the towers around it to provide storage and shelter from missiles.

Plate 42   Saone: wall-head defences on tower at 4, looking south. Perhaps the most complete surviving example of Crusader wall-head defences, this shows a two-tier system with arched openings at roof level surmounted by a wall walk with crenellations: note the arrow slits in the merlons.

arrow slits in the merlons. Only in a few places (the postern by the great trench and on towers 4 and 9) are three corbels which could have supported either stone machicolations or simple wooden hoarding. In fact, while some provision is made for flanking fire from within the towers, the wall-head defences remain very simple.

The architectural features of the castle pose some interesting problems. The Byzantine fortifications used a variety of tower shapes and masonry techniques. The east wall of their fortress, subsequently overbuilt by the Frankish work, used round towers (unless, of course, this is an early phase of Frankish work). Such round towers also appear, in Crusader masonry, on the east front, as we have seen. However they are effectively unknown from other Crusader castles of the pre-Hattin period. Are all the round towers Byzantine work, or at least on Byzantine foundations? A further problem relates to the three towers on the south side of the village enclosure. In general design these rectangular towers are typical of twelfth-century Crusader work, including the straight stairs and the clearly Crusader wall-head defences, yet they are constructed in a smooth, but not regular, ashlar masonry, which is not the same as either the Byzantine or the Crusader work on the main fortress. Furthermore, in the interior of one of them, there is an arch built with the thin bricks typical of Byzantine work. These features led Deschamps to suggest that the three towers of the castletown enclosure and at least the foundations of the round towers on the east wall (and therefore the edge of the great ditch) were Byzantine work. But this need not necessarily be so. It is probable that the Crusader occupation was quite peaceful and that the inhabitants of the village, Greeks and possibly Armenians, continued to live there under new masters. It is also likely that the Franks used some locally recruited labour. In these circumstances, it is only natural to see Byzantine or Armenian characteristics in work of the Crusader period.

As so often, we have the fullest literary descriptions of the castle when it was besieged. In this case Arab historians give us a number of accounts of the fall of Saone which have been carefully analysed by G. Saadé.[18] Saladin's assault began on 27 July 1188, when he and his son al-Malik al-Zahir arrived with their forces; Saladin camped and set up his siege engines on the plateau opposite the east front while his son established himself across the valley from the weakly defended north side of the lower enclosure. The bombardment began; some of the stone balls used, weighing between 50 and 300 kg, can still be seen on the site. The bombardment lasted all the next day and much of the fabric was damaged. On Friday, 29 July, Saladin gave an order for a general attack. Zahir's men stormed the castletown (*rabad*), where the inhabitants fled to the castle, leaving their meals uneaten. The Muslims continued their advance and it was then that they made use of the point by the north wall where the ditch separating castle and village had not been completed. They soon stormed the walls and found themselves in the courtyard of the castle itself, where they seized beasts and other supplies. The garrison had by now retired to the donjon. By the end of the day they had been allowed to ransom themselves and been granted safe-conduct. It had taken just three days. The castle was strong and well provisioned but the garrison was probably inadequate and they seem to have lacked siege engines of their own or any other means of retaliating actively against their assailants.

Like Kerak, Saone played an important role under Muslim rule. Saladin entrusted Saone and Bourzey to one of his amirs, Mankawar, who held it as a fief in 1229. He was succeeded by his son and grandson until the castle was handed over to Sultan Baybars in 1272 by his great-grandsons who took up posts in the Mamluke administration (an interesting example of Mamluke centralism replacing Ayyubid 'feudalism'). Still later, in the 1280s, a Mamluke amir, Sunqur, made Sahyun the centre of a small semi-independent emirate until it was finally taken by Qala'un's commander in Syria in 1287 and incorporated in the province of Tripoli. The Muslim rulers repaired the walls and added some more luxurious residential accommodation in the court of the castle, including a mosque and some fine baths, but otherwise made few major alterations.

Nor was the castle completely unknown to the Franks; in 1225 a Venetian ambassador, Foscarini, was received at Saone and signed a commercial treaty with the amir. But there are also more gloomy associations. About 5 m above the bottom of the great trench, excavated into the rock, there is a prison, a windowless cavern whose roof is supported by a single pillar. Among the unfortunates confined here was Pierre de Queivilliers. We know of him because a letter, dated to May 1227, has survived from his son to the Hospitallers, who had been negotiating for his release, telling them that he had died in captivity. It may well have been in this dismal, sunless hole that Pierre passed his last days, dreaming no doubt of the open meadows and broad, slow rivers of his native Picardy, and it may even have been he who carved the crude cross which can still be seen on one of the walls.[19]

The Crusaders occupied the County of Edessa between 1097 and 1144 when the city fell to Zengi. They are known to have built and repaired castles in the area but there is no construction that can reliably be assigned to the Crusader period.[20] The citadel at Edessa itself has been frequently modified from antiquity onwards and while there are some features, like rock-cut ditches and bossed masonry, which have parallels in Crusader work elsewhere, there is no evidence to substantiate this. The castle at Tell-Bashir, the second most important in the country and home of the Courtney family, is no more than a few stones on the summit of a giant tell.

There is, however, one castle in the northern fringes of the states which seems to have an interesting and very early Crusader provenance. This is at the castle at Anavarza in Cilicia, already noted for its fine Armenian round towers. In the narrow waist of this large fortified plateau, there are the substantial remains of a large square donjon, built in the squared, bossed masonry which is characteristic of much Crusader building further south. The donjon is separated from the rest of the castle by rock-cut ditches. The surviving chambers of the interior show fine groin vaulting. These, and other factors, have led Edwards[21] to assign this building to the brief Frankish occupation during and immediately after the First Crusade (1098–1110). If this is correct, it is, as he notes, 'perhaps the first known example of Crusader military construction in the Levant'. It is interesting in being a square donjon placed in an existing enceinte and showing at this early stage typically Crusader techniques of vaulting.

The Crusader building in the northern Syrian hills is astonishing both in quantity and quality. Apart from Antioch itself, the area between the Orontes and the sea had never been very rich or prosperous; even in antiquity its cities were modest compared with those in other parts of Syria and Palestine. Only in the two centuries of Crusader rule did this area produce architecture of world class, and the steep slopes and narrow valleys must have rung almost unceasingly to the sound of masons' hammers.

5

SIEGE WARFARE IN THE CRUSADER LANDS

MOST Crusader castles were designed to resist armed attack by large forces for a considerable length of time. The builders who constructed them were keenly aware of the weapons available to the assailants and tried to devise ways of countering them. The development of castle architecture must be seen as the result of a continuing dialectic between attack and defence which gave the advantage sometimes to one, sometimes to the other. Only by examining techniques of attack can we come to a real understanding of the architecture of defence.

The most basic way of taking a castle was by blockade and starvation of the defenders; simply by surrounding the place and preventing anyone getting in and out famine would complete the task at minimum risk to the attacking army. In practice, forcing surrender in this way was usually impractical and it could only be achieved in special circumstances. The problems for the attacking army were numerous. To begin with, it was not only the defenders who had to eat; the besieging army had to be supplied and this often caused major problems. When the Crusaders blockaded Muslim-held Antioch through the grim winter of 1097–8, their forces suffered terribly from hunger and they were forced to send off foraging parties further and further into the already ravaged countryside; even so, famine among them almost caused the collapse of the whole project. The defenders, by contrast, seem to have been comparatively well provided for and it was treachery, not starvation, which finally led to the fall of the city. Lack of water was a very severe problem for the Crusaders during the siege of Jerusalem in the summer of 1099 but the defenders of the city seem to have had no such problems.[1]

The anonymous author of the treatise on the construction of the castle at Saphet puts the position clearly: 'It [the castle] cannot be besieged without a very large army but such an army would not have supplies for long since it would find neither food nor water, nor can such a very great number be near at the same time and, if they are scattered in remote places, they cannot help one another.'[2]

Castles were often very well provided with food. Margat held supplies for a five-year siege. When Kerak was besieged by Saladin, it is said to have had plenty of food but to have been short of arms. When the Muslims occupied Gastun (Baghras) in 1269 after the garrison had fled, they 'found no-one in it except for one old woman but the place was discovered to be full of grain, provisions and everything else which is stored in such forts'.[3] Large castles were equipped to prepare large amounts of raw grain; at Crac des Chevaliers there were ovens, huge oil jars and a windmill on one of the towers. Two massive ovens survive in the vaults at Margat. At Saphet 12,000 mule loads of barley and corn were consumed each year and there were windmills, ovens and twelve watermills outside the castle. In most cases, starving these castles out was a forlorn hope.

They were equally well supplied with water. There were three ways of providing this. The first was to dig wells to fresh water. At Montreal a steep passage leads far down in the rock on which the castles stand to a spring-fed well. During the rebuilding of Saphet, water supply proved very difficult until an old, spring-fed well was discovered and opened up. There were three wells of fresh water at Chastel Pelerin and one very deep well was unearthed at Crac during restoration work. No doubt other castles had wells which are yet to be discovered.

Covered cisterns were a common way of providing a water supply. Often these were under the main block or donjon of the castle, as at Giblet or Chastel Blanc where they were under the main keep. On a more modest scale, the hall-house at Calansue and the keep at Caco both had underfloor cisterns, the one at Caco being filled by water collected on the roof and led down through an earthenware pipe in the thickness of the wall.[4] The small keep at Tukhlah in the County of Tripoli was similarly equipped.[5] At Crac des Chevaliers there are no less than nine cisterns, again filled by water collected on the flat roofs. At Saone there are two magnificent cisterns with vaulted roofs, the one in the courtyard being 36 m long and covered with a plain pointed tunnel vault in smooth ashlar masonry which makes it look at first glance more like a church than a public utility.

The third way of keeping water was in an outside cistern known as a berquilla (from the Arabic *birkah*), a great tank open to the sky. Such open cisterns would probably be less suitable for drinking water as dust would blow in and algae grow more easily than in the covered ones. They often formed an integral part of the defences since sappers would find that digging a tunnel underneath a cistern full of water added another hazard to an already perilous operation. At Kerak, Beaufort, Gibelacar and Margat they were placed on the narrow ridge which formed the most vulnerable aspect of the castle. At Crac des Chevaliers the berquilla lay between the outer and inner walls but this was an unusual arrangement. Sometimes, as at Crac and Gastun, they were filled by aqueducts but more usually water was channelled into them from the nearby hills and the terraces of the castle. The systems were ingenious and successful: surprisingly, given the arid nature of much of the area occupied by the Crusaders, there does not seem to be a single recorded example of a Crusader castle falling through lack of water.

An attacker also faced the problem of keeping the besieging army in the field for long periods with little prospect of booty to keep morale high. After the fall of Gastun in September 1188, Saladin wished to move on to the siege of nearby Antioch but 'he was aware that the determination of his troops, especially those from far away, had weakened and their zeal for the Holy War had flagged and they only wanted to return to their countries and rest from fighting',[6] so he abandoned the project, intending to return next year. In fact, he never came back and the city remained in Christian hands for the next eighty years. The campaigning season was normally limited to the spring and summer, and a winter spent in soggy tents and muddy trenches was not an appealing prospect. Saladin conducted a winter campaign in 1188–9, but it was not easy going. He began the attack on Saphet in October: 'He was not deterred by the fact that he was leaving his family, his children and his home during a month when everyone, no matter where he may be, is anxious to return to the bosom of his family' and this determination to pursue the expedition at this time of the year is seen as evidence of his exceptional dedication to the Holy War. It was no picnic: 'Saphet is a very inaccessible fortress, the ground all round being broken up by deep ravines. The army invested the place and placed its mangonels in position ... rain was falling in torrents and the ground became a swamp but this did not affect the Sultan's determination,' in the end the engines did their work and the castle surrendered on 6 December.[7] This problem was largely solved by Sultan Baybars and his Mamluke successors. Partly because of the increasing professionalism of the Muslim armies and partly because of the more efficient use of artillery, sieges became much shorter and castles fell within a few weeks or not at all. No major Crusader castle in the late thirteenth century survived a siege of more than six weeks, Arsuf (1266), Saphet (1266), Crac des Chevaliers (1271), Margat (1285) and Acre (1291), all of which are said to have resisted for about six weeks, being the longest.[8]

The difficulty of forcing surrender by starvation was made clear in the case of Belvoir after the main Crusader army had been destroyed at Hattin in July 1187. This was held by the Hospitallers and was well supplied but the garrison must have been sadly aware that here was very little prospect of relief. Despite this the blockade proved ineffectual. The force which had been left to prevent supplies from reaching the castle had been surprised in a night attack so, despite the snow and the cold, Saladin was obliged to come in early March 1188 to retrieve the situation. He soon realised the task was impossible and he abandoned the siege in May: 'He saw that it would be necessary to employ a great number of troops to reduce this place, for it was very strong, most amply provisioned and garrisoned by determined men whom, so far, the war had spared.' The next winter, after the fall of Saphet, he returned to Belvoir and once again the attack turned into an endurance test:

> The walls [of the castle] built of stones and clay afforded perfect protection to those behind it so that no one could appear at the entrance of his tent without putting on his armour. Rain fell without ceasing and the mud was so thick that it was impossible to get about, either on foot or on horseback. We suffered terribly from the violence of the wind and the heaviness of the rain, as well as from the proximity of the enemy who, from their position necessarily commanded our army, killing and wounding a great number of men.

In the end it was the undermining of the walls, not hunger, which led the garrison to ask for terms. The limits of the effectiveness of blockade were clear: only a very ill-prepared defence could be starved into submission during a summer season while maintaining a siege through the winter was well-nigh impossible.[9] Even Baybars, the most determined and skilful exponent of siege warfare in the entire Crusader period, only campaigned on a seasonal basis, returning to the citadel in Cairo for the winter.

The occasions when shortage of supplies did force surrender were when the defence was damaged by other factors. When Zengi blockaded King Fulk at Montferrand in 1137, starvation played an important role in the King's surrender because 'the Christians were obliged to use their horses for food, since there was nothing else. After these were gone there was no food of any description, so even the strong and robust grew weak from hunger and feebleness, induced by famine, ravaged the strength of even the most vigorous.'[10] But the circumstances here were unusual: not only had the king and the royal army taken refuge in this frontier fortress, but there were many other refugees who had brought no supplies with them and stores which might have supplied the normal garrison for a long time were soon consumed. When Saladin attacked the castle at Kerak in 1183, the defenders were short of arms but, despite a great influx of refugees from the town, they had sufficient food.[11]

Starvation was also decisive if there was no hope of relief. After the battle of Hattin had destroyed the Crusader field army, the castles of Outrejourdain were left completely isolated from any hope of help. The fate of these garrisons is described in one version of *L'estoire d'Eracles*

When [Saladin] had taken all the cities and all the castles of this side of the river Jordan, he went on to attack le Crac [Kerak]. He firmly believed that it would surrender on his arrival. There were good people inside the castle who did not wish to disgrace themselves or harm the Christian cause. They held out and defended it vigorously for so long that they ate dogs and cats and all the animals in the castle ... He also laid siege to Montreal which is 36 miles from Crac. Montreal is in Idumaea and Crac in Moab. They endured the siege so long that they sold their wives and their children to the Saracens to get bread. And those in Montreal lost their sight, so that they could no longer see, for lack of salt which they did not have, not wanting to do any harm [*meschief*] to the castle. So they waited day after day for God to send them help. Saladin several times offered them sufficient money and safe conduct to Christian territory, but they refused.

Kerak surrendered in October/November 1188 and Montreal in April/May 1189, and Ernoul says that Saladin restored their families to them.[12]

Simple blockade was resource-consuming and ineffective: more active methods of attack were developed to speed things up. As far as we can tell, the technology of siege warfare was very primitive in western Europe at the time of the First Crusade. The Bayeux Tapestry shows attempts to storm castles using ladders and to set fire to the wooden palisades with firebrands. When Louis VI of France, a very experienced warrior, attacked the castle of Le Puiset in 1111 his siegecraft consisted of little more than rushing at the walls and attempting to scale them, and the use of primitive incendiary devices to set fire to the wooden palisade.[13] It is not until the middle of the twelfth century that artillery was used effectively at the siege of Lisbon in 1147. From 1151 we have the famous account of Geoffrey the Fair, Count of Anjou, at the siege of Montreuil-Bellay when, after reading the work of the Roman military theoretician Vegetius, he had a catapult constructed to hurl a cauldron of hot oil at the wooden gates of the castle.[14] Not until the beginning of the thirteenth century were siege engines and sapping regularly and effectively used in western Europe.

In the Levant in the early twelfth century it would seem that the technology of building siege engines was much more developed than in the west and that the Crusaders soon adopted it. It is striking that the Crusaders seem to have been unable to make use of either artillery or sapping in the long siege of Antioch in 1097–8 but that by the time that the Crusaders attacked Jerusalem in the summer of 1099 they were using both catapults and tall siege towers. Construction of the siege engines was entrusted to Gaston de Béarn, who may have had experience of Muslim warfare in Spain; the army was aided in this by the arrival of Genoese sailors who used their skill with wood and rope to build engines.[15] Despite these advances, the Crusaders seem to have lagged behind in technical expertise in both sapping and the construction of artillery.

Not until the arrival of Richard Cœur de Lion and Philip Augustus at the siege of Acre in the summer of 1191 do the Crusaders seem to have been able to use artillery to destroy large-scale fortifications. When Richard came to attack the small castle of Darum in 1192, he hired sappers from Muslim Aleppo whom he recruited at Acre, to do the work for him.[16]

The Franks did continue to use devices which were peculiar to them, notably the protected battering rams known as sows or cats which were unknown to the Muslims and the great movable siege towers. These had been used to great effect at the siege of Jerusalem in 1099 and, despite the fact that they were both costly and clumsy, continued to be employed by the Franks. They could be very effective in the right conditions: William of Tyre describes one in use against the city of Banyas, besieged by the Crusaders and their Damascene allies in 1140:

> Soon an engine of great height towered aloft, from whose top the entire city could be surveyed. From this vantage point, arrows and missiles of every sort could be sent, while stones hurled by hand would also help to keep the defenders back. As soon as the engine was ready, the ground between it and the walls was levelled off and the machine was brought up to the ramparts. There, as it looked down upon the whole city, it seemed as if a tower had suddenly been erected in the very midst of the place. Now for the first time the situation of the besieged became intolerable; they were driven to the last extremity, for it was impossible to devise any remedy against the downpour of stones and missiles which fell without intermission from the movable tower. Moreover there was no safe passage within the city for the sick and wounded, or where those who, still strong and vigorous and sacrificing themselves in the defence of others, could withdraw for rest after their labours. In addition, they were now debarred from passing back and forth about the ramparts and could not, without peril of death, carry aid to their comrades who were falling. For the weapons and modes of assault used by those fighting below could be considered little or nothing in comparison with the manifold dangers to which they were exposed from the fighters in the tower. In fact, it seems to be rather a war with gods than with men.[17]

This was the theory, and at Banyas, a small, poorly defended city on a comparatively level site, it worked. At the siege of Acre and elsewhere, however, the towers proved vulnerable to incendiary attack. The filling in of ditches in front of the ramparts often proved a major problem. It is not surprising that this form of attack was not favoured by Muslim armies.

Muslim siege techniques were based on undermining the walls (sapping) and the use of siege engines, at both of which they proved greatly superior to their Christian opponents.

An early detailed account of mining is provided by Usamah b. Munqidh from the siege of Kafartab (a town across the Orontes briefly held by the

Crusaders) in 1115 and it is perhaps worth quoting in full for its vivid first-hand description.

> It occurred to me to enter the underground tunnel and inspect it. So I went down in the trench, while the arrows and stones were falling on us like rain, and entered the tunnel. There I was struck with the great wisdom with which the digging was executed. The tunnel was dug from the trench to the *bashurah* [the usual Arabic term for an outerwall]. On the sides of the tunnel were set up two pillars, across which stretched a plank to prevent the earth above it from falling down. The whole tunnel had such a framework of wood that extended as far as the foundations of the *bashurah*. Then the assailants dug under the wall of the *bashurah*, supported it in its place, we went as far as the foundation of the tower. The tunnel was narrow, it was nothing but a means to provide access to the tower. As soon as they got to the tower, they enlarged the tunnel in the wall of the tower, supported it on timbers and began to carry out, a little at a time, the bits of stone produced by boring. The floor of the tunnel was turned into mud because of the dust caused by the digging. Having made the inspection, I went on without the troops of Khurasan [where the miners came from] recognizing me. Had they recognized me, they would not have let me off without the payment of a heavy fine.
>
> They then began to cut dry wood and stuff the tunnel with it. Early the next morning they set it on fire. We had just at that time put on our arms and marched under a great shower of stones and arrows to the trench in order to attack the castle as soon as its tower tumbled over. As soon as the fire began to have its effect, the layers of mortar between the stones of the wall began to fall. Then a crack was made. The crack became wider and wider and the tower fell. We had assumed that when the tower fell we would be able to go in and reach the enemy. But only the outer face of the wall fell, while the inner wall remained intact. We stood there until the sun became too hot for us, and then returned to our tents after a great deal of damage had been inflicted on us by stones, which were hurled at us.

In the end the Muslims did enter the castle by climbing up the ruined wall, but only after a hard struggle. An interesting feature of this account is that Usamah finds the mine unusual and interesting. Furthermore the miners came not from Syria but from Khurasan in northeast Iran. This may mean that the technology was a comparatively new import to the area, brought by Iranians employed by the Saljuks and their successors.

Another account showing the devastating effect of mining comes from 1123 when Fulcher of Chartres is describing the adventure of King Baldwin II at Kharput, north of the County of Edessa. The king had been sent to the castle as a prisoner, but with the aid of some local Armenians had succeeded in taking it over. The Muslim lord Belek was furious and began to attack it:

> He immediately ordered the rock on which the castle was situated to be undermined and props to be placed along the tunnel to support the works above.

> Then he had wood carried in and fire introduced. When the props were burned the excavation suddenly fell in, and the tower which was nearest to the fire collapsed with a loud noise. At first smoke rose together with the dust since the debris covered up the fire but when the fire ate through the material underneath and the flames began to be clearly visible, a stupor caused by the unexpected event seized the king[18]

and he and his companions soon surrendered. This account reads as if it is based on an eyewitness description and offers a textbook example of the effectiveness of undermining.

Mining played a significant part in the sieges after the battle of Hattin. In 1188 Saladin was able to take the castle of Trapesac in the Principality of Antioch after one tower had been brought down. It was also important in the fall of the city of Jaffa (the Crusaders held the citadel) during the Third Crusade. Here a section of the wall was undermined and 'fell with a fall like the end of all things' but the defenders were ready. 'A cloud of dust and smoke arose from the fallen wall that darkened the heavens and hid the light of day, and none dared enter the breach and face the fire. But when the cloud dispersed, it disclosed the wall of halberds and lances replacing the one that had just fallen'[19] and the Muslims still had a hard struggle to force an entry.

In the thirteenth century both mines and countermines were used. At the siege of Saphet in 1266 Baybars is said to have ordered the digging of a number of tunnels one of which was intercepted by a Frankish countermine and fierce fighting ensued. Later the saps were used to make breaches in the outer (bashurah) walls which caused the garrison to retreat to the inner citadel where they finally surrendered,[20] under the sad delusion that they had been given safe conduct. Our understanding of the siege at Saphet is made more difficult by the fact that there is no archaeological evidence of the position and effect of the mines. In the case of Crac des Chevaliers, besieged and taken by Baybars five years later in 1271, we are on firmer ground. Here the Muslim miners brought down one of the massive towers in the outer wall from which the area between the inner and outer lines of defence was entered. As at Saphet the fall of the outer defences meant that the garrison asked for terms, although Baybars may have deceived them with a forged letter purporting to come from the Grand Master ordering them to surrender.

The final fall of Margat in 1285 was also achieved by mining. In this case numerous tunnels were dug under the citadel with Sultan Qala'un supervising in person. It seems that the tower of the spur of the lower enceinte settled into one of the towers and crushed it but that the defenders realised that the position was hopeless and opened negotiations which led to the final surrender.[21]

Mining was clearly very effective on occasion but it had drawbacks. The work was skilled, dangerous and time consuming. It also required large numbers of men: Sultan Qala'un brought 1,500 miners with him for the final assault on Tripoli in 1289 though in the event they were not needed. Nor were all castles able to be attacked in this way. Some were built on solid rock; 'Imad al-Din comments that the rocky terrain at Kerak prevented mining.[22] The citadel at Caesarea was impossible to undermine because, when St Louis had reconstructed it, he had placed classical columns horizontally through the walls (a similar technique can still be seen in the walls of the citadel at Giblet) but also because the sea flowed around the moat which would have flooded the workings. Furthermore, mining at this time seems to have been done using short tunnels from the base of the wall.[23] Saladin's mine under the tower of the castle at Le Chastellet in 1179 was only 30 cubits long (15 m) and 3 cubits (1.5 m) wide under a wall which was itself 9 cubits (4.5 m) thick.[24] This meant the workings were easily detected and destroyed by the defence. Mining, in short, was effective if the circumstances were right. Catapults by contrast could be used in almost any situation.

It is easy to imagine that medieval siege engines were slightly ridiculous, rather Heath-Robinson affairs, worked, so to speak, by string and rubber bands and that it was only with the coming of gunpowder that artillery posed a serious threat to castles. Consider now this description[25] of the siege of the castle of Montferrand in 1137:

> Meanwhile, Zengi continued his vigorous attacks upon the besieged with unremitting zeal. The very walls shook under the impulse of his mighty engines. Millstones and huge rocks hurled from the machines fell into the midst of the citadel, shattered the houses within, and caused intense fear to the refugees there. Great fragments of rock and all kinds of whirling missiles were hurled with such violence against them that there was no longer any place of security within the walls where the feeble and wounded might be hidden. Everywhere was danger, everywhere hazard, everywhere the spectre of frightful death hovered before their eyes. Apprehension of sudden destruction and a sinister forboding of disaster ever attended them. With this very object in view, their cruel foe redoubled his assaults. He arranged his men in alternative divisions and, by using successive relays, renewed his strength. When the first detachment became weary, fresh men were brought into line, so that the battle seemed continuous rather than begun anew. Insufficient numbers prevented the Christians from enjoying these refreshing changes, yet they sustained with unswerving exertion not only the earlier but also the later attacks. But some succumbed to severe wounds and others to illness of various kinds so that day by day our ranks decreased. One failing was common to all, the impossibility of enduring constant engagements. Their nights devoted to keeping watch, were sleepless, while during the day their strength was further exhausted by never ending combat.

This sounds more like the battle of the Somme than a chivalric romance and the author shows not just the physical destruction caused by the catapults but the psychological stress which resulted.

The history of siege engines is complex and is made much more difficult by the vagueness of medieval descriptions. It is usually said[26] that three types of siege engines were in regular use, the mangonel, the petrary and the trebuchet, the first two using torison or twisted ropes to propel a missile, the third using a counterweight. In fact there is little if any evidence for the use of torsion catapults in crusading warfare and by far the most important artillery piece was the swing beam engine, known in Arabic as a manjaniq and in the west as a trebuchet. This engine consists of a long beam placed over a fulcrum so that one end projects much further from the fulcrum than the other. A stone or other ammunition is placed in a sling at the end of the long end. Then the short end is brought down sharply, causing the tip of the long end to rise much faster to a vertical position. The sling at the end of the long end whips round to release the projectile at great speed.

The swing beam siege engine was probably invented in China and the first clear description of it in the Mediterranean lands comes from a description of the Avar attack on Thessaloniki in 597 in the miracula of St Demetrius.[27] It was widely used in the Islamic world from the time of the Prophet onwards and appears in the Latin west during the 885–6 Norse assault on Paris, though the technology seems to have fallen into disuse there until the second half of the twelfth century. In these early trebuchets, manpower was used to bring the short end of the beam down: men would hold on to cords hanging from the short end, and, on a given instruction, pull it down with as much force as they could muster. This system meant that the engines were simple, effective and comparatively easy to transport, and they were widely used in the Mediterranean world in the twelfth century, from the Crusader states to Portugal, whence there is a full account of their effectiveness in the Christian conquest of Lisbon in 1147.

During the twelfth century a new and more effective version of the swing beam engine was developed. This used a heavy counterweight rather than manpower to bring the short end down. At first this counterweight was a net full of stones but in the thirteenth century it was more often a wooden box full of rock or sand. While this was more difficult to transport and construct, it had a number of advantages over the manpowered version. It could be operated by a much smaller crew and it could maintain a constant aim, enabling the same piece of castle wall to be hit time after time. These new-style trebuchets seem to have been invented by the Byzantines and are first recorded in use in 1165. Fortunately, we have an Arabic treatise, with illustrations, on these new weapons written by one Mardi b. ʿAli al-Tarsusi and presented to Saladin around 1180.[28] This makes it clear that the counterweight machine was then known to the Muslims so it is likely that it was used, at least in a limited scale, in Saladin's campaigns between 1187 and 1189 when so many Crusader castles were reduced. Thirteenth-century and later Arabic treatises describe a number of different trebuchets, ranging from small, hand-operated ones mounted on single poles to heavy artillery.

The range and power of this artillery was formidable. The ammunition often consisted of specially rounded stones. Some of these survive at Saone castle and weigh between 50 and 300 kg, and projectiles of up to 200 kg are known from literary sources. Tarsusi says that the maximum range for a traction trebuchet was about 120 m but there is evidence that it could be as much as 200 m. By comparison, the maximum range of bow-shot was about 140 m. Counterweight trebuchets probably had a longer range still. It may have been this increased range which was the undoing of the defenders of Saone in 1188; they had expected to be attacked by engines firing from across the great trench to the east and had fortified the site accordingly, but they seem to have been unprepared for engines firing across the valley from the north, a distance of perhaps 200 m.

The development of this new and improved artillery fundamentally changed the balance between attack and defence. The engines became so effective that, given uninterrupted firing time, they would reduce any fortress to rubble. It was no use sitting behind castle walls and trusting in their strength: unless the defenders took active measures to neutralise the artillery, the fortress they had built would be destroyed as surely as the incoming tide washes away the children's sandcastle.

Accounts of the sieges at Kerak and Saone show that Saladin had mastered the effective use of artillery but his efforts were on a fairly modest scale, six or eight engines. The real master of the craft was Sultan Baybars (1260–76). His success was due to his ability to organise and deploy these clumsy and costly machines as much as in the actual firing of them, though, like Saladin, he saw that his personal involvement in the fighting was essential if real progress was to be made. His first major success was against Caesarea in 1265.[29] The walls of the town fell easily when his men used their horse pegs and bridles to create makeshift rope-ladders and haul themselves to the top. The Citadel, recently fortified by St Louis, was said to be the most formidable on the coast. Undermining was impossible because the workings would be flooded with seawater. Trebuchets played a vital part in reducing the castle and Baybars also used the covered shelters mounted on wheels which the Arabs called *dababat* (which is also the modern Arabic word for tanks) and which were used to approach the base of the wall, the sultan himself sheltering under one to see how digging was progressing. He gave robes of honour to the commander of the siege engines, 'Izz al-Din al-Afram, for the work he had done.

Trebuchets were equally decisive in the capture of Arsuf which followed immediately afterwards.[30] They were brought ready made from Damascus and were carried shoulder high over difficult stretches of the route. Before the trebuchets could be deployed effectively, the ditches which protected the castle had to be filled in and this proved the most difficult part of the operation. When the engines had made gaps in the wall, the Muslim stormed the outerworks (bashurah) and negotiations for surrender began. Once again. 'Izz al-Din al-Afram was decorated for his efforts.

During the siege of Saphet later in 1266,[31] the trebuchets were again brought to the site, probably from Damascus, and their arrival signalled the beginning of real operations. The sultan sent 'Izz al-Din out to meet them. They were brought on camels as far as Jacob's Ford on the Jordan but had to be carried or dragged from there, the sultan himself lending a hand, and his biographer comments on his endurance. In 1268 it was the turn of Beaufort.[32] Once again, beams for the trebuchets were brought from Damascus, two began bombardment the day after the sultan arrived on 4 April and twenty-six were in operation by the end of the siege. The enemy soon stormed the new bastion constructed by the Templars to the south of the main castle and the sultan used it as an observation post and a base for his artillery. His governor of Egypt had sent a gift to help the campaign and this was used to pay the crews of trebuchets in his name. The Franks seem to have suddenly lost their nerve and on 15 April asked for terms, chivalrously accepting that the men would be made prisoner while the women and children were allowed to depart to Tyre.

The last phase of Baybars' conquests in 1271 shows the same reliance on artillery. After mining had brought down a section of the outer wall at Crac des Chevaliers, it was the arrival of his siege engines within striking distance of the great towers of the inner wall which induced the garrison to surrender. Immediately afterwards, on 29 April, he set about taking the castle of Gibela-car with his usual determination, riding on the carts which carried the timbers for the mangonels and helping dig and level the land around this mountainous site so that they could be set up. By 11 May the garrison had prudently decided to surrender.

Trebuchets were central to Baybars' achievement and played a vital role in every one of his successful assaults on Crusader castles. His achievement depended on his vigour and skills as an organiser and the almost industrial system he seems to have developed for erecting large numbers of prefabricated siege engines in a short period of time. But despite their formidable power, the engines had their limitations. Only leaders prepared to commit massive resources and determination could really use them effectively; a Saladin or a Baybars could, but when the much more feeble Ayyubid, al-Malik al-Mu'azzam attempted to deploy them against the newly erected Templar castle at Chastel Pelerin in 1220, he found that they would not reach the main walls and, making no effort to fill up the ditches or destroy the outer defences, he moved off.[33]

The Crusaders who came to the Levant in the twelfth century found siege techniques, notably mining and artillery, much more advanced than those in their homelands. In the two centuries which followed, artillery continued to develop rapidly in terms both of technical innovation and of more effective methods of deployment. But although they were very formidable weapons, there were still ways in which a castle architect could frustrate them. They needed level access close to the walls; they were vulnerable to sallies from the garrison which could destroy or burn them and the fire from engines and archers from within the castle which could impede or cut short their work. It was these limitations that castle architects tried to exploit in order to render their castles impregnable.

Castle builders responded with skill and ingenuity to the growing threats posed by mining and siege engines, threats which was made cruelly apparent in the fall and destruction of Le Chastellet in 1179 and the subsequent failure of most castles to survive Saladin's attacks from 1187 to 1189. The designs of the twelfth century had to be substantially modified and improved to face these new challenges.

Attacking the besiegers and preventing them digging their mines or setting up the engines was an attractive proposition. The Muslims showed themselves masters of this, as was demonstrated on several occasions at the siege of Acre (1189–91) when swift sorties from the garrison led to the destruction of carefully constructed battering ram engines by fire.[34] The Crusaders were less successful in arranging sorties, at least in part because they never seem to have mastered the technology of incendiary devices, notably the crude oil-based inflammable materials which the Arabic sources call *naft* and which are usually described as Greek Fire in modern literature. The Muslims used it to good, but ultimately unsuccessful, effect during the 1099 siege of Jerusalem which shows that the technology was already well developed in the east. It was *naft* which allowed the defending garrison to wreak such havoc on the Crusader machines at Acre.

Nonetheless Crusaders did make sorties to attack their tormentors, as when the garrison at Belvoir successfully broke the blockade by a sortie during the first siege in 1188, killing the Muslim commander. Sultan Baybars was almost killed in the trenches when taken by surprise by a Frankish sortie during the siege of Arsuf, 1266.[35]

There were perils, however, in making sorties, not least of which was the return to the castle. The defenders of Banyas found this out to their cost in 1157.

> One day, while the foe [the Muslim army commanded by Nur al-Din] was pressing them more fiercely than usual, the besieged opened the city gate and made a sally against the enemy outside. Since they offered battle without due caution, however, they roused a multitude of the enemy against them. The Turks rushed upon them, and the citizens, unable to maintain their position,

tried to withdraw into the city. The gate could not be shut, however because the pressure of the crowd trying to enter was so great. Consequently the enemy, intermingling with the townspeople, entered in such large numbers that the town was taken by force.[36]

At Jaffa in 1197 the defenders had actually refused to let the sortie party back in when they were obliged to retreat.[37]

In order to reduce the danger of losing a castle in this way, and to increase the element of surprise, castles were equipped with a number of special postern gates. Typically, this gate was small, low (no need for horses to enter here) and in the re-entrant angle between tower and curtain wall where it could be concealed from enemy view and completely covered by the defenders' fire. At Belvoir, a state-of-the-art fortification of the 1170s, four postern gates can be identified, each either in or beside a tower. At Chastel Pelerin, built in 1218, each of the three projecting towers of the outer land wall (the direction from which attack would come) had two posterns, one on each side, defended by machicolations above.[38] That the provision of postern gates continued to be an important consideration can be seen at Crac des Chevaliers, where one of the last Hospitaller constructions was a postern gate of the second half of the thirteenth century opened in the re-entrant angle of one of the towers when Nicholas Lorgne was castellan (at some time between 1254 and 1269.[39] As well as having towers on each side, this was defended by a portcullis and almost certainly machicolations, though the present ones are Muslim rebuilding after the originals had been damaged in the assault of 1271.

But launching sallies was not always possible and architects also devised ways of defence which were less risky. The main purpose of these devices was to keep both miners and siege engines away from the walls and so prevent them from inflicting serious damage.

An obvious way of doing this was the use of natural or artificial ravines. Many Crusader castles were built on craggy hills so the ground sloped away steeply on most sides. Montreal is on an isolated summit and it probably survived its epic two-year siege (1187–9) because there was no angle from which siege engines could be brought up against the walls. More common was the spur which left one vulnerable side where the castle could be approached. In the case of Beaufort and Crac des Chevaliers the successful assault was launched from this side because it provided the only access. Where natural escarpments were lacking, artificial substitutes were created. At Kerak and Saone these took the form of stupendous rock-hewn chasms (the one at Saone survives to its full depth, 30 m; the one at Kerak, apparently originally just as deep, has since been almost completely filled up). Another form of protection was the *berquilla* or cistern (discussed above) which could be dug out of the rock and which served the dual purpose of providing a water supply in normal conditions and an extra line of defence in times of emergency. The struggles of Saladin at Kerak in 1184 and Baybars at Arsuf in 1266 to fill the moats before a serious assault could begin, show how effective they were.[40] Since freshwater moats were impossible on most Syrian sites, seagirt castles were the best protected against mining. No one could sap the walls of the sea castle at Sidon on its island and one of the strengths of Chastel Pelerin was that it only needed to be defended on one short, landward side, since it stood on its own little peninsula. However strong the Muslims were on land, the Franks had almost unchallenged command of the seas; only once, at Ascalon in 1247, did the Muslims attempt to attack a Christian strong point from the sea.[41]

Earthworks were tried in some places. At Beaufort and Crac des Chevaliers, separate outer defences were built on the neighbouring hill. These seem to have been of earth and stones rather than worked masonry. In both cases they turned out to be a mistake; with the very limited manpower available, they could not be held, and Baybars used them as platforms for the very siege engines they were supposed to be keeping at a safe distance.

An outer line of stone walls was both more usual and more effective, giving rise to what is somewhat misleadingly called a concentric castle (misleading because none of these castles is actually round). The idea of putting a low outer wall in front of a higher inner one was not new with the Crusades. It had been employed in the Theodosian walls of Constantinople in the fourth century, advocated by Procopius in the sixth and employed at Korikos in the early twelfth. On occasion, where the terrain suited, it was used by Crusader builders. In fact a complete double circuit of walls was quite rare. In some cases the outer line of walls simply protects a lower area of the castle which might otherwise be used as a base of attack. Both Beaufort and Kerak have lower baileys along one side of the main citadel (although in both cases the surviving masonry dates from the Muslim period) and Rochefort (Bourzey) has a small, well-defended lower enclosure, but this does not make them concentric castles and at Kerak the vulnerable approaches were protected by a single wall only. The Templar castle at Gastun (Baghras), on a rocky knoll, is another castle where the steep slope of the site meant that lower and upper walls were required. Saone boasts a complex pattern of multiple walls (no less than five according to Muslim observers) but in this case it was a result of enclosing an inner Byzantine castle with an outer Crusader one. As at Kerak, the important consideration was to enclose the whole of the summit of the ridge and so deny access to enemy siege engines; along the flanks, there was only a single line of walls. Nor can castles like baronial Giblet or Templar Chastel Blanc, with their great stone keeps protected by walls around the bailey, be properly described as concentric.

This leaves a small minority of castles where the landscape and the resources available meant that a complete double circuit of walls was both practical and desirable. One of the earliest of these was the mid-twelfth-

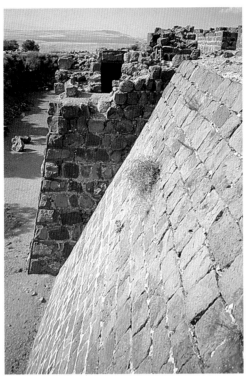

1 Belvoir, western moat looking north

2 Bourzey, general view from the southwest

3 Saone, great trench looking north

4 Chastel Pelerin, general view from the east

5 Chastel Blanc, donjon from the east

6 Crac des Chevaliers, general view from the southwest

7 Margat, general view from the south

century Hospitaller castle at Belmont, just west of Jerusalem, where the outer circuit is polygonal. More clearly dated is another Hospitaller castle, Belvoir, built in the 1170s and destroyed in 1188. Here the outer walls were lower but more massive than the inner ones and clearly designed to bear the brunt of attack with a pronounced splayed base all round. In the thirteenth century, literary descriptions and the fragmentary archaeological evidence suggests that the castle of Saphet had two complete circuits of walls. The two clearest examples of concentric fortifications are the great Hospitaller castles of the north, Crac des Chevaliers and Margat. At Crac the outer line of defences dates from the early thirteenth-century rebuilding but they may have replaced an earlier structure. Margat has an outer line of walls enclosing the whole of the summit of the ridge and an inner citadel at one end so the 'concentric' aspect is much less apparent.

Whether they were strictly speaking concentric or not, the outer walls were of fundamental importance. At Arsuf, Saphet and Crac des Chevaliers, the fall of the outer walls led directly to the surrender of the castle which could not hold out without them.

The walls themselves had to be protected and miners and engines alike kept away from their bases. There were a number of ways of doing this, by building towers to provide flanking fire along the sides of the walls from archers within the towers, by elaborating the wall-head defences, by creating shooting galleries inside the curtain walls and by making artillery platforms on which the defenders could mount their own engines.

The earliest datable Crusader castle wall, Raymond of St Gilles' building at Tripoli, has slightly projecting towers which are little more than buttresses, but during the twelfth century the Crusaders developed a very distinctive style of boldly projecting, square tower with interior chambers and arrow slits in the sides and face. Such towers can clearly be seen at Kerak, Saone, Arima, and Rochefort (Bourzey) and it is clear that from the shelter of their walls archers could command the approaches to the line of the curtain. The projecting towers at the corners of the bailey wall at Giblet and other castrum plans had the same effect.

At the end of the twelfth century, this design was abandoned and replaced by new designs of flanking towers. There is no contemporary comment on when or why these changes are made. Circumstantial evidence suggests that they were incorporated in castles built or strengthened after the campaigns of 1187–9. Historians of military architecture have suggested that square towers have two significant disadvantages. The first is that their projecting corners were particularly vulnerable to mining. When Belek undermined the castle of Kharput in 1123, it was a tower which collapsed; at Le Chastellet in 1179, again, it was the tower which was brought down; and the castle of Trapesac fell to Saladin when one of the towers was undermined. Equally the corners and flat faces of the towers would make an easy target for siege engines. Clearly towers to provide flanking fire for the walls were a vital part of the defences and yet they were also among the most vulnerable points. The second disadvantage of the square tower was that there was a considerable area of 'dead' ground immediately in front of the outer face, an area which could not be covered by archers firing from the curtain wall and where an enemy could begin mining operation or set up siege engines.

Two different designs emerged to cope with these difficulties. The first, which seems to have been favoured by the Templars, was to make towers oblong, with the longer sides of the rectangle attached to the curtain walls. These projected sufficiently to allow archers and artillery to cover the ground in front of the walls but not so far that they were vulnerable. Such oblong towers can be seen clearly at Chastel Pelerin (1218), at the thirteenth-century work at Tortosa and, it would seem from the fragmentary evidence, from the outer walls at Safita.

The other response was to build round towers. These had the advantage that they lacked vulnerable corners. In Roman times, Vitruvius had understood this: 'The towers', he writes, 'must be either round or polygonal. Square towers are sooner shattered by military engines, for the battering ram pounds their angles to pieces; but in the case of round towers they do no harm, being engaged, as it were, in driving wedges to their centre.'[42] The area of dead ground in front of them was considerably reduced because it was more easily covered by archers on the walls on either side. However, round towers did have their disadvantages too. For a start, they required more skill to construct them as the stones have to be precisely shaped: it would have been very difficult to build round towers with the crude, almost boulder-like masonry which was used at Kerak. Round rooms are much less convenient than square ones for living in and when towers were used, as at Crusader Saone or Muslim Bosra, as residential quarters, square towers were preferred. At Margat they solved this problem by having square chambers in the great round donjon, while at Crac des Chevaliers the round tower in the centre of the south wall has a large rectangular accommodation block on its inner side. Round towers were also less suitable for mounting siege engines, an important consideration in the thirteenth century. It was probably these limitations which led all Muslim architects and some Crusader ones to prefer rectangular towers throughout the thirteenth century.

It is by no means clear where this use of round towers originated. It has already been shown that there was a long Armenian tradition of building round towers, of which the 1122 tower at Edessa was actually built under Frankish rule. They had also been used in the gates at Cairo only a decade before the arrival of the First Crusade in the Levant. But round donjons also appeared in western European castles before any datable Crusader examples, the earliest of which is probably that built by Henry I at Chateau-sur-Epte *c*.1130–5. On the other hand there are no examples of round mural interval towers before Richard I's Château Gaillard (1197–8).

The earliest examples of round towers in Crusader building are probably to be found in five towers (including the two which flank the postern gate) on the wall of the castle at Saone overlooking the great trench, where they seem to grow out of the natural rock which is also shaped in semi-circular projections. Though smaller in diameter than thirteenth-century examples, these are clearly round towers with hollow interiors and slits for archers to aim fire along the wall. They are Crusader work (i.e. before 1188) and probably date from the early twelfth century. Deschamps[43] suggests that the semi-circular rock projections on which these towers stand date from Byzantine times and that the Crusaders simply imitated the plans laid down by their predecessors. Equally, Saone lies right in the north of the Crusader states, in an area of strong Armenian influence, and it may well be that there is Armenian influence here, although the masonry of which these towers were built is typically Crusader.

Thereafter, there are no further examples of Crusader round towers before the great Hospitaller building projects at Crac des Chevaliers and Margat around the beginning of the thirteenth century. Both these cases are interesting in that the castles had been built in the twelfth century with square towers but were systematically changed in the rebuilding so that almost all the towers present rounded fronts to the enemy. The builders obviously saw advantages in this. In the outer, west wall of Crac is the finest example of the systematic use of regularly spaced round towers to be found in Crusader building. Unfortunately the exact chronology of these rebuildings is uncertain (see below).

Wall-head defences were a useful addition to flanking fire from projecting towers as a means of protecting the walls from attack. The underlying principle was to put structures on the tops of the wall which would project and enable the defenders to cover the vulnerable base of the wall without exposing themselves to enemy fire. Two types of these defences were developed, wooden hoardings and stone machicolations.

Wooden hoardings were more widely used but are much less easy to study than stone machicolations since there are no surviving medieval examples. They can only be investigated from manuscript illustrations and more exactly from holes for inserting timbers frequently found around the wall heads of western European castles. The reconstructed example at Carcassonne gives a clear idea of the appearance of such structures. Evidence for the use of wooden hoardings in Crusader castles is very scarce. During the siege of Saphet in 1266, Ibn al-Furat recounts how the Franks burned the *sata'ir* on the *bashurah* (outer wall) to prevent the Muslims from storming it. The word 'sata'ir' can mean any sort of wooden projection and could refer to hoardings.[44] There seem to be no examples of holes in the masonry of a sort which might have supported wooden hoardings in the western manner but there are examples of stone corbels (*breteches*) which must have supported either timber or stone machicolations. Twelfth-century examples of these can be found at Saone where they survive at three places, all overlooking gates,[45] and at Burj al-Arab over the window. The same device is used at Margat, above the main gate and over the window in the great round donjon.[46] More striking is the use of these *breteches* on the four-square guard house (Burj al-Sabi) which commands the coast road below Margat and was probably built around 1200. Here they are disposed regularly all around the top of the tower at the level of the roof terrace and the defences must have stood out in front of the crenellations.

Stone machicolations are comparatively rare. There are twelfth-century examples of what Edwards calls 'slot machicolations' (and which he sees as characteristically Armenian devices)[47] over gates at Saone, Bourzey and Beaufort.[48] As the name suggests, these were open slots leading from an upper chamber down into the gate passage. The descriptions of the building of Chastel Pelerin (1218) and Saphet (1240)[49] both mention '*propugnacula*' as part of the defences of the main walls. These are distinct from the towers and the outer walls and may well be stone machicolations.

It is only at Crac des Chevaliers, however, that we can trace the development of the true machicolation. In the twelfth century large slot machicolations were constructed along the front of one of the surviving square towers of the inner bailey[50] and they may have been constructed to protect the base of the wall before the outer enceinte was built in the late twelfth or early thirteenth century. This tower also had a postern gate in one side, which was defended by a *breteche* similar to those found at Saone. This seems to be a unique survival of the twelfth-century system of defence. Later the three large slot machicolations were replaced by a gallery of machicolations sustained by corbels which ran along the head of the wall.

Further development of the machicolation can be seen on the late twelfth-/early thirteenth-century west and south walls of the outer enclosure.[51] Along the south wall, and above the postern gate in the north wall mentioned above, there are (or rather were) regular spaced box machicolations, each standing on three projecting corbels and having two slots in the floor over the base of the wall and an arrow slit in the face. Each is reached independently from a covered wall walk. These have no parallel in other surviving Crusader work but are strikingly similar to early thirteenth-century Muslim work at Damascus and Aleppo, but we know they are of Frankish construction because of the masons' marks. After the Muslim conquest in 1271, the southeast corner was rebuilt and the separate box machicolations were replaced by a continuous, covered gallery of machicolations, in many ways like the *chemin de ronde* of later medieval French military architecture.

Most wall heads were defended not by machicolations but by more simple crenellations. Surviving examples of Crusader wall-head defences are comparatively rare. On the twelfth-century donjon and other towers at Saone, the roof is surrounded by a wall some 4 m high. There are arrow slits at roof level, designed to facilitate downward fire. These arrow slits are covered by flattened pointed arches which support, about 3 m above the level of the roof terrace, a wall walk, protected by simple merlons.[52] This seems to have been the most common form of wall-head defences; the same system can be seen at Chastel Rouge (twelfth century)[53] and, from the thirteenth century, at Chastel Pelerin[54] and Margat. In the case of Chastel Blanc (c.1200) there is no wall walk but simple crenellations with arrow slits in the merlons.[55] Most of these examples all occur on inner fortifications where command of the base of the wall was not so vital since the outer lines of defence should have seen to that. A rather different pattern can be seen on the inner walls at Crac and Tortosa, where there are arrow slits and larger rectangular openings whose purpose is not at all clear.[56]

New wall-head defences were complemented by new defences within the walls. The simple curtain wall of the twelfth century was replaced by much more careful designs and it became a complex fighting platform. The main intention was to provide direct fire outwards at or near the bottom of the wall from a sheltered position. This is apparent in the defences of the citadel at Margat where the walls either have passages with arrow slits (as in the outer western wall), or, more commonly, vaulted halls leading to arrow slits, as on the inner western and eastern fronts. The surviving fragment of the main wall at Tortosa shows that it had vaulted halls or passages behind it giving access to arrow slits at many different levels. This was not new: there are halls and galleries in the walls at both Kerak (north front) and Saone (west front) dating from the twelfth century. However, these arrangements seem to have become more systematic in the thirteenth.

Evidence for this can be found at Tortosa and Crac des Chevaliers, in both of which solid twelfth-century walls were developed to provide more opportunities for fire. In Tortosa this took the form of a gallery, plentifully supplied with loopholes, around the base of the solid twelfth-century donjon. At Crac the twelfth-century inner enclosure was surrounded on the west and south by a thirteenth-century outer wall. In part this was to push the wall out at the base so that the exterior was a steeply sloping glacis rather than a vertical wall. Between the twelfth- and thirteenth-century walls, there ran a gallery, from 1 m to 3 m in width, which gave access to numerous arrow slits. There can be no doubt that one of the reasons for this apparent duplication of wall building was to increase the fire power near ground level.

Siege engines were one of the main methods of defence as well as attack. They had been used by the Muslim defenders of Jerusalem in 1099 and the failure of the Christians to set one up when Saladin besieged Kerak in 1183 was a major cause of their loss of morale. When he returned the next year, the defenders were much better prepared and their siege engines prevented Saladin's men approaching the trench outside the castle walls until he had built elaborate shelters for them: the delay was long enough for the main Crusaders army to relieve the siege. At Bourzey in 1188 a siege engine in the castle made life very difficult for Saladin's troops. In the thirteenth century their use became more common. When Baybars heard that the Franks at Jaffa had erected engines on the citadel 'in spite of the fact that they were at peace' he made his displeasure known.[57] The castle at Saphet had a staff of no less than 300 *balistarii* to work the siege engines. The Crusaders sometimes used them to good purpose in battle. At the siege of Beaufort in 1268, three people close to Sultan Baybars were killed by a Frankish stone shot by the defenders, though he himself was unscathed.[58] At Gibelacar in 1271, Frankish engines did considerable damage to the attackers and killed one of the Muslim commanders when he was at prayer, and the fall of Margat in 1285 was preceded by an artillery duel between the engines of the attackers and the defenders.[59]

The need to provide platforms for these engines affected Crusader castle architecture considerably. The siege engines, particularly the new, counterweight trebuchets, required strong towers with ample space at roof level. They also needed solid stone vaults to keep them up and as much height as possible to increase the range. The castle at Saphet was so designed that the engines of the defenders were invisible from outside the castle. A new style of tower building was developed and the small, flanking towers of the twelfth century were replaced by these much larger artillery platforms. It is probable that the first fortress specifically built for this new artillery was the citadel in Damascus, built by al-'Adil in the first decade of the thirteenth century (see below, pp. 181–2) Christian builders soon adopted the new techniques: the massive towers at the south end of the inner defences at Crac, the round tower and connected structures at Margat and the huge rectangular towers at Chastel Pelerin and Tortosa all show these features. The lack of them at crucial places could be disastrous. Baybars clearly saw that Crac des Chevaliers had been vulnerable because there was nowhere to mount artillery at the south end of the outer enceinte, and he built a vast square tower to fill this gap. In addition, there was the need to house and feed the large numbers of men required for the engines. Increasingly important as well was the provision of shelters within the castles, so that defenders could be protected against incoming missiles (see above, pp. 92–3).

The need to defend the castle against the two threats of mining and bombardment must have been the foremost consideration of all Crusader castle builders. They responded to the challenge with scientific ingenuity, both when they designed the fortifications originally and when they modified their existing defences in the light of experience. Every feature has purpose and nothing happens by chance. It is this pattern of developing response to challenge which makes the architectural history of these castles so intriguing, just as the response of architects in twelfth- and thirteenth-century France to the challenge of building great churches makes the early history of Gothic architecture so satisfying.

6

NOBLES, TEMPLARS AND TEUTONIC KNIGHTS IN THE THIRTEENTH CENTURY

THE defeat at Hattin and the subsequent fall of so many castles to
Saladin had a traumatic effect on Crusader castle architects. The
castles which were founded or remodelled in the thirteenth century
differed from their twelfth-century predecessors in ownership, distribution
and design.

By this time very few castles remained in the hands of the lay nobility
except in the coastal cities where some families like the lords of Sidon and
Caesarea and the Ibelins in Beirut managed to maintain at least a shadow of
their former status. None of their buildings survives from this period and the
thirteenth-century fortifications which do survive at Sidon and Caesarea were
not built by the lords. We do, however, have one record from this time which
sheds a rather surprising light on the life-style of these nobles. In 1212 the
aristocratic German traveller Wilbrand of Oldenburg passed through Beirut
and has left a description of the castle of John of Ibelin.[1] One tower, newly
built since the reconquest of the city by the Crusaders in 1197, had a chamber
overlooking the sea on one side and gardens on the other, which was luxu-
riously decorated with marble panels like lightly rippling water on the floor
and painted clouds 'which seemed to move' on the ceiling. In the middle there
was a richly decorated tank with a fountain shaped like a dragon whose
waters cooled the air and beside which, the no-doubt travel-weary writer says
he would 'willingly sit for all his days'. The whole passage gives an idea of the
luxury which could be found in some Crusader castles, an aspect of their
architecture whose physical traces have almost entirely disappeared.

Outside the coastal towns, the castles of the Kingdom of Jerusalem show a
marked discontinuity between the twelfth and thirteenth centuries. Many
were lost, never to be retaken. The mighty fortresses of Oultrejourdain were

Plate 43   Sidon, sea castle, thirteenth-century: general view from southeast.

gone for ever, Belvoir was not recovered, the castles built in Fulk's reign around Ascalon were left in ruins; never again would Frankish knights crouch in the cave at al-Habis to survey the northern plains. Frankish settlement was now confined almost exclusively to the coastal plains and, while the cities were refortified, few independent castles were constructed. Even when Jerusalem was reoccupied by Frederick II from 1228, little attempt seems to have been made to strengthen its defences and no castles were constructed in the Judaean hills.

The castles of the coastal towns were certainly strengthened during the thirteenth century but only at Sidon, centre of one of the most important lordships in the Kingdom of Jerusalem, are there still significant remains.[2] In the twelfth century the castle of Sidon had stood, like Giblet, at the apex of the land walls on the site of the ancient acropolis. The town fell easily to Saladin's troops on 29 July 1187 and ten years later a party of Crusaders found it 'sine habitatore et rebus'. The town seems gradually to have been repopulated and 2,000 Christians were massacred in a surprise Muslim attack in June 1253. When St Louis, who was then engaged on the refortification of Jaffa, heard the news, he hurried to Sidon and, after burying the putrid corpses of the victims, set about rebuilding the fortifications. The site of the castle is known but, like Toron, it was almost completely rebuilt by the Amir Fakhr al-Din in the seventeenth century and virtually none of the Crusader work survives.

A second castle was built on a reef which protects the harbour some 100 m from the shore (plate 43). There seems to have been no building on the site in the twelfth century but in 1227–8 a party of French, English and Spanish pilgrims awaiting the arrival of Frederick II on Crusade began construction. The contemporary *L'estoire de Eracles* explains:

> The pilgrims who were not at Acre, not wanting to be idle, took counsel and agreed that they should go to Saete [Sidon] to fortify the city and the castle. When they arrived, they realised that it would be too much work to undertake the fortification of the town and castle. They saw an island in the sea beyond the harbour and they knew that they could make a better and more secure fortification there in a short time. They set to work and built two towers, one large and the other medium, and a length of wall between the two towers. They worked at this between St Martin's Day [11 November 1227] and the middle of Lent [2 March 1228].

This new island castle served as a refuge for the garrison in 1253 when it was held by Simon de Montceliart, chief of Louis IX's crossbowmen, and in 1260 when the town was sacked by the Mongols, provoked by Julien of Sidon's foolish attack on their camp. After 1260, Sidon, along with Julien's other properties at Beaufort and the Cave de Tyron passed to the Templars. They continued to hold it until 1291. After the fall of Acre on 18 May, some of them escaped to Sidon where they hoped to hold out in the sea castle and it was here that they elected a new master, Thibaut Gaudin, to replace William of Beaujeu who had been killed at Acre. It soon became clear, however, that assistance was not going to arrive and the Mamluke sultan began the construction of the causeway to the island. Finally, at dead of night on the 13 July, the Templars took ship and, abandoning their castles, set sail for Cyprus.

The archaeology of the castle is not at all clear and the plans published by Rey, Deschamps and Müller-Wiener are all significantly different. The site is not large and construction is on a fairly small scale. The latest and most detailed discussion (fig. 15), by Kalayan, distinguishes no less than four stages, based on different types of masonry work but bearing in mind that the original builders hailed from at least three different countries it would not be surprising if different kinds of stone dressing were used at the same time. It is most likely that we should see the initial work as the square towers A–B and C, which were later strengthened by Simon de Montceliart who enveloped both A and C in more massive constructions. The final phase probably represents Templar work. This consisted of enclosing the square towers with a vaulted shooting-gallery well provided with arrow slits, very much as they did in the donjon at Tortosa. It was probably the Templars as well who were responsible for the vaulted Gothic hall at the seaward side of the main fortifications. It is noticeable that at Sidon, as at Chastel Perlerin, the fortifications

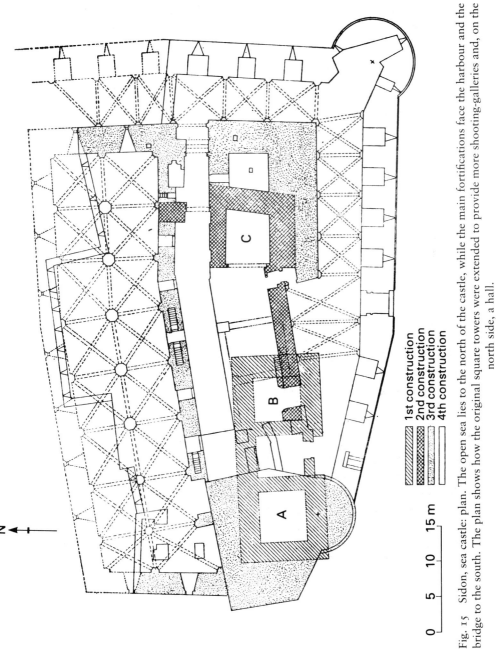

1st construction
2nd construction
3rd construction
4th construction

0 5 10 15 m

Fig. 15 Sidon, sea castle: plan. The open sea lies to the north of the castle, while the main fortifications face the harbour and the bridge to the south. The plan shows how the original square towers were extended to provide more shooting-galleries and, on the north side, a hall.

are directed against attack from the land whereas the sea side is much less strongly defended.

Outside the coastal towns, new work of the thirteenth century was confined to the north of the old Kingdom of Jerusalem, to Chastel Pelerin on the coast, Montfort, Judin and Saphet in the hills of Galilee, and Beaufort in the south of Lebanon. Saphet and Beaufort were only recovered by the Franks in 1240 and were lost again in 1266 and 1268 respectively. All the castles which were built belonged to the Military Orders. Chastel Pelerin, Beaufort and Saphet to the Templars, Montfort to the Teutonic Knights; none was built by laymen or by the Hospitallers who seem to have devoted their energies to the defence of the northern Crusader enclaves (apart from the development of their head-quarters in Acre). Only a small proportion of the Templar castles which had existed in the twelfth century were refortified in the thirteenth. Le Toron des Chevaliers (Latrun) and La Fève in the Vale of Jezreel, for example, never seem to have been rebuilt. The rectangular enclosure plan, which had been commonly used by the Military Orders in the twelfth-century kingdom, was also abandoned and all castles were built on sites defended by steeply sloping ground or by the sea. It is apparent too that all the large-scale new construc-tions in the Kingdom of Jerusalem (Chastel Pelerin, Sidon and Saphet) were undertaken on the initiative of pilgrims from outside the kingdom. Only in Tripoli and Antioch were the Templars, like the Hospitallers, able to call on sufficient revenues from land, booty and tribute for large construction projects.

Templar work of the early thirteenth century was on a massive scale. As a result of accidents of survival, the great Hospitaller works at Crac des Cheva-liers and Margat now look vastly more impressive than anything constructed by the Templars but examination of the remains at Chastel Pelerin and Tortosa and the descriptions of Saphet make it clear that their work was of similarly huge proportions. There were also marked differences in style: in contrast to the Hospitallers, but like their Muslim contemporaries, the Tem-plars consistently preferred rectangular to round towers.

Chastel Pelerin (1218) was the earliest of these projects.[3] Unlike most twelfth-century castles, we know a good deal about the circumstances of its construc-tion from the contemporary account in the *Historia Damiatina* of Oliver Scho-lasticus. The immediate stimulus was the fortification of Mount Tabor by the Muslims which posed a threat to all the Christian communities on the coast. The seaside road was left very exposed, and the old tower of Le Destroit which served as a place of refuge on this stretch was no longer adequate (plate 44). The initiative was taken by a visiting lord from Flanders, Gautier d'Avesnes, who gathered knights from the Templars and the Teutonic Order and a large number of pilgrims. They decided to fortify a rock spit on the coast between Caesarea and Acre which could provide security and a good anchorage.

Plate 44   Chastel Pelerin (Athlit): view from the old Templar tower at Le
Destroit which the new castle replaced. The coast road ran where the railway
and sheds are in the foreground.

The work began in February with the digging of a ditch across the promontory which was completed by Easter (15 April), the whole enterprise taking
only six weeks. The great inner wall with its two massive oblong bastions was
completed in the next six months.[4] The plentiful supply of volunteer labour
from the pilgrims must have helped speed the process. We are also told that
there was an ancient wall on the site, which we now know to have been Phoe-
nician, and the builders were able to re-use much of the ancient masonry,
which accounts for the very large size of some of the blocks, much bigger than
those normally found in Crusader work. Equally encouraging was the discovery of a horde of ancient coins of a sort unknown to the builders which
was soon put to good use buying supplies. After its completion the castle was
entrusted to the Templars who held it as long as it remained in Crusader
hands, becoming their most important base in the Kingdom of Jerusalem.

The main defensive work consists of a mighty rampart across the landward
end of the spit (fig. 16). There is a ditch with counterscarp, then an outer
wall, 6 m thick and about 16 m high (the outer west wall at Crac des Chevaliers is about 9 m high). This wall was crowned by a covered chemin de ronde
provided with numerous casemates and arrow slits. Above this there were
crenellations on the wall head but there is no trace of machicolations or projecting wall-head defences. Instead the dead ground at the foot of the wall was
covered by three projecting square towers. The central and southern towers
each had two small gates, one in each re-entrant angle, defended by portcull-
ises within and simple, two-corbel machicolations over. Behind this outer wall
there was a thin bailey, enclosed at the north and south ends by walls with

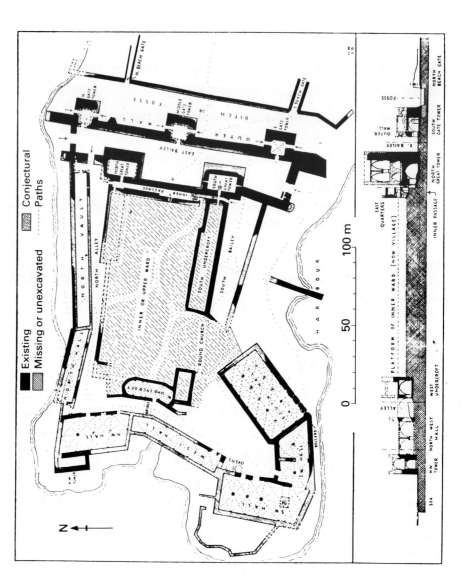

Fig. 16   Chastel Pelerin: plan and section.

covered corridors in them so that the outer wall could be reached from the main castle without exposing the defenders to enemy fire. Behind this bailey stood the inner wall. None of this survives to full height but it must have overlooked the outer wall. This was strengthened by two great towers, placed so that they commanded the curtain walls between the towers in front. Enough of one of these towers survives to show that it had three floors, of which the top was a lofty hall with fine ribbed vaults, and stood to a height of more than 34 m, only slightly lower than the highest towers of the inner enceinte at Crac. These towers were connected by internal passages 'so wonderfully contrived' as Jacques de Vitry wrote, 'that armed horsemen can go up and down the steps'.

Behind these mighty walls, the interior of the peninsula was occupied by a number of extensive crypts and halls, mostly very ruinous now, which must have provided accommodation of the scale and elegance found in the Hospitallers' work at Crac des Chevaliers in the same period. The main hall (*palatio*) was used to feed 4,000 men daily in the siege of 1220. Naturally, since the castle was occupied by a Military Order, there was a fine chapel of almost octagonal plan, whose vaulted roof was supported by a slender central column. In both the strength of its defences and the extent of its living quarters, Chastel Pelerin was among the most impressive of thirteenth-century Crusader works.

Outside the castle proper a small town was founded with a church and baths and enclosed by an unimpressive wall. In 1220 the castle, defended by no less than 4,000 combatants, faced a major assault by al-Malik al-Mu'azzam who brought with him seven siege engines: his artillery could not even reach the great towers of the inner enceinte, one engine was destroyed by the artillery of the defenders and the attack was a fiasco. He withdrew after a month and the hastily constructed castle had proved its worth. As long as it could be supplied by sea and was adequately garrisoned it was virtually impregnable: even the mighty Baybars, conqueror of Crac des Chevaliers, left it alone when he sacked the town in 1265. It was never taken by assault and it was not until after the fall of Acre in 1291 that the much reduced garrison was finally forced to abandon it. Apart from some slighting of the defences immediately after the Muslim occupation, the castle seems to have remained largely intact until Ibrahim Pasha used it as a quarry to rebuild the walls of Acre in 1838, since when the fabric has deteriorated rapidly.

The Templars played a central role in the defence of inland Galilee as well. In 1240 a Crusade of French barons led by Thibault IV of Champagne made a treaty with the Sultan Isma'il of Damascus whereby Beaufort, which had been held by the Muslims since its capture by Saladin in 1190, was returned to the Crusaders. The garrison refused to hand it over and Isma'il was put in the embarrassing position of having to undertake a full-scale siege so that he could enforce the terms of the treaty. The castle was then returned to the lords of Sidon to whom it had belonged in the twelfth century. It was one of them, the courageous but reckless Julien, whose stupidity caused a fatal breach between the Crusaders and their Mongol allies, who was obliged to sell Beaufort and Sidon to the Templars in 1260.[5] It marked the end of an era: Beaufort was the last rural castle of any importance in the Levant to remain in baronial hands. Having acquired this outpost the Templars set about modifying it. The castle itself was still strong and the Muslims had more than made good the damage done in 1190. The Knights added a vaulted hall, so characteristic of the architecture of the Military Orders, to the inner bailey. They also built an outer work on the plateau to the south of the castle, where Saladin had set up his engines and which they rightly saw as the vulnerable angle. Unhappily for them, these new defences proved their undoing. When Baybars besieged the castle in 1268, they were forced to abandon their new work which the sultan then used as a base for his artillery. Finally on the 15 April the 480 men defending the castle, of whom twenty-four were knights, were forced to surrender; their women and children were allowed to escape to Tyre but they themselves were handed over to the soldiers of the besieging army.

The Templars also took over the castle at Saphet. Saphet is an interesting case in that we know a good deal about it from written sources, indeed the anonymous tract called *De Constructione Castri Saphet* is the fullest account we have of the building of any castle, but the physical remains are very scanty. According to late medieval travellers, the fortress was one of the most magnificent constructed by the Crusaders and was certainly one of the great glories of the Templars. They had built a fortress on the site in the twelfth century which was taken by Saladin in 1188. It remained in Muslim hands, like Beaufort, until 1240 when it was restored to the Templars. They do not seem to have felt able to undertake any restorations on their own initiative but, as at Chastel Pelerin, they were prodded into action by a visiting pilgrim from the west, in this case, Benoît d'Alignan, Bishop of Marseilles, who persuaded the Master, Armand de Périgord that the work should be undertaken. With the use of Arab prisoners as forced labour, the castle is said to have been completed in three years. Despite its strength, it fell to Baybars in 1266, two years before Beaufort. After a failure to take the citadel by force, Baybars tricked the Templars into surrendering in return for being allowed to retire to Acre but they were led out and executed: according to western sources, 150 Templars, 767 other fighters and two friars were killed. The Syrian Christians seem to have been spared.[6]

The castle survived and was used as a local centre of government until a disastrous earthquake in 1837 left it a pile of shapeless ruins. The evidence has recently been re-examined by Pringle using old travellers' accounts and the plan published by Conder and Kitchener when the site was more open than it is today. The inner enceinte, according to the *De Constructione*, was no less than 44 m high with seven, probably rectangular towers, which rose another 4 m above that. Outside this there was a ditch and then an outer wall, 22 m high, again strengthened by towers, although in this case they may have been round. This outer wall was provided with casemates so that the defenders could fire missiles without being seen and it was connected to the inner bailey by underground passages. The *De Constructione* does not mention a donjon. It seems that a great round tower was built on the summit of the hill by Baybars and this may have replaced or incorporated a Templar chapel. All these features can be paralleled in other, surviving Templar work, although the use of round towers is unusual, and it is clear that the castle was constructed on an immense scale.

The Teutonic Knights were comparative newcomers to the Kingdom of Jerusalem in the thirteenth century. The German hospital seems to have become militarised in about 1198 when German Crusaders returning home wanted to establish a permanent base in the Levant. In 1226 they acquired a substantial lordship in the hills of Galilee some 16 km northeast of Acre. The arrival of a sizeable contingent of German pilgrims in 1227 and the Emperor Frederick II in 1228 boosted their workforce and their funds. The original centre of the lordship had been at Chastiau dou Rei, a twelfth-century enclosure. The knights, however, seem to have decided that this site was too low lying and exposed and they sought a situation with more natural defences. It was probably in 1227 that work began on the castle which was to be known as Montfort, German pilgrims working on the site while the French, English and Spanish were working at Sidon. In 1228 Bohemond IV of Antioch Tripoli agreed to contribute 100 bezants a year to the construction and in 1229 the Master, Hermann of Salza, wrote to Gregory IX for financial support for their 'castrum novum'. By the 1240s, the castle was functioning as an administrative centre for the Knights but its prosperity was short lived. It fended off a Mamluke attack in 1266 but the lands around were so ravaged that in July 1270 the Hospitallers lent the Teutonic Knights some lands to sow grain on. In June 1271 Baybars himself led the attack on the castle, on the 11th the Muslims took the castletown and the next day breached the outer walls, and the Knights were obliged to retreat to the keep from which they negotiated their surrender. Led by their Master, Johan von Sachsen, they were allowed to retire to Acre.

Compared with Saphet or Crac des Chevaliers, the castle was built on a modest scale. It lies along the crest of a ridge (fig. 17). At the east end, where the ridge joins the hills, it was defended by a rock-cut ditch and a D-shaped keep on top of a cistern. To the west, there are the remains of a long undercroft which probably supported a hall and a chapel; fragments of stained glass

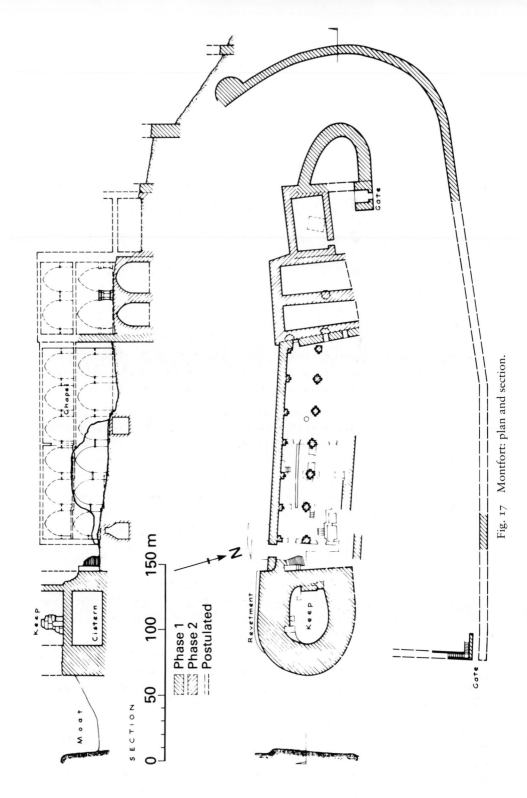

Fig. 17 Montfort: plan and section.

Plate 45   Judin: view from the highest Crusader tower looking west along the
ridge, with the wooded hills of Galilee in the foreground and the plains of
Acre in the distance.

were found here. At the west end, where the ground fell away, there was
another undercroft of two bays which must have supported a chamber above.
This lightly defended structure was enclosed on the north and west sides by a
wall some 30 m down the slope. By the river which ran along the north edge
of the ridge there was a mill, which was converted into an elegant guest house
in the mid-thirteenth century.

The Order constructed a second castle about 7 km to the south at Judin.
Here again, they chose a rocky, ridge-top site (plate 45). The remains of the
castle were substantially rebuilt in Ottoman times but recent work has shown
that the castle of the Knights consisted of two square towers some 20 m apart,
enclosed in a curtain wall running along the edge of the ridge. Between the
towers there was a courtyard which may have contained more buildings. Circumstantial evidence suggests that the whole structure dates from the period
of occupation by the Teutonic Knights after the 1220s.

Both Montfort and Judin seem to owe more to German traditions of military architecture than Crusader practice. The free-standing keep at Montfort
strongly resembles a German *Bergfried* while the two towers enclosed by a
curtain wall at Judin are very reminiscent of contemporary German castles
like Munzenburg. None of the innovations in planning and defence we see in
Templar and Hospitaller building of the thirteenth century seem to be found

in either building. The choice of sites is equally striking. Chastiau dou Rei lies in a village overlooking an open valley surrounded by fields and orchards, a very productive area. The Teutonic Knights seem to have abandoned this for sites which are more remote, inaccessible, and in the midst of rough and rocky forest land. Perhaps this is a sign that in the thirteenth century, even in an area so close to Acre (Judin is only about 16 km from the city which can be seen from the tops of its towers), defence had become more important than economic opportunities when it came to siting castles. In the event, neither Montfort nor Judin proved strong enough to withstand the assaults of Mamluke artillery for very long.[7]

TRIPOLI, ANTIOCH AND THE NORTH

There was considerably more continuity between twelfth- and thirteenth-century castles in the northern Crusader states than there was in the old Kingdom of Jerusalem. Saladin's reconquest of 1188 had been less complete here and Military Orders remained in possession of some of their main strongholds, the Templars at Safita and Tortosa, the Hospitallers at Margat and Crac des Chevaliers throughout. In the thirteenth century, increasingly close, if sometimes strained, relations with the Armenian Kingdom of Cilicia meant that the Orders expanded their influence into areas they had not entered in the twelfth century. In other ways, however, trends in the north mirrored those further south. Apart from coastal towns, like Nephin and Giblet, the Patriarch of Antioch's castle at Cursat and of course the capitals at Antioch and Tripoli, baronial castles had virtually disappeared by the thirteenth century and castle building was almost entirely in the hands of the Military Orders.

The Templars' main base in the north was at Tortosa (fig. 18),[8] a small town on the Syrian coast which they had probably acquired in the 1150s and which they proceeded to strengthen by building a massive castle. The pleasant little city is built on a flat site, offering no natural defensive features, and it still boasts the most complete surviving twelfth-century Crusader cathedral, a work of great beauty and restrained dignity. At first glance little remains of the castle which was the headquarters of the Templars but closer examination shows that substantial sections of the fortifications have survived, embedded in the structure of houses of the town. As at Cluny, where the surviving fragments of the great abbey church provide enough information for a convincing reconstruction of the vanished whole, so at Tortosa there is enough left to rebuild the castle in the mind's eye.

The chronology of the military architecture is not entirely clear. Accounts of the attack by Saladin in 1188 when the town fell but the Templars held out in the donjon make it clear that it was already a strong fortress. Saladin laid

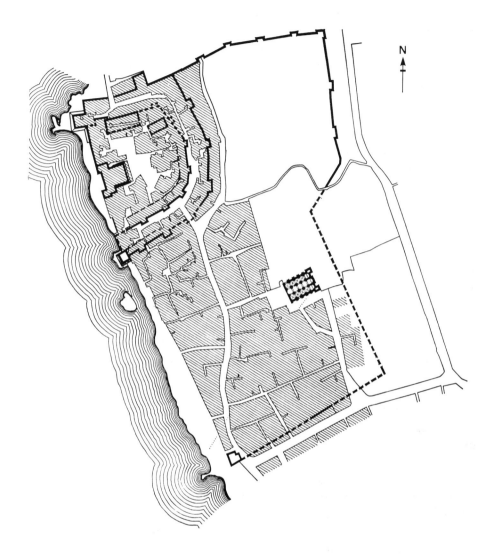

Fig. 18 Tortosa: plan of castle and city. The castle lies at the northwest of
the city walls and the cathedral can be noted centre right.

waste the town outside the castle and in 1202 Tortosa was struck by the same
earthquake which inflicted such damage at Crac des Chevaliers and Chastel
Blanc. In 1212 Wilbrand of Oldenburg passed through on his way from Beirut
to Antioch: 'It is a small city', he wrote, 'not much fortified and situated by
the sea. At the centre it has a very strong castle with an excellent wall with
eleven towers as if crowned with eleven precious stones ... this castle is very
well guarded by the Templars since it belongs to them.' This suggests that the

Plate 46   Tortosa (Tartus), probably thirteenth-century: eastern side of outer
enceinte. The large rectangular blocks on the bottom four courses of the
towers and curtain walls are Crusader work. Note the rectangular towers, the
ditch and the traces of the counterscarp visible at the extreme right.

castle had been rebuilt between 1202 and 1212 and most of the surviving
fabric probably dates from this rebuilding. The castle thus strengthened
remained in Templar hands to the very end of the Crusader era and was not
finally surrendered to the Mamlukes until 3 August 1291, two months after
the fall of Acre itself.

The castle stood at the northwest corner of the city wall with direct access
both to open country to the north and to the sea, which then came right up to
its western flank where there is now a new road. Coming from the city, the
visitor was confronted by a ditch and then the outer enceinte defended by projecting oblong towers (plate 46) of considerable size (about 15 m long as
opposed to the 20 m of the towers of the outer walls at Chastel Pelerin). Within
this there was another ditch and then the inner line of walls whose oblong
towers commanded the outer circuit completely (fig. 19). One small section of
the inner walls still survives to its full original height, which is no less than
25.5 m (higher, Braune notes, than the great round tower at Margat). The wall
is constructed, like all the other fortifications at Tortosa, of finely cut bossed
masonry. The inner side of this fragment (plate 47) shows signs of vaulted
chambers which would have provided both shooting galleries and firing platform. As in the inner enceinte at Crac, the upper defences are provided with
rectangular openings, perhaps for siege engines, as well as arrow slits.

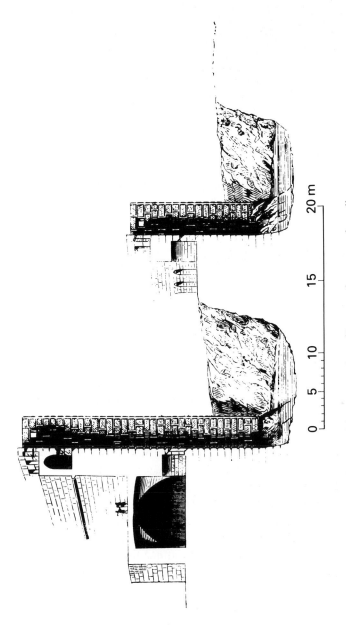

Fig. 19   Tortosa: section of inner and outer castle walls.

Plate 47   Tortosa: surviving fragment of inner wall seen from interior (west)
side. At 25m in height, this was as large a fortification as any built by the
Crusaders. Note the traces of wall walks at the upper level giving access to
arrows slits and rectangular openings.

Inside this inner enceinte was a bailey much of which is still the square of
the modern town. Around this were arranged the main conventual buildings.
These included a chapel of which two bays with fine Gothic ribbed vaulting
still survive, though now only covering a squalid yard (plate 48), and a rectangular chapter-house on an undercroft; here again traces of fine vaulting can
be distinguished. Along the sea side there was another hall with a central row
of pillars. Altogether the conventual buildings clearly reflected the wealth of
the Order and the importance they attached to Tortosa.

At the core of the castle lay the donjon which now only survives to first-
floor level (plate 49). The original donjon seems to have been a typical piece of
twelfth-century Crusader work, square, with the basement divided into two
rectangular chambers. This was perhaps the donjon which Saladin failed to

Plate 48 Tortosa: interior of chapel, south wall. Compare the squared ribs of
the vault with those of the Templar hall at Chastel Blanc (plate 51).

take in 1188. Later it was strengthened to add shooting galleries at ground
level by surrounding it with a vaulted passage provided with numerous arrow
slits. Further provision for flanking fire was made with the addition of two
oblong towers where the donjon met the sea-wall of the fortress. The changes
of design here are a good example of the modification of a plain twelfth-
century donjon to cope with the more active defensive techniques required in
the thirteenth. We know nothing of the circumstances of the construction of
this great work but there are striking similarities with the much better documented Templar work at Chastel Pelerin. These include the site with direct
access to the sea, cut off from the land by two ditches and two lines of walls,
the use of very large square-cut masonry, the distinctive oblong towers projecting only a short distance from the walls (in contrast to the almost square,
boldly projecting towers we find in twelfth-century work like Saone or the

Plate 49   Tortosa: donjon from the sea (west) side. Originally the sea came up to the foot of the castle walls. The wall in the centre is the side of the first donjon, probably twelfth-century. The two projecting wings visible on the right and left were added later to provide additional flanking fire.

round towers beloved by the Hospitallers) and the way in which the towers of the inner enceinte are placed between the towers of the outer wall to command them completely. The vaulted hall in the interior also has parallels with Templar work in Chastel Pelerin and Beaufort. These distinctive features seem to add up to a Templar style with its own characteristics and its strength is shown by the fact that, like Chastel Pelerin, it was never taken by the Muslims but only abandoned by the Templars after the fall of Acre in 1291.

The other major Templar building in the county of Tripoli was Chastel Blanc (Safita).[9] Even today the great, gaunt tower of the Templars dominates the pretty little Syrian hill town which the locals call Burj Safita, the tower of Safita (plate 50). The castle belonged to the County of Tripoli and, like nearby Arima, was probably handed over to the Templars in about 1171 after it had been sacked by Nur al-Din and then damaged by an earthquake. Saladin did not feel strong enough to attack the castle in 1188 but in 1202 the tower was described as 'prostrata' by the earthquake. It is probable that the building in its present form dates either from the 1170s or from after 1202, and it is said, by an Arab source, to have been strengthened by St Louis during his stay in the Crusader states. In 1271 Baybars began a systematic reduction of the fortifications of the County of Tripoli; the 700-strong garrison of Chastel Blanc

Plate 50   Chastel Blanc (Safita), late twelfth- or early thirteenth-century:
general view from southeast. The massive donjon dominates the village. The
surviving wall of the hall can be seen to its right.

were determined to resist him but the Master of the Temple in Tortosa
ordered them to surrender and they left in exchange for their lives.

The appearance of the castle today is slightly misleading as it looks like an
isolated tower in the middle of the town. In Crusader times there were two
enceintes, an oval, outer one about 165 × 100 m and an inner which was
probably rectangular. The outer one was defended by at least two typically
Templar oblong towers and contained a variety of vaulted chambers, including a large hall building on three storeys (plate 51). The surviving springing of
the arches shows that this had fine Gothic vaulting, similar to that found in
the chapel and chapter-house at Tortosa. The donjon (plate 52), however,

Plate 51   Chastel Blanc: wall of hall from east. Note the gate leading into the
bailey, the high ground-floor undercroft with groin vaults and the springings
of the ribbed vaults of the upper floor. This must have been a magnificent
Gothic hall.

must always have been the most striking feature and it reflects with marvell-
ous clarity its role as a home for fighting monks (fig. 20). It is the tallest of the
surviving Crusader donjons (27 m; Giblet, 21 m; Saone, 22 m; Chastel
Rouge, 12 m) and quite different in design from these other purely military
structures. The lower main floor consists of a simple but rather grand chapel,
now a well-kept and much-used church, with a barrel-vaulted roof which
suggests a twelfth-century date, and an apse inscribed in the east wall; only the
arrow slits in the walls reveal its military aspect on the interior (plate 53). The
upper floor is reached by a staircase in the thickness of the massive walls and
leads to a hall, divided by a line of pillars and roofed with groin vaults (plate
54). Above this is a flat roof edged with simple merlons and arrow slits but

Plate 52   Chastel Blanc: window in south wall of donjon. This is both arrow
slit and church window in the great cliff of masonry 27 m high.

showing no indication of machicolations or of holes in the stonework to
support hoarding. It is tempting, and probably accurate, to regard the upper
hall as a dormitory for the knights who were supposed to live a communal,
monastic existence. The interior masonry work, while not rich in ornament,
has a fineness and polish which distinguish it from the more functional work
in other donjons. No other building in the Latin east shows so clearly the
interrelation between religious commitment and military activity in the
twelfth century as this mighty fortress church.

The Templars had other properties in the County of Tripoli, the castles
at Arima and Chastel Rouge, but it is not clear how much of the fortification at these places was built by them and how much by their baronial
predecessors.

In the Principality of Antioch, the Templars seem to have been responsible

Fig. 20   Chastel Blanc (Safita): section. Note the under-floor cistern, the large chapel which occupies the main bulk of the tower and the upper chamber, possibly the knights' dormitory.

for the construction of three castles in the Amanus mountains, Gastun (Baghras), Calan (the Crusader La Roche de Roissol or possibly La Roche de Guillaume) and Trapesac.[10] The Amanus range, though not very high, is rugged and in many areas heavily forested. Only a few passes across it connect the Principality of Antioch to the south and east with the Cilician kingdom of Armenia to the north and west. Control of these routes was of considerable importance and, though none of the castles is in a position actually to block the passes, they would form a secure base for attacking hostile forces trying to cross the range. The Templars seem to have acquired these sites in the mid-twelfth century (1153 in the case of Gastun), and this mountain area was dominated by them until the time of Saladin's conquests in 1188 when Gastun and Trapesac fell. Gastun was occupied by the Armenians in the thirteenth century while Trapesac remained in Muslim hands despite a Templar expedition from La Roche Guillaume in 1237 to regain it. La Roche de Roissol/

Plate 53   Chastel Blanc: window in south wall of church from interior. Note
the simplicity of design combined with very high-quality masonry work.

Guillaume seems to have remained in Templar hands throughout until it was
abandoned around the time of the fall of Antioch in 1268.

These castles are markedly different in character from the Templar fortresses of the Kingdom of Jerusalem and the County of Tripoli. They are all
on mountain sites, La Roche spectacularly sited on top of a peak, and relied
heavily on topography to provide natural defences. The masonry work is
poor, consisting of small, irregularly shaped stones and completely lacking the
finely finished stonework we find at Chastel Pelerin or Chastel Blanc. The
Templars here must have been relying on local masons and architects familiar
with the Armenian tradition of mountain-top fortresses.

Only at Gastun (Baghras) are there substantial remains of Templar building.[11] Here a rocky knoll is encircled and crowned by fortifications on two
levels. The fabric is of small coursed rubble and there are rounded towers and

Plate 54 Chastel Blanc: interior of first-floor chamber from southeast. The
squared pillars and ribs are used to support a groin vault.

corners, very much in the Armenian style but quite unlike other known
Templar work, and a fine enclosed defensive gallery with arrow slits on the
lower level. The Knights built two large, well-lit halls as was their custom.
The castle is compact and craggy and was to become a major political issue. It
was retaken from the Muslims in 1191, not by the Crusaders of Antioch but
by the Armenians, and their possession of this outpost so close to Antioch
itself soured relations between these two Christian powers for much of the
early thirteenth century until it, like Antioch itself, fell into Baybars' hands in
1268.

The remains of La Roche de Roissol/Guillaume (Calan) are very scanty.[12]
The isolated hill-top was defended by a curtain wall and divided into upper
and lower baileys. The surviving curtain wall and towers cling to the edge of
the precipice. In the upper bailey there are some remains of a hall and rather
more substantial ones of a simple apsed chapel about 15 m long. If it was
intended to accommodate the garrison for worship, it can never have
amounted to more than a small detachment. At Trapesac the site is still more
ruinous and, in this case, built over so that even the redoubtable Edwards has
been unable to devise a plan.[13]

7

THE HOSPITALLERS IN TRIPOLI
AND ANTIOCH

T HE Hospitallers were the partners and rivals of the Templars in the defence of the Crusader states.[1] The order had begun in Jerusalem and before 1187 they had had properties in the city and castles in the rural areas. After the battle of Hattin their castles at Belmont, Belvoir and Bethgibelin were lost and never subsequently refortified by the Christians. They still retained estates in the area of Acre and a fortified palace within the city but no castles (with the exception of the fortified commanderie at Calansue which they regained in 1191 and held until 1265.[2] Instead they devoted their resources, both from their local estates and from their ever greater holdings in western Europe, to the defence of their great castles in the County of Tripoli.

The Hospitallers' serious connection with the County of Tripoli began in 1144. In this year Count Raymond II of Tripoli granted them what amounted to an independent principality in the east of his county. It included the small towns of Rafanea and Montferrand on the eastern slopes of the mountains looking towards Homs and the Orontes valley, considerable properties in the Buqai'ah (the plain between Homs and Tripoli and separates the mountains of Lebanon to the south from Syrian hills to the north), a number of small fortifications in this plain, fishing rights in the Lake of Homs and a castle on a spur of the Syrian hills, looking both east and south, which the Arabs referred to as Hisn al-Akrad, the Castle of the Kurds. This gift brought with it both assets and problems. On the positive side the lands were rich and fertile, being well watered by streams and by rainfall; on a cold, grey winter day when the rain sweeps in from the Mediterranean, the hills can seem more Scottish than Levantine. The bad news was that these lands were very exposed to Muslim attack from Homs, which was never captured by the Franks, and further afield: it had no natural defences. Yet even this proximity had its advantages

Plate 55   Crac des Chevaliers, twelfth- and thirteenth-century: general view
from southwest, showing outer and inner enceintes. The round southwest
tower of the outer enciente and the square tower on the extreme right of the
picture were rebuilt after the castle was captured by the Mamlukes. It was
from this side that Sultan Baybars mounted his assault in 1271 and the
original Crusader fortifications were damaged in the attack.

for it meant that the neighbouring Muslim settlements could be raided or put
under tribute for the benefit of the Knights. It could also be used to attract
pious donations: when the Master of the Hospital Raymond du Puy heard
that the king of Bohemia, Wladislav II, was coming on Crusade in 1160, he
offered him the keys of the castle 'situated on the frontier with the pagans'
and the king rewarded him generously.[3]

They decided to establish their main base overlooking the plain at the
Castle of the Kurds, so called because an eleventh-century Amir of Homs had
established a Kurdish garrison there, and they processed to create the finest
and most elaborately fortified castle in the Crusader Levant (plate 55) to
defend the eastern frontier of the County of Tripoli and to serve as an
administrative centre of their great estates.[4]

The defensive role can be seen during the various invasions of the County
of Tripoli by the Muslims. In 1180, for example, Saladin ravaged the County,
and all its defenders, not daring to challenge him in the field, shut themselves
up in their castles, the Hospitallers in Crac.[5] This meant of course that when
the raid was finished, the Knights could emerge again to take over and revive
their ravaged lands which could not be protected from being damaged by the

enemy but could be protected from being permanently occupied. The same happened in May 1188, in the aftermath of the battle of Hattin, when Saladin came to prospect the fortress but decided it was too strong and passed on to Tortosa and Margat where he had no more luck. The possession of the castle meant that in the first half of the thirteenth century, the Hospitallers 'principality' of Crac was the only significant inland area of the Crusader states which remained continuously in Frankish hands: the value of a great castle could not be more clearly illustrated.

The offensive function of the castle at Crac is perhaps more unexpected. The golden age came in the first half of the thirteenth century, a period when most of the other Crusader enclaves in the Levant were struggling to survive but when Crac had a garrison of 2,000 and lorded it over the surrounding areas. Most of the evidence for this comes from Muslim sources which, naturally, tend to dwell on their own successes and pass over the less encouraging aspects. Reading between the lines, however, it seems clear that the Knights at Crac extracted tribute on a fairly regular basis from the Muslims of Homs and Hama and the neighbouring districts and that this went on as long as the various members of the Ayyubid family who had divided Saladin's domains up amongst themselves were in covert or open rivalry. As early as 1203 raids were being launched on Hama and Montferrand, now under Muslim control. In 1207–8 the Franks of Tripoli and Crac were attacking Homs. In 1230 the Amir of Hama refused to pay his tribute and a combined force of 500 knights and 2,700 footsoldiers, both Hospitallers from Crac and Templars, set out to take it by force. On this occasion they were rebuffed but in 1233 they assembled a punitive expedition including, in addition to their own forces, the Master of the Templars, Walter of Brienne, with a hundred knights from Cyprus, eighty knights from the Kingdom of Jerusalem led by Pierre d'Avalon, John of Ibelin, lord of Beirut (the great lawyer and senior member of the local aristocracy) and Henry, brother of Bohemond V of Antioch, with thirty knights from the principality. It was as great a show of force as the Crusaders of the Levant could manage at this time, testimony to the prestige of the Knights of Crac and the central role of the castle in the Crusader east. They ravaged the lands of Hama unchallenged and after this the prince of Hama agreed to pay his tribute. The Isma'ilis (Assassins) of the Syrian mountains were paying tribute at the time of Joinville's visit in 1250–1, and as late as 1270 they were still complaining to Baybars about the tribute they had to pay to the Franks.[6]

Crac was also visited by many passing Crusaders who, we may presume, left donations. In 1218 King Andrew II of Hungary came there and was received with royal honours by the castellan, Raymond of Pignans. The king was extremely impressed by the work of the Knights in what he called the 'key of the Christian lands [terre clavem christiane]' and endowed them with income from his own properties in Hungary, 60 marks per annum for the Master and 40 for the brothers. A less affluent but equally chivalrous visitor was Geoffroy de Joinville, a baron from one of the leading families of Champagne, who had been given the right to quarter his arms with those of England by Richard Cœur de Lion on account of his knightly prowess. He joined the Fourth Crusade, many of whose members went on to sack Constantinople in 1204, but he broke away from the mob and came to Syria to fulfil his crusading vows. He died at Crac in 1203 or 1204 and was buried in the chapel, and his shield, along presumably with many others, was hung on its frescoed walls. We know about this because his nephew Jean, the biographer of St Louis, went to Crac in the early 1250s in the course of St Louis' stay in the Levant, and took the shield back to France. There it hung in the collegiate church at Joinville until stolen by some German mercenaries in 1544. Geoffroy's bones probably still lie beneath the paving of the austere and dignified chapel with its simple apse and plain vaulted roof to the present day.[7]

Crac is an exceptional castle. It owed its glories to the wealth the Knights acquired from their own rich lands, from extracting tribute from the neighbouring Muslims and from the generosity of visiting Crusaders.

The good times came to an end after 1250. In 1252 a horde of Turkmans, estimated by the treasurer of the Hospital at Acre as 10,000 in number, ravaged the fertile lands around the castle and after this there are signs that the financial position was deteriorating. In 1254 St Louis finally left the Levant where he had spent so much money strengthening fortifications, and in 1255 Pope Alexander IV replied favourably to a request for exemption from tithes because of the expenses incurred by the Hospitallers in maintaining the castle and a permanent garrison of sixty Knights in the heart of enemy country. In 1268 the Master Hugh Revel complained that the lands on which 10,000 people had lived were now deserted and that no revenues whatever were collected from Hospitallers properties in the Kingdom of Jerusalem. Early in 1270 Baybars allowed his horses to graze on 'the meadows and crops of Crac and this was one of the reasons why it was captured since its only provision came from its crops and these were all used for pasture by the Muslim troops at this time'.[8]

Financial decline was compounded by political changes on the Muslim side with the seizure of power by Baybars in 1260, which meant not only that no more tribute was paid but that a united Muslim army, supported by all the resources of Egypt, now faced the Franks. The Hospitaller garrison dwindled: Hugh Revel in his 1268 letter says that there were only 300 brothers left in the east. Early in 1270 Baybars made a foray in the area of Crac but returned to Cairo on hearing the news that St Louis was launching another Crusade. St Louis died the same year in Tunis and early in 1271 Baybars was free to devote his whole attention to the castle. He left Cairo on 24 January

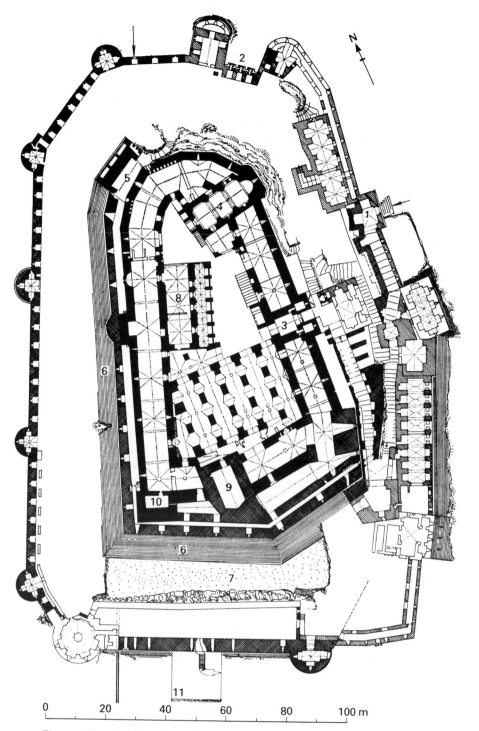

Fig. 21 Crac des Chevaliers: plan at ground level. Twelfth-century Crusader work is in black, thirteenth-century work is hatched and cross-hatched, Muslim work unshaded. 1. Outer gate; 2. postern; 3. gate of inner enceinte; 4. chapel; 5. northwest tower; 6. glacis; 7. tank; 8. hall; 9. residential tower; 10. Warden's Tower; 11. Baybar's Tower.

and, after taking Chastel Blanc and a number of other small forts, appeared outside Crac on 3 March.

Literary and archaeological evidence suggests that the main Muslim attack came from the south front.[9] Here Baybars set up his siege engines on the outer defensive work which the Knights had built to guard against precisely this eventuality. By 29 March, the outer walls had been breached by a combination of bombardment and sapping. The stretch of wall which was brought down and subsequently rebuilt by the Muslims can be traced in the fabric and Baybars subsequently constructed a massive new square tower to guard this weak point. The garrison retreated to the inner defences and at this point peace negotiations were opened. According to some sources the Franks were tricked into surrender by a forged letter from the Master of the Order in Tripoli but the truth is that once the Muslims had set up their engines inside the outer walls, it was only a matter of time before they took the whole castle. The Knights were allowed to retire to Tripoli and on 8 April they finally abandoned the fortress they had defended so stubbornly. Many of their local allies among the mountain people were not so privileged and were taken prisoner.

The castle stands on a spur of the mountains (figs. 21 and 22). As so often in Crusader castles, there was one side, the south in this case, where the natural defences were non-existent and it was here that the architects of Crac constructed their most elaborate and massive works. There were two main phases of Frankish building. Between the Hospitallers' takeover of 1142 and earthquake of 1170 an enclosure castle was built, much of which is incorporated in the later fabric. It was defended by square towers which do not seem to have projected far beyond the line of the curtain walls. There was a main gate between two small square towers on the east side and a smaller gate in the side of the northwestern tower. In the interior there were vaulted chambers lining the courtyard and possibly a hall for the Knights. It was not dissimilar from other courtyard castles constructed by the Hospitallers in the twelfth century, although the irregular site gave it a distinctive shape.

In 1170 it was damaged by an earthquake and an Arab source mentions that the chapel was demolished. It was probably after this that the present chapel was built, since it interrupts the line of the earlier defences. With its pointed barrel vault and simple apse it is clearly related to the chapel at Margat which we know was built after 1186, though the style would have been considered old fashioned in most parts of France by this period.[10] The twelfth-century walls of the inner court are now largely invisible behind the later work but in the northeast section of the defences two stretches of twelfth-century curtain walling can be seen with the outside of the chapel apse projecting between them. In both chapel and walls, the masonry is distinguished by large rectangular blocks laid in courses with the typical bossed centres and flat margins of twelfth-century work. Further twelfth-century work survives in the north-

Fig. 22   Crac des Chevaliers: reconstruction, seen from the northeast.

Plate 56   Crac des Chevaliers: tower at northwest of inner enceinte from
west (6). This is the only one of the square twelfth-century towers to survive
in its original form. Clearly visible are the three arches of the slot
machicolations. Above them are a line of small openings which must have
given access to a projecting machicolation, probably added in the thirteenth
century. The sloping glacis on the right is another thirteenth-century addition.
On the far side, this tower shelters a postern gate in the re-entrant angle (not
visible here).

west tower of the inner enclosure (no. 5 on the plan), a complex building
which shelters a postern gate in one flank (comparable with some in Saone)
and three slot machicolations on its front (plate 56). If these are twelfth-
century work, as seems likely, they are very early examples and certainly
predate the rather similar slot machicolations which were found on Richard
Cœur de Lion's donjon at Château Gaillard, 1197–8.

In 1202 the castle was again damaged by earthquake and it may have been
after this that it was completely remodelled and assumed its present appearance. This was a period of great military activity in Crac and also a time of

Plate 57   Crac des Chevaliers: west wall of outer enceinte looking south.
These round towers were part of the early thirteenth-century rebuilding. Note
the corbels for the box machicolations; the continuous machicolation on the
far tower is probably Muslim work, added after the 1271 conquest.

great prosperity, and this is reflected in both the scale and the quality of the
work. An outer circuit of walls was constructed (there may have been one in
the twelfth-century castle but, if so, no trace of it remains). This outer circuit
went round the whole castle, but can best be seen on the long west side (plate
57) where the Frankish work is virtually unaltered. This outer wall by itself
would form a substantial castle, being 9 m high and defended by prominently
projecting towers. In contrast both to twelfth-century Hospitallers work and
contemporary Templar building, towers are rounded. It is not just the shape
that is new. There are archery slits in the turrets and curtain, so positioned
as to minimise the area of dead ground and staggered so they are not directly
above each other (plate 58). From these the archers could command the area
before the walls in almost complete safety. These wall-head defences were
the most elaborate and developed anywhere in the Latin east. There was a

Plate 58 Crac des Chevaliers: tower and curtain on west wall of outer
enceinte. Note the corbels which originally supported the box machicolations.
Also visible are the long arrow slits with stirrup bottoms to facilitate downward
fire; they are not placed above each other, to avoid weakening the wall.

stone-vaulted chemin de ronde which gave access to box machicolations
boldly projecting on corbels with holes in the floor for dropping missiles and
arrow slits in their faces (plate 59). Inside, these machicolations are curiously
cramped and claustrophobic (plate 60); the archers who manned them were
obliged to squat or kneel and for all the weight of stonework which surrounded them, they must have felt a bit like the tail gunner in a Lancaster
bomber, very isolated and vulnerable. The whole structure is a brilliantly
designed and superbly built fighting machine.

These box machicolations are an interesting architectural puzzle. Simple
corbels at Saone and Margat show that some form of machicolation or hoarding was used by the Crusaders before the end of the twelfth century but there

Plate 59   Crac des Chevaliers: box machicolations on west wall of outer
enceinte. Note the sloping roof and the corbels, and that each machicolation
has an arrow slit in the centre of the outer face.

are no Frankish parallels, either then or later, for the highly developed box
machicolations at Crac. There are, however, clear parallels in Muslim work.
Some of this is at Crac itself. According to Deschamps, the southwest corner
of the outer walls was rebuilt after the siege of 1271 and the builders used
both box machicolations and a continuous covered machicolation. These
could simply have been imitations and developments of the Frankish work,
but more significant are the appearance of such machicolations, identical even
to the arrow slits in the front, in the citadels at Aleppo (plate 61) and Damascus, both to be dated to the first decade of the thirteenth century, exactly
contemporary, in fact, with the work at Crac. It is difficult to know exactly
what to make of this. The similarities are too close to be accidental. It could
be that one side copied the others work or that the same group of masons

Plate 60   Crac des Chevaliers: interior of box machicolation with castle wall
to the left and outer face to the right. The interior space is extremely narrow
and cramped and the defenders must have had to crouch in positions of
great danger and discomfort.

were working for both Christian and Muslim patrons in this period. Unfortunately the uncertainty about the exact dating of the work at Crac makes it
impossible to know which came first but the evidence for cross-cultural trans-
mission of military technology is indisputable.[11]

Work on the outer enceinte continued through the thirteenth century. At an
unknown date the enclosure was extended at the southeast corner using a
rubble masonry greatly inferior to the earlier work. In the north wall a
postern gate was added: an inscription records that this was the work of
Nicolas Lorgne who was probably castellan in the late 1250s before being pro-
moted to be Marshal of the Hospital in 1269 and finally Grand Master

Plate 61   Aleppo citadel, first decade of thirteenth century: machicolation on
south façade of entrance tower. The wall above the machicolation is a
fifteenth-century addition: the machicolation was originally at or near
the wall head. Note the sloping roof, the corbels and the arrow slit in the
centre, all strikingly similar to the example at Crac of approximately the same
date: nothing similar is known from earlier castle building. Who copied whom
and how did the transfer of technology take place?

between 1278 and 1284. This was perhaps the last improvement the Knights
made before the loss of the castle in 1271.[12]

The entrance was greatly strengthened at this time. From the outer gate the
visitor proceeds up a long vaulted tunnel (plate 62), dominated at all points by
defensive positions. Half-way along, this tunnel does a hairpin bend and
doubles back to reach the entrance to the inner bailey. Should you go straight
on at the bend, you will emerge and find yourself between the two circuits of
walls and completely overlooked from the inside. The whole structure is one
of those 'bent entrances' beloved of Byzantine builders and historians of military architecture but elaborated and developed beyond anything seen before.

Plate 62   Crac des Chevaliers: entrance tunnel. The long covered passage
leading from the main gate to the interior is overlooked for the whole of its
length by murder-holes and other vantage points from which the defenders
could attack intruders.

The area in between the circuits is quite narrow and was not used as an
outer bailey to provide accommodation. Most of it was dry, but on the
vulnerable eastern side there was a great open water tank, fed by an aqueduct
from the neighbouring hill, which provided both a water supply and a moat.

And so to the massive inner walls which followed the line of the twelfth-
century circuit but were built slightly outside it. On the west and south sides,
this meant that there was a narrow passage between the old and the new
which was developed as a shooting gallery in the thickness of the wall. Only
on the north and at some points on the west was the old work visible at all.
The south and west fronts are the most impressive. Here the inner wall rises
up from a mighty glacis, a steeply sloping cliff of stonework designed to make
the wall more stable in the face of siege engines and earthquakes (plate 63). It

Plate 63   Crac des Chevaliers: south façade of inner enceinte from south. The
figures in the foreground are standing on the inside of the outer walls.
Between them and the foot of the great glacis lies the berquilla or open water
cistern. Above stand the two western towers of the south façade with the
'Warden's Tower' on the left. Note the arrow slit half-way up the glacis on
the right-hand side, showing that there is a passage along the interior to
provide more firing positions.

totally dominates and overlooks the outer wall (plate 64). Out of this glacis
spring four round towers, one in the centre of the west front, three huge ones
on the south (plate 63). These are immensely impressive, not just because of
their size and the way in which they seem to grow almost organically out of
the glacis but also because of the superb ashlar masonry. The thirteenth-
century Frankish work is mostly constructed in limestone taken from a quarry
a couple of kilometres away. Unlike the bossed stonework characteristic of
twelfth-century work, this is flat ashlar, so finely and exactly cut that the
mortar is almost invisible. The wall-head defences have mostly disappeared
but traces along the southern wall show that there were no machicolations

Plate 64   Crac des Chevaliers: southwest tower of inner enceinte, the
'Warden's Tower', from south. Note the large window upper right giving
light to the great round chamber within and the superb masonry work where
tower and glacis meet.

Plate 65   Crac des Chevaliers: western wall of inner enceinte from south. The
photograph is taken from the top of the outer wall. The 'Warden's Tower' is
on the right, the twelfth-century tower 2 (see plate 56) at the left end.

but arrow slits interspersed with window-like rectangular openings in the
parapet, presumably so that the engines mounted up there could fire through.

The interior of the courtyard is comparatively small since three quarters of
it is built over (plate 66). The chapel stands at one end and a great raised
esplanade at the other (plate 67), supported by squat piers and heavy stone
vaults. Like the similar but smaller hall at Saone, this was no doubt designed
to provide storage and stabling but also as a much-needed place of shelter
from missiles. Along the western side stands the hall of the Knights. This was
probably of twelfth-century origin but the interior vaulting, with its roll-
moulded ribs, is thirteenth. The most striking feature is the gallery on the
courtyard side (plate 68), which probably dates from the 1230s;[13] elegant, with
delicate, slender pillars and tracery, it shows all the refinement of the high

Plate 66   Crac des Chevaliers: entrance to inner court looking west. The
gallery of the Knights' Hall can be seen in the background.

Gothic of the thirteenth century (plate 69) and is a perfect complement to the
massive fortifications. There is a short Latin verse inscribed on one of the
arches:

> Sit tibi copia
> Sit sapiencia
> Formaque detur
> Inquinat omnia sola
> Superbia si comitetur

(Have richness, have wisdom, have beauty but beware of pride which spoils all
it comes into contact with). It may not be fanciful to imagine that this verse
was inscribed to warn the Knights against glorying in their magnificent fortress.

The great towers in the southern wall were developed as living accommodation for the sixty or so Knights, the aristocrats of the castle community. The

Plate 67   Crac des Chevaliers: interior of inner court, looking south. The gallery of the Knights' Hall is to the right. Ahead at ground level are the arches of the vast stores and shelters which occupy most of the area of the court. In the distance can be seen the rear of the centre tower of the south façade.

centre tower boasts large airy chambers with rectangular mullioned windows looking down into the court (plate 71) (the outside face, of course, being sternly military). The southwest tower has a large, elegantly vaulted circular chamber. Originally this was military in character and had arrow slits to provide flanking fire along the east and south walls but the slits were later blocked and a large pointed window inserted. It was probably designed in its present form as the lodgings of the Grand Master, away from the other Knights. It has a large arched window from which he could survey the lands which owed him tribute and the direction from which his enemies might approach. There are remains of a small watchtower on top, over which Rey envisaged the standard of the Grand Master, snapping in the stiff Syrian breeze.

Crac has a sister, similar in size, if not in refinement. The great Hospitaller castle at Margat stands on an isolated, triangular 360 m hill overlooking the Mediterranean sea (plate 73). In the political geography of the Crusader states, it lay at the south of the Principality of Antioch but there were close links between the Knights at Margat and those at the sister castle of Crac des Chevaliers, only 60 km away over the hills as the crow flies. As we have seen it was in the years after 1130 that the Mazoir family made Margat the centre of

Plate 68   Crac des Chevaliers: gallery of the Knights' Hall looking south.
Note the fine rounded pillars and ribs in contrast to the squared ribs favoured
by the Templars at Tortosa and Chastel Blanc (plates 49, 51 and 54).

their extensive properties. When the Hospitallers bought the castle in 1186, they also acquired the small seaside town of Valenia, a number of lesser castles and a patchwork of estates, most of them nearby but some as far away as the Amanus mountains, northwest of Antioch. Margat, like Crac, was developed as the administrative centre of vast lands which amounted virtually to an independent principality.[14]

Of the Mazoir castle only some stretches of curtain wall with typically twelfth-century square towers now remain but the castle was obviously formidable in 1188 when Saladin looked at it and passed by to find easier prey: 'Recognising that Marqab was impregnable', says Abu'l-Fida, 'and that he had no hope of capturing it, he passed on to Jabala.'[15] Like Crac, Margat enjoyed its greatest power and prosperity in the first half of the thirteenth century and the Knights of the two castles often joined expeditions against Hama and

Plate 69   Crac des Chevaliers: gallery of the Knights' Hall, detail.

other Muslim towns. In response to this, Margat was attacked in 1204–5 by troops sent by the Sultan of Aleppo, al-Malik al-Zahir; they destroyed some of the towers but the Muslim general was killed by an arrow and his army retired. Margat was strong enough to extract tribute from the neighbouring Muslims for most of the thirteenth century and it was not until after the fall of Crac in 1271 that Baybars obliged the Knights to renounce all the revenues and rights they enjoyed in Muslim territory.[16] The garrison at Margat retained their offensive capability almost to the final disappearance of the Crusader states and as late as 1280 200 Knights from the castle launched a successful pillaging raid to the Buqai'ah plain near Crac des Chevaliers, by then, of course, in Muslim hands. The Knights also controlled the north–south coastal road below their stronghold. In addition to the main castle, the Knights built a guard tower, square and massive near the shore, and a wall to connect it to the castle: no-one could pass along the coast road without paying.

Plate 70   Crac des Chevaliers: interior court looking north from centre tower of south façade. In the foreground is the roof of the shelter. At the far end of the court is the chapel with its entrance loggia in front, to the left the Knights' Hall. The square, box-like tower in the distance is the rear of tower 2.

The functions of the fortress were not purely military. By the beginning of the thirteenth century the bishop of the little seaside town of Valenia had abandoned the city and had transferred his see to the castle, where the chapel must have doubled as his modest cathedral. Between 1204 and 1206 a General Chapter of the Hospitallers was held at Margat and the archives (*escris et recordations*) of the Order were collected and kept in the castle.[17] The German traveller Wilbrand of Oldenburg saw it in its prime in 1212.

> It is a huge and very strong castle, defended by a double wall and protected by several towers. It stands on a high mountain. This castle belongs to the Hospital and it is the strongest in the whole of this country. It confronts the numerous castles of the Old Man of the Mountain [the Isma'ili Assassin leader] and of the Sultan of Aleppo and has put such a check on their tyranny that it can collect an annual tribute of 2,000 marks from them. Every night four Knights of the Hospital and twenty-eight soldiers keep guard there. The Hospitallers provide for a 1,000 people there apart from the garrison. Every year, the lands around the castle produce harvests of more than 500 carts. The provisions stored there are sufficient for five years.[18]

Writing in the 1220s, the Muslim geographer Yaqut observes more succinctly, 'Every one says it is a castle whose equal has never been seen.'

Plate 71 Crac des Chevaliers: wall of centre tower of south façade facing
onto court. The exterior of this tower is rounded and fortified (plate 63), the
interior has large, rectangular windows lighting spacious, airy chambers
which may have been the living accommodation of the Knights, the aristocrats
of the castle community.

Margat lacks the style and grace of Crac.[19] This is largely because it is built
of the local black basalt, which is hard and unyielding and cannot be shaped
and dressed with ease. It is ruggedly impressive rather than beautiful. It stands
on a hill commanding extensive views over the Mediterranean far below and
the narrow coastal plain to north and south. Inland too the terrain drops
steeply and, beyond the valley, the castle surveys the hills where the Assassins
lived. It is a harsher and bleaker landscape than the smiling countryside of the
County of Tripoli to the south and the building seems to reflect this more
austere environment. Only to the south was there a narrow neck of land connecting the castle plateau with the neighbouring hill. The architects rightly saw
this as the danger point and protected it with a rock-cut reservoir to discourage

Plate 72   Crac des Chevaliers: wall-head defences on south front of inner
enceinte immediately east of the central tower. Note the arrow slit with the
steeply sloping stirrup base to allow downward fire and the rectangular
opening which may have been designed for use by ballistas.

undermining (as in a similar situation at Kerak) and all the fortifications that
money and artifice could devise. The castle walls enclose the flat top of a triangular plateau. As at Kerak and Saone, this area is divided into two sections, a
fortress proper and a castletown, divided by a well-fortified ditch and wall.

The long walls which run round the edge of the plateau were defended by a
dozen towers, of which all but four are round and seem to date from after the
Hospitaller takeover of 1186. The defences of the castletown vary greatly. On
the east front there are a series of round towers which protect an outer wall
which is essentially a giant hillside terrace. Inside this there was an inner wall
crowning a low glacis. It is not clear how far round this inner wall extended
and there seem to have been no towers on it. On the north end there is a single
wall defended only by one square tower, probably of twelfth-century work.

Plate 73   Margat (Marqab), mostly thirteenth-century: general view from
southeast. The isolated plateau on which the castle stands is clearly visible; on
the other side the land drops steeply to the Mediterranean. The south
provides the only slightly level approach. The small patch of trees below the
main tower marks the position of the berquilla or open cistern wich provided
water defences on this vulnerable side. The citadel stands at this (south) end
of the enclosure and is dominated by the great round donjon with its northern
edge marked by the conspicuous round tower to the right. Further to the right
can be seen the lower but still formidable walls of the castletown. The tower
on the wall of the outer enceinte immediately below left on the donjon is the
Tour de l'Eperon undermined by the Muslim attacks in 1285 and
subsequently rebuilt.

On the west side, overlooking the sea far below, the original enclosure was
strengthened in the early thirteenth century by the addition of a fine series of
four round towers (plate 74), which Deschamps compares with the round
towers on the outer west wall at Crac des Chevaliers, though the finish is not
nearly so fine and the wall-head defences are lost.

The main castle lay at the southern end of this enclosure (fig. 23). It is
approached through a square gatehouse in the outer walls. Above the entrance
arch, there are corbels which must originally have supported a simple machicolation and there is a groove for the portcullis. As at Crac, though in different ways, the entrance system at Margat offers the visitor a variety of choices
(fig. 24). It is impossible to go straight through the outer gate and there is no
access to the upper floor. The visitor has to make a 90 degree turn to the left,
which takes him to the castletown, or the right, in which case he approaches
the citadel. In both cases he has to go along an open walk, between inner and
outer walls, overlooked by the latter. The visitor to the fortress then makes
another 90 degree turn to the left into a gatehouse in the inner walls. The door
leads into a long, sloping passage. At the top of this he can either go straight

Plate 74   Margat: western wall of castletown enclosure looking north. These great round towers were added by the Hospitallers in the late twelfth or early thirteenth century and can be compared with those on the west outer wall at Crac des Chevaliers (plate 57) though these have lost their wall-head defences and there is no sign that they ever had machicolations (the box machicolations so noticeable at Crac have no parallels at Margat). Note the rugged black basalt of Margat which contrasts so strongly with the smooth white limestone of Crac.

on, which leads him to the corner of the castletown enclosure, or turn right, through yet another fortified gate, into the court of the citadel itself. It was the only entrance and offered no opportunity whatever to the attacker.

The citadel is defended by double walls except on the castletown side where there is a single wall and ditch. On the west (sea) side the outer walls are defended by three square towers which probably date from the time of the Mazoirs before the Hospitaller takeover (plate 75). The wall which connects them is defended by a covered shooting gallery (or 'fortie cooperte' as the

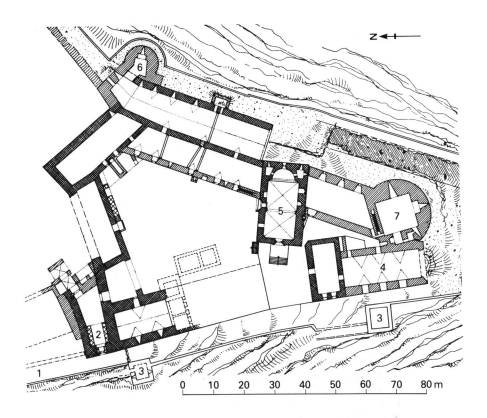

Fig. 23 Margat: plan of citadel (the castletown lay to the north). 1. Path
from outer gate; 2. inner gate; 3. twelfth-century towers; 4. hall; 5. chapel; 6.
northeast tower; 7. donjon. The Tour de l'Eperon lies off the plan to the
north.

account of the building of the castle at Saphet calls these defences in the base
of the walls). On the other side, the outer wall has no towers, perhaps because
the ground drops away so steeply. At the southern apex of the triangle there
was a tower which the Crusaders called the Tower of the Spur (Tour de
l'Eperon). It was here that the Muslims undermined the walls and the present
structure is a Muslim replacement. As at Crac, the outer walls would be a
formidable castle on their own but they are overlooked at all points by the
great cliffs of masonry which surround the inner court (plate 76). These are
seen at their most impressive on the east side where the huge, plain wall of
black stone remains unbroken to the wall head (plate 77). The inner court is
surrounded by great vaulted halls, some of them two storeys, for shortage
and shelter. On the southwest there is one with more elegant vaulting which

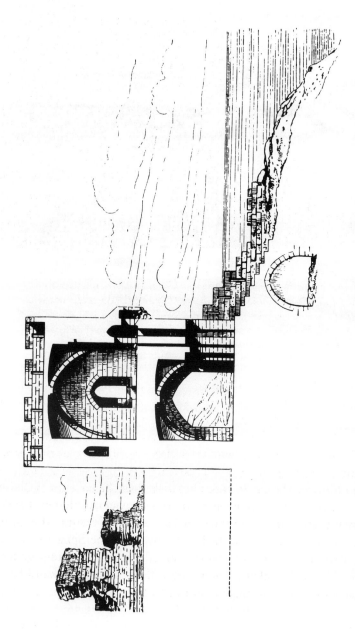

Fig. 24   Margat: section of entrance tower. Note the machicolation and groove for portcullis. There is no direct communication between the ground-floor entrance and the guard chamber above.

Plate 75 Margat: west wall of citadel looking north. The square towers on
the outer wall may date from the fortress built by the Mazoir family from
whom the Hospitallers bought it in 1186. In the centre is the outer gatehouse.
Both the outer and inner walls of the citadel are provided with passages and
casements at lower levels (the 'fortie cooperte' of the account of the building
of Saphet) to give access to arrow slits near the ground.

was probably the Knights' hall. There was also a grand, austere chapel (plate 78)
whose chevet, as at Crac, was incorporated into the defences. It is larger than
the chapel at Crac and is divided into two large bays with groin-vaulted roof. It
was decorated with frescoes of which traces survive in the side chapels.[20]

The dating of these various elements is not clear. It is likely that the chapel
was built soon after the Hospitallers acquired the castle in 1186. From the fact
that several windows were blocked, we can assume that the halls on each side
of it are later. There seem to have been numerous changes of plan and additions: in such great castles of the Military Orders, we should think of masons
continuously at work, perhaps a new project every year, modifying and developing the fortifications, a new turret here, an additional shooting gallery
there. It could be this piecemeal approach, rather than one or two major campaigns, which accounts for the ingenious but rather confusing plan of the
defences.

The most impressive defensive works were two massive rounded towers.
The smaller of these, at the northeast corner of the inner fortress, still retains
its wall-head defences (plate 79). As at Saone, these consist of a lower level
with arrow slits, and in one case a larger rectangular opening, and above that

Plate 76   Margat: east walls of citadel from the north. The steeply sloping
ground is used to create a massive outer line of defences. The round donjon
can be seen at the far end of the inner wall.

a wall walk with merlons, each pierced by an arrow slit. At the south end,
where the natural defences are at their weakest, the Hospitaller builders constructed a great rounded donjon 20 m in diameter and 24 m in height which
dominates the southern bow of the castle like the bridge of an ocean liner (fig.
25). This can be compared with early thirteenth-century circular donjons in
the west: it was larger than Philip Augustus' early thirteenth-century
Villeneuve-sur-Yonne (diameter 15 m, original height 27 m) and Pembroke

Plate 77   Margat: east wall of citadel looking north. The north tower of the
citadel can be seen in the foreground, the walls of the castletown beyond.

(diameter 16 m) and almost identical to Bothwell (diameter 20 m, height
27 m); all of these were dwarfed, however, by the vast circular donjon at
Coucy-le-Château (1225–45), wantonly destroyed by the Germans in 1917,
which was 31 m in diameter and 55 m in height. It is noticeable that the
round donjon at Margat is lower in proportion to its diameter than the
western examples, just as the square donjons of the Crusader states tend to
be squatter. It also differs from the western parallels in that the interior
chamber is not round but square, meaning that the walls are up to 10 m
thick in places.

The castle is remarkable for the number of superimposed halls and vaults,
all provided with arrow slits to make them shooting galleries. Exploring them
is like a tour of a vast, three-dimensional maze; narrow straight stairs in the
thickness of the wall, often pitch dark, lead you to yet another cavernous,

Plate 78   Margat: west façade of chapel, showing the basalt structure and
limestone detailing: note that the upper part of the façade has been rebuilt,
perhaps after earthquake damage.

sombre hall, only lit by thin bright shafts of sun through the arrow slits
(plate 80). These halls are roofed with crude rubble vaulting, always in the
hard black stone. None of them seems to have any specialised function,
although there are two large ovens in one and others were no doubt used as
stables. The rest must have served variously as stores and barracks. They also
supported an extensive roof terrace, as much as 15 m wide, which is now
covered with grass and scrub so that it is hard to believe that you are walking
25 m above ground level. These great terraces must have been designed to
support siege engines. We know that engines within the castle played an effective part in the defence against the Muslims in 1285 and it was presumably
here that they were mounted. There are also parallels within the terraces at

Plate 79   Margat: thirteenth-century wall-head defences on northeast tower
of citadel. This is the only part of the fortress where the wall-head defences
have survived. They are on two levels with casemates on the lower and a wall
walk above giving access to the crenellations (compare with the
twelfth-century examples from Saone, plate 42).

Crac and the ruined vaulting shows that the inner walls at Tortosa and Chastel
Pelerin also supported terraces on the inside.

In the early 1280s, a decade after Crac had been lost, the castle was still
heavily defended. In 1281, Nicolas Lorgne, sometime castellan of Crac and
now Master of the Order, wrote to Edward I that the castle was 'bien garni de
frères et d'autres gens d'armes' but he appealed for funds to maintain it. For
Burchard of Mount Sion, passing in 1283, it was still 'a strong fortress situated
on a very high mountain'.[21] Despite the ten-year truce then in force, Qala'un
began a siege on 17 April 1285, but it was a hard task his men faced and
many were killed by the defenders' engines and arrows. On 23 May they

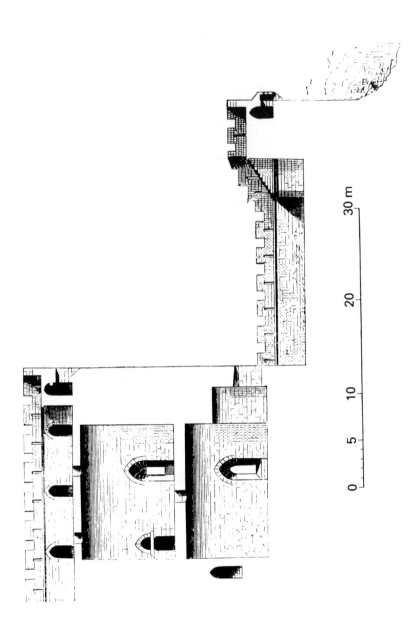

Fig. 25   Margat: section of donjon and Tour de l'Eperon. The Tour de l'Eperon in its present form was rebuilt after the Muslim conquest of 1285.

Plate 80   Margat: vaults in citadel, east side looking north. Like all major
Crusader castles, Margat had vast vaults for storage and shelter.

undermined the Tower of the Spur[22] at the southern end of the outer defences, but it seems to have collapsed into the mine, causing great damage to the assailants. Nonetheless, it soon became apparent to those inside that there were many other mines and the next day the garrison asked for terms. Qala'un wanted the fortress intact and the terms were lenient; the garrison was allowed to retire to Tripoli and Tortosa, twenty-five of the most senior riding out in full armour.

Six and a half centuries later, Deschamps found vivid evidence of the ferocity of the last stand at Margat.[23] Around the arrow slits of the castle defences, there were arrowheads still stuck in the mortar between the stones, showing where the attackers had tried to shoot in at their stubborn opponents. Saphet, Beaufort, Chastel Blanc, Crac and numerous smaller fortresses had all fallen; Margat was the last Crusader castle to endure a major siege and its fall marks the end of an era when ingenuity of design, excellence of craftsmanship and courage in defence could compensate for lack of men and lack of money.

8

MUSLIM CASTLES OF THE TWELFTH AND THIRTEENTH CENTURIES

As was pointed out in chapter 1, castles as they existed in the west, or even in Byzantium, were hardly known in Muslim Syria at the beginning of the twelfth century.[1] Perhaps surprisingly, the arrival of the aggressive Crusaders does not seem to have inspired defensive fortifications on the Muslim side, though the major earthquakes of 1157 and 1170 may have destroyed much of the evidence. Nur al-Din (1146–74) rebuilt the city walls of Damascus and Homs and the curtain wall of the citadel at Aleppo, and added a tower to the exterior of the cavea of the Roman theatre at Bostra. His work is very much in the twelfth-century style; the towers are small and comparatively far apart (though he did construct round towers on the city walls of Damascus and Homs),[2] and the defences, both arrow slits and at the wall head, were comparatively simple.

Nur al-Din also rebuilt or repaired a number of fortresses along the marches between the Crusader Principality of Antioch and the territories of Aleppo. Among these were the fortifications on the tell at Harim,[3] which must have resembled Aleppo in their time but which have now almost completely vanished, and the tell of Qal'at al-Mudiq.[4] This was the citadel of the ancient city of Apamea which was taken by the Crusaders in 1106 and retaken by the Muslims in 1149. As at Harim, the curtain wall, embellished with rectangular towers, circles the top of the tell but we cannot really be sure how much of the building dates from the time of Nur al-Din and how much is earlier or later.

On the Orontes north of Hama lay the castle of Shayzar, built along a narrow ridge, and protected on one long side by the gorge of the river and on the other by the steep slope of the land to the rift valley.[5] This castle had been the family home of the Banu Munqidh, one of whose members, the famous Usamah, has left us a volume of memoirs which gives a vivid and engaging picture of his life and times. Unhappily it seems that none of the surviving structure can be attributed to this illustrious family who resembled so closely the nobility of western Europe in status and attitudes. The earthquake of 1157 destroyed both castle and dynasty (though Usamah, who had left the family home, survived). Nur al-Din then assigned the castles to one of his Amirs, Ibn al-Daya, whose family held it until 1233. The defences are best preserved at the north end of the ridge, where a bridge allows access from the valley, and at the south end, where a donjon and rock-cut ditch defend the ridge from the adjoining mountain. Very little of this work can be dated, but it is likely that much of the curtain wall and possibly the entrance were the work of Nur al-Din. The donjon at the south end carries an inscription in the name of the Sultan Malik Aziz Muhammad who took the castle from the Banu' l-Daya in 1233. Van Bercham suggests that the inscription was added to an already existing building, possibly of the late twelfth century, but the elaboration of the plan with its vaults and numerous arrow slits is strongly reminiscent of early thirteenth-century Muslim work. Without further investigation, the castle at Shayzar will remain too enigmatic to tell us much about the Muslim fortifications of the time.

We are on much firmer ground in the case of the castle at Ajlun, investigated and published by C. N. Johns.[6] The castle stands well away from any urban centre, in the wooded hills of northern Jordan, commanding fine views across the Jordan valley to the Crusader-held west bank. It is not on any trade route but may have been designed to counter incursions from the recently constructed Hospitaller castle at Belvoir which lay opposite it on the other side of the Jordan valley. There seems to have been no existing building on the site when the castle was founded by the Amir 'Izz al-din Usamah in 1184–5. The design is an irregular but compact quadrilateral with a small central courtyard and square towers at each corner. There is no donjon. The castle was enlarged in the early thirteenth century but enough remains from the twelfth century to show how similar in technique and design the castle was to Frankish work of the same period.

The early thirteenth century saw major developments in military architecture in the Muslim lands, developments which are the more obvious because of the Ayyubids' helpful practice of leaving dated building inscriptions on their castles. (It would answer a lot of intriguing questions to find one on the outer west wall at Crac.) With the possible exception of Subeibe, this activity does not seem to have been a response to the Crusades but a result of the in-fighting between members of the Ayyubid family after Saladin's death in 1193. The details of the making and breaking of alliances do not concern us here but the most important development was the establishment of al-'Adil as ruler in Damascus in a series of struggles between 1193 and 1201 against the bitter opposition of other members of his family. In the course of these struggles the citadel at Damascus was attacked no less than five times and on two occasions the attacks were very hard fought and nearly successful.[7]

When he finally established his power, al-'Adil was determined to fortify the citadel[8] and other castles under his control so that he could never again be threatened in this way, and in the years before his death in 1218 he transformed Muslim military architecture. This was partly a result of the importance siege warfare assumed in these conflicts which centred round possession of strong points rather than campaigns in the field (in contrast to the inter-Muslim disputes of the ninth and tenth centuries for example), but it was also a result of the increased efficiency of siege engines and the need to defend against them. Cheveddin[9] argues that the most important change was the need to provide towers, not just for flanking fire along the walls, but as bases for trebuchets with which to bombard an attacking army. While this remains a hypothesis, it does account for the marked change in style of military architecture. The towers of these early century fortresses are more massive (up to 30 m along each side as opposed to the 3.5–6 m typical of twelfth-century and earlier fortification) and more closely spaced.[10] In addition the towers are much more solidly built in finely drafted masonry and the chambers are strongly vaulted. Wall-head defences are also much more developed. In both Damascus and Aleppo we see the development of box machicolations which have no parallel in the architecture of the twelfth century but which are strikingly close in date and design to the ones at Crac des Chevaliers.

It is now clear that there was no citadel in Damascus in Roman or early Islamic times and that the first fortifications on the site were built in around 1077 by the Turkish adventurer Atsiz and continued under Saljuk rule.[11] Little trace of this earliest phase survives and the citadel was rebuilt by Nur al-Din in the second half of the twelfth century. After his final establishment in Damascus in 1201, al-'Adil began a major rebuilding which lasted from 1203 to 1216. He called on all the minor princes of the Ayyubid house to contribute a tower, and one inscription survives showing that one of the towers was built by the prince of Hama. Despite this various patronage, the plan of the citadel seems to have been remarkably consistent with the curtain wall being surrounded by thirteen massive towers, only a few of which still retain their original appearance. These towers have stone vaults, and numerous arrow slits entered from the interior chambers. The wall-head defences consist of merlons with arrow slits in them and box machicolations supported on three stone corbels with sloping roofs.

Clear evidence of new techniques of fortification at the beginning of the thirteenth century can be found in the citadel at Cairo. Here Creswell notes that two of Saladin's round towers, finished before 1183/4, were completely enclosed by much larger round towers constructed by his son al-'Adil before

Plate 81   Bosra, citadel, twelfth- and early thirteenth-century: west side from
southwest. The citadel stood around the Roman theatre from the end of the
eleventh century onwards. Here the high but fairly small twelfth-century
tower (upper centre) can be contrasted with the massive early
thirteenth-century ones (left and right).

1207/8. Besides being about three times the diameter of the father's work,
al-'Adil's towers also have stone machicolations, which Saladin never used.
Nothing could illustrate the change in castle building more clearly: a state-of-
the-art fortification of the 1180s required complete remodelling only twenty-
five years later in the first decade of the thirteenth-century to provide a more
active defence.[12]

Closely related to the citadel at Damascus was the citadel at Bosra in the
Harwan, also built during the reign of al-'Adil (plate 81).[13] Here the basis of
the castle was the massive Roman theatre (which remains one of the best-
preserved examples of a classical theatre anywhere). The earliest fortifications
were two small towers added in 1088 by the orders of the Saljuk governor
Kumushtakin. In 1147–8 another tower was added to the exterior by the ruler
of Damascus, probably in anticipation of Crusader attacks. As with Damascus, however, the whole was vastly strengthened in the reign of Al-'Adil.
Between 1202 and 1218, eight massive towers were erected, the largest of
which measures no less than 25 × 37 m. All are stone vaulted and some
contain almost palatial chambers. Interestingly, the roofing system is not in
the local Hawrani style found elsewhere in the building but seems to have

been the work of masons from Damascus. Unfortunately, the wall-head defences are very dilapidated but some brackets for machicolations survive.

Another classical monument fortified in the early thirteenth century was the enclosure of the temples of Bacchus and Zeus at Baalbek. The builder here was a minor Ayyubid prince, Bahram Shah, who added a series of towers between 1213 and 1224 and a curtain wall to connect and improve the classical structure. It is noticeable that Bahram's work is on a much smaller scale than al-'Adil's and the dimensions of the tower much more restricted.[14]

In 1228–30 a younger son of al-'Adil's, al-Aziz 'Uthman, built the castle of Subeibe which Kitchener in his *Survey of Palestine* described as 'the finest ruined castle I have seen in the country'.[15] The castle stands on a ridge above the one-time Crusader town of Banyas and was probably constructed in response to the threat posed to Damascus by the arrival of Frederick II's Crusade. The castle was designed to act as an obstacle (indeed the only military obstacle, as the Bishop of Marseilles noted) on the road from the Crusader lands to Damascus. The first fortress was rectangular, built round a courtyard, with square corner towers, somewhat similar in design to the castle at Ajlun. Before 1230 this had been expanded to take in the whole of the ridge, the curtain wall being defended by rectangular towers of fairly modest dimensions, perhaps because here, unlike Damascus or Bosra, the site was on a mountain top which afforded natural protection. The castle was further strengthened after 1260 by Baybars who added much larger towers including, unusually, three round ones, at strategic points.

But perhaps the most impressive example of Ayyubid fortification comes from Aleppo.[16] The citadel on the ancient tell which overlooked the town had certainly been fortified in the late tenth and eleventh centuries and new, fairly small towers had been added to the enceinte by Nur al-Din. In 1209–10 Saladin's son, al-Zahir Ghazi, constructed a new and much more massive gate with a stone bridge across the moat, defended at its outer end by a small tower. Ghazi's work was vastly extended by the Mamlukes in the fifteenth century when a palace was constructed on top of it, and the massive and austere cliff of masonry which is such an impressive feature of the site today dates from this later phase. Ghazi's building was impressive enough. Two great square towers flanked the gate, each well provided with arrow slits so that the defenders could command the entrance from the chambers inside. This led not directly to the interior but to a series of oblong halls at right-angles to each other, making the entrance passage twist and turn so that an assailant could be trapped and harried. The whole work is on a different scale, the masonry much finer than the towers of the twelfth century and earlier. The merlons on the wall head disappeared when the building was heightened, but the box machicolations still survive, now rather incongruously half-way up the façade. They are stone built, resting on four corbels, with arrow slits on the front and a sloping roof, strikingly similar in design to the almost contemporary examples in the citadel at Damascus and the outer west wall at Crac des Chevaliers.

The similarities between the Muslim and Crusader architecture of the early thirteenth century are striking. Most obviously there is the increased size of towers, the great towers of the citadel at Damascus being paralleled by the oblong ones at Chastel Pelerin and the round ones at Crac and Margat. The use of box machicolations of virtually identical design at Crac, Aleppo and Damascus is too clear to be coincidental. There is also the use of finely cut stone, pointed arches and vaults which often makes it difficult to distinguish Crusader from Muslim work except by date and context. But there were differences as well. Apart from Baybars' work at Subeibe in the 1260s, the Muslims never used the large round towers which are so characteristic of Margat and Crac. The Muslims also made little use of multiple lines of defence and nowhere in their building do we find the careful interrelation of outer and inner walls we find at Crac or Chastel Pelerin; there is nothing in the Muslim architecture of the period which could possibly be considered as a 'concentric castle'. Finally the domestic accommodation is much less developed. The most important Muslim strongholds, Aleppo, Damascus and Bosra, were urban fortifications, and while they contained palace buildings for the ruler, the garrison probably lived in houses in the town except in time of war and there is nothing to compare with the halls, chapels and chambers of the castle-convents of the Military Orders.

9

POSTSCRIPT: CRUSADER CASTLES AND THE WEST

T WOULD be natural to assume that changes and developments in the architecture of castles in the Crusader east would be reflected in western Europe, whence most of the Crusaders had come and whither at least some of them returned. In fact the evidence for this is at best ambiguous. The first problem is that castle building in western Europe varied widely: the tradition of castle buildings in the German Empire, for example, remained radically different from that in northern France. When Frederick II embarked on an impressive display of castle building in southern Italy in the first half of the thirteenth century, he made almost no use of the round towers which were universally adopted in Capetian France and Britain at the same time. Instead, at Bari, Trani, Melfi, Gioia del Colle he used high square or rectangular ones, and octagonal at the elegant and ornamental Castel del Monte, though curiously his two surviving castles in Sicily at Catania and Syracuse have round towers. It is in France north of the Loire, and by extension in England, that we should look most profitably for comparisons with Crusader work. This may be partly because, from the mid-twelfth century onwards, the vast majority of the Crusaders came from these areas. A more important reason was that, between c.1180 and c.1220, these areas were the theatre for a prolonged conflict between two powerful and developed states, the Angevin Empire and Capetian France. This was a war in which the control of fortresses played a major part and there were memorable and well-recorded assaults on castles using professional engineers and the most effective siege techniques available: Château Gaillard (September 1203 to 6 March 1204), Rochester (11 October–30 November 1215), Dover and Berkhamstead (both in 1216).

The technologies of assault were very similar to those used in warfare in the

Latin east; indeed it is likely that the use of trebuchets and possibly mining were originally learned during the Crusader wars. Certainly Richard I used men from the Crusader states among his artillery men.[1] It is not surprising, therefore, that the architects of defensive works adopted some similar designs to thwart these new methods of assault.

The most obvious of these was the abandonment of the donjon as the most important feature of the defences. As late as the 1180s Henry II made the great square donjon at Dover the centrepiece of his castle, though there were extensive outerworks to protect it. Château Gaillard has a donjon as a place of last resort, though, again, it is well protected by outer walls. There had been Crusader castles in the twelfth century like Coliath and Belvoir without donjons. Equally both Margat and Crac have towers which are significantly larger than the rest and which might be considered as donjons while the early thirteenth-century castle at Safita is dominated by the vast rectangular donjon. Muslim castles of the early thirteenth century, notably Damascus and Bosra, had no donjons and a pattern of regularly spaced towers of approximately equal size around a perimeter wall. In England, a castle without a donjon is found at Framlingham in the twelfth century. In the early thirteenth this plan became much more common: one of the best early examples is the castle at Fère-en-Tardenois, built by Robert of Dreux around 1205, where seven round towers of equal size project boldly from the polygonal curtain wall. The pattern can also be seen clearly in the castles of Philip Hurepel, Count of Boulogne, at Boulogne (1231) and Hardelot (1228–34). In England we can point to the castles of Ranulph de Blundeville, Earl of Chester, at Beeston (1225), which has an almost Syrian feel with its curtain walls following the edge of the ridge and its rock-cut ditch, and Bolingbroke (1220s), a regular hexagon with round towers at each corner. Donjons did not of course disappear; when Enguerrand de Coucy rebuilt his ancestral castle at Coucy-le-Château between 1225 and 1245, a vast circular donjon was the dominant feature.

The abandonment of the donjon, so vulnerable to artillery and sappers, as the main form of defence was accompanied by the emergence of the concentric castle, with several layers of fortifications so that the outer walls kept the sappers and catapults away from the main fortification. Such a design can be seen at Belvoir in the 1180s and again at Crac in the early thirteenth-century rebuilding. As has been noted, Muslim military architects do not seem to have used this plan extensively but in the west it can be clearly seen in Henry II's work at Dover in the 1180s. But the 'concentric' castle was always a rare (and expensive) exception and only those prepared to make a massive investment in fortification, like Edward I at Beaumaris in the 1290s, could really undertake it.

A much more general change in the west was the adoption of round rather than square towers. Round towers had been used in the twelfth century: the fine circular donjon at Chateaudun is a good example. Richard I had used exclusively round towers in his building at Château Gaillard and from 1200 in northern France they completely replaced square ones. Philip Augustus' castle building shows this especially clearly; not only did he construct new round donjons for such urban castles as Vernon-sur-Seine or Villeneuve-sur-Yonne, but he also took pains to add round towers to castles already well provided with square ones, which he clearly felt were now out of date. Examples of this can be seen at Falaise, where a high round tower was added at one corner of the massive square donjon of the early twelfth century, and Gisors, where a large round tower was added to an enceinte already well provided with square ones.

In Britain too the round tower soon became the norm. At Pembroke (c. 1200) William Marshal built a great round donjon; almost at the same date a large round tower was erected to provide flanking fire along the walls of an older enceinte at Barnard Castle. King John added round towers to the square defences at Dover and Corfe while at Rochester damage caused by the siege of 1215 was made good by building a round tower onto the square keep. The triumph of the round tower was much more complete in Britain and France than in the Middle East. Its use became widespread in both east and west in the two decades between 1190 and 1210 but we cannot say which came first or point to any direct influence one way or the other.

While the shapes of the towers show some similarities, the scale was different. In the west, the towers tended to remain smaller than the massive artillery platforms we find at Crac, Chastel Pelerin, Damascus or Bosra. At Chastel Pelerin the great towers of the inner walls were 28 m long by 18 m deep and over 34 m in height; al-'Adil's towers on the citadel at Damascus were some 30 m long by about 12 m deep; at Bosra the Ayyubid towers are around 20 m along each side. The largest of the round towers which flank the walls of the castle at Château Gaillard are no more than 10 m in diameter and the early thirteenth-century round towers at Dover are, if anything, even smaller. The round mural towers at Fère-en-Tardenois are only about 10 m across. Furthermore, the mural towers of these western castles were always wooden floored as opposed to the stout stone vaults which were universal in the Middle East. This suggests that these towers were not designed for use as artillery platforms in the way in which the ones in the Middle East were. This explanation is given added force by the literary evidence, or absence of it: trebuchets mounted on towers do not seem to have been widely used to defend castles in the way they were in the Crusader wars.

Wall-head defences developed rapidly in the Middle East and we have noticed before the use of stone-built box machicolations from the first decade of the thirteenth century in both Christian and Muslim work. Stone machicolations are rare in the west before the end of the thirteenth century. The great

tower at Château Gaillard seems to have been provided with slot machicolations somewhat similar to those in the late twelfth-century tower on the
northwest of the inner enceinte at Crac. There are certainly stone corbels projecting from the wall heads at both Fère-en-Tardenois and Coucy but the wall
head has been destroyed and these may well have been to provide support for
wooden hoards. Wooden hoarding, rather than stone machicolation,
remained the norm in the west but was almost unknown in the east, either
because of the lack of timber or because the Muslim facility with Greek Fire
made it vulnerable.

As Fossier recognised, the Crusaders brought back from the east new
methods of attacking castles, not new theories of military architecture. In both
east and west, architects and builders tried and adapted, coming up with solutions which were sometimes the same and sometimes different; experiment
and experience, rather than architectural influences from the other end of the
Mediterranean, were the deciding factors.

APPENDIX

INTRODUCTION

This short pamphlet records the reconstruction of the castle of Saphet by the Templars from 1240 onwards. The narrative centres on Benoît d'Alignan, Bishop of Marseilles from 1229 to 1267, who visited the Holy Land twice in 1239–40 and 1260–2. He seems to have been the inspiration for the rebuilding of the castle, as the pamphlet makes clear. The text exists in two copies, one in Paris of the fourteenth century and the other an undated Italian manuscript in Turin. Both are bound in with other Crusader texts including the *Historia Occidentalis* of Jacques de Vitry. The pamphlet must have been written between 1260 when Benoît visited Saphet for the second time and 1266 when the castle fell to the Muslims. Its anonymous author may have composed it simply to commemorate the bishop's work but it seems more likely that this is a fund-raising treatise, designed to be read or used as a basis for sermons and appeals. The emphasis on the cost of the castle, its continuous usefulness to the Christians and, in the final section, its role in protecting well-known Holy Places, suggest that this is a strong possibility. Whatever the motivation of the author, however, the treatise remains one of the fullest and most circumstantial accounts we have of the building of a medieval castle and provides a fascinating insight into what contemporaries thought on the subject.

DE CONSTRUCTIONE CASTRI SAPHET [1]

Since it is our firm and steadfast intention to be always zealous in those things which are to the honour of God and to dwell continually and chiefly on those which we perceive to be for the exaltation of the Faith and the Church, the edification of those around, the salvation of souls and the support of the Holy Land, we propose to set forth specially and principally when and why the castle of Saphet was begun and how it was built.

Why, when and how the building of the castle at Saphet was begun

A great army of Christians, among whom were the King of Navarre and Count of Champagne, the Duke of Burgundy, the Count of Brittany, the Count of Nevers and Forez, the Count of Montfort, the Count of Bar, the Count of Macon and many other counts and barons, arrived to support the Holy Land.[2] In this army the knights with military equipment numbered more than 1,500 in addition to those who did not have sufficient military equipment and an almost uncountable multitude of crossbowmen[3] and footmen. When they arrived at Jaffa and Ascalon and debated how they ought to proceed, certain nobles, trusting in their own strength and disregarding the advice of the Templars, Hospitallers and other churchmen and nobles of the country, left the army by night. And since they did not give glory to God, to whom victory belongs, but instead tried to take it for themselves, they were ignominiously defeated, many of them were captured and killed and the army was driven back to Jaffa in great confusion. There, in order to alleviate and mitigate the disaster, it was decided to rebuild the castle of Saphet, since they could not construct such a good work in the whole land. And so that the Master of the Temple could begin the work, they promised to give him 7,000 marks to pay for it and that the army would stay there for two months so that it could be built more safely and easily.

But when they returned to sandy Acre they forgot their promises and they did not go to build nor did they contribute anything towards it. When a truce was made with the Sultan of Damascus, the king and the great army returned to their country. The bishop of Marseilles, in fact and in name Benedictus, went to St Mary of Saidnaya[4] on pilgrimage with the Sultan's permission. While he was waiting for some days in Damascus as commanded by the Sultan, many people frequently inquired of him if Saphet was to be rebuilt. When he asked them why they inquired so insistently, they answered that with the building of the castle of Saphet, the gates of Damascus would be closed.

Therefore when the bishop returned from Damascus, he carefully observed the land as far as Saphet and he did not see any fortress apart from Subeibe which was held by the nephew of the Sultan.[5] When he reached Saphet he found there a heap of stones without any building where once there had been a noble and famous castle and there he was received with great joy by brother Rainhardus de Caro who was at that time the castellan there. But they had nowhere there to lay their head except *garbelarias* [cloaks of wool-linen union or perhaps jabalas] which the servants of the brothers carried on which they made the beds of their masters.

When the bishop had inquired carefully about the surroundings and district of the castle, and why the Saracens were so fearful of it being built, he found that if the castle were constructed, it would be a defence and security and like a shield for the Christians as far as Acre against the Saracens. It would be a strong and formidable base for attack and provide facilities and opportunities of making sallies and raids into the land of the Saracens as far as Damascus. Because of the building of this castle, the Sultan would lose large sums of money, massive subsidies and service of the men and property of those who would otherwise be of the castle and would also lose in his own land casals [villages] and agriculture and pasture and other renders since they would not dare to farm the land for fear of the castle. As a result of this, his land would turn to desert and waste and he would also be obliged to incur great expenditure and employ many paid soldiers [*stipendiarios*] for the defence of Damascus and the surrounding lands. In brief, he found from common report that there was no fortress in that land from which the Saracens would be so much harmed and the Christians so much helped and Christianity spread.

When the bishop heard this and similar opinions, he came to Acre and visited the Master of the Temple, Armand de Périgord, who was lying sick, and the Master asked him what he had seen and heard in Damascus. The bishop told him about what seemed more significant to him, what he had seen and heard about how the Saracens were in fear and trembling and seeking reassurance about the building of the castle at Saphet. So with reference to what he had said, he began to persuade him forcefully and insistently that they should devote all their strength to build it quickly during the time of truce. But the Master said to him with a sigh, 'Lord Bishop, it is not easy to build Saphet. Did not you yourself hear what the King of Navarre, the Duke of Burgundy and the counts and barons of the army promised about going to Saphet so that it could be built more securely and more rapidly, and how they would stay there for two months and give 7,000 marks for the building? In the end they did not pay a single penny for the building and you are saying that we should build the castle without a help from anyone?'

Then the bishop said, 'Master, stay resting in your bed and give your good will and your verbal support to the brothers and I have faith in the Lord that you will do more from your bed than a whole army with a multitude of armed men and the abundance of their riches.' Since the bishop persisted, the great men who were there said, 'Lord Bishop, you have said what seems good to you and the Master will take counsel and respond to you.' When the bishop had withdrawn from the Master, he summoned the senior members of the council and convinced them of what he had said to the Master and satisfied them completely and they replied that he should come the next day and get the Master to place this before them in council.

How the bishop of Marseilles persuaded the Master of the Temple and his council to build the castle of Saphet

The following day the bishops came to the Master and asked him to call his council because he wished to speak to them about something important to him. When they came the bishop said to them,

'Lords, I understand that your Order[6] was first begun by holy knights who dedicated themselves totally to the protection of the Christians and attacks on the Saracens. Since they kept to this firmly and faithfully, the Lord exalted and favoured your Order with the Apostolic See and with kings and princes and today your Order is greatly celebrated and renowned with God and men. It seems to me that you should now follow the example of those holy knights. When I was in Damascus, I found out from many people that there is nothing else that the Saracens would fear as much as the building of Saphet, since it is said that with the building of that castle, the gates of Damascus are closed. We ourselves have seen and inspected the site and it is commonly known that it is not possible to build a castle or fortress in this land, by which Christianity can be so well defended and the infidelity of the Saracens attacked, as Saphet. Because of this I as your faithful friend, mindful of the honour of God, the salvation of souls and the promotion of your Order, ask, advise and demand that you, as faithful servants of God and devoted and strong knights, look back to the example of those first holy knights, who founded your Order and that, following the example of your founders, you offer you and yours to build the castle of Saphet, which will always remain such a threat to the infidels and such a defence to the faithful. I however do not have the money which would be sufficient for you for this work but I offer myself to make a pilgrimage there, if you want to build it. If however you don't want to, I will preach to the pilgrims and go there with them to build of rubble because there is there a big pile of stones, and I will make there a wall of dry stones to defend the Christians from the attacks of the Saracens!'

When he had heard this, the Master, as if laughing replied, 'You are clearly determined what should be done!' and the bishop added, 'May you and yours take good counsel and may the Lord be with you.' And so he withdrew from them. The Lord, however, directed their council and they unanimously decided that the said castle should be rebuilt now while they were at truce with the Sultan of Damascus, because if it was put off, the building could easily be delayed.

The joy at the building of the castle at Saphet

When it had been decided that Saphet should be built, there was great joy in the House of the Temple and in the city of Acre and among the people of the Holy Land. Without delay an impressive body of knights, serjeants, crossbowmen and other armed men were chosen with many pack animals to carry arms, supplies and other necessary materials. Granaries, cellars, treasuries and other offices were generously and happily opened to make payments. A great number of workmen and slaves [*operarii et sclavi*][7] were sent there with the tools and materials they needed. The land rejoiced at their coming and the true Christianity of the Holy Land was exalted.

The bishop of Marseilles himself came with those pilgrims he could bring and pitched his tents on the site of the synagogue of the Jews and the mosque of the Saracens so that by this he indicated and clearly showed that the castle of Saphet would be rebuilt to weaken the unfaithfulness of the infidels and strengthen and defend the faith of Our Lord Jesus Christ. When everything that was required for the beginning of so glorious a work was ready, after the celebration of Mass, the bishop came and gave a short sermon to encourage the devotion of those present, called on the grace of the Holy Spirit and, with a blessing and due solemnity, laid the first stone to the honour of Our Lord Jesus Christ and the exaltation of the Christian faith. On the stone he displayed a silver gilt jar full of money to support subsequent work. This was done in the year of the Lord 1240, on the third of the ides of December [11 December].

How a well of fresh water was found within the castle of Saphet

Since there was a lack of water there and since it was brought from afar by many pack animals with labour and expense, the bishop sought for several days to find small springs to make a cistern [*berquilla*] to collect water in. A certain old Saracen man said to the bishop's steward, 'If your lord gives me a tunic, I will show him a spring of fresh water within the castle.' When he had promised him the tunic, he showed him the place where there is now a well over which there were ruins of towers and walls and many piles of stones. When they asked him again for a clear sign, he said that they would find a sword and a helmet of iron in the mouth of the well and so it was found to be. Because of this, they worked more determinedly and strenuously there until at length excellent flowing water was discovered in great abundance for the whole castle. The bishop stayed there until the castle was firmly established so that it could defend itself against the enemies of the faith. When he returned home he gave to the castle as if to his dearest chosen son, all his tack, tents and furnishings and, having given his blessing, he entrusted the guardianship and progress of the work and the workmen to Our Lord Jesus Christ to whose honour it was begun and to whose name it was dedicated.

The wonderful construction of the castle of Saphet

When, however, the same bishop returned to support the Holy Land against the Tartars on 4 of the Nones of October [4 October 1260], and came to visit Saphet, he found that, between the one journey when the bishop returned to Marseilles and the other by which he returned to Saphet, by the grace and providence of God and the energy and prestige of the brothers of the Temple, the castle had been built with such industry and such wonder and magnificence that its exquisite and excellent construction seemed to be made, not by man but rather by almighty God.

To understand this more fully and make it clearer: the castle of Saphet is situated almost half-way between the cities of Acre and Damascus, in Upper Galilee on a spur entirely surrounded by mountains and hills, sheer precipices, crags and rocks. From most directions it is inaccessible and impregnable because of the difficulties, hardships and narrowness of the roads. In the direction of Damascus, however, it has the river Jordan and the Lake of Genasereth (also known as the Sea of Galilee and the Sea of Tiberias) like a rampart and these are like natural fortifications at a distance. There are however there both inner and outer wonderful manmade fortifications and buildings to be admired.

It is not easy to convey in writing or speech how many fine buildings there are there: what fine and numerous defences and fortifications with ditches, which measure 7 cannas [15.4 m, a canna is 2.2 metres] in the depth of rock and six in width: what inner walls, 20 cannas [44 m] high and a canna and a half [3.3 m] thick at the top: what outer walls [antemuralia] and trenches [scama], 10 cannas [22 m] in height and 375 cannas [825 m] in circumference: what underground tunnels between the outer wall and the [inner] ditch with underground chambers round the whole castle for 375 cannas [825 m]: what casemates, which are called fortie cooperte, which are above the ditches and underneath the outer wall, where there can be crossbowmen with great balistas which defend the ditches and things near and far and cannot be seen by others from outside where they can be safe without any other protection: what towers and battlements [propugnaculis] where there are seven towers, of which everyone is 22 cannas [48.4 m] in height, ten (22 m) in breadth, with walls two cannas [4.4 m] in thickness at the top: how many offices for all necessities: what number, size and variety of construction of crossbows, quarrels, machines and every sort of arms, and what effort and amount of expense in making them: what number of guards every day, what number of the garrison of armed men to guard and defend and repel enemies who were continually required there: how many workmen with different trades, how much and what expenses are made to them daily. It is not suitable to pass by in silence such famous, such exceptional, such magnificent and such necessary works done and needing to be done for the honour of God and the exaltation of the Christian name, for the bringing down of the infidel and the building up of the faithful but at least to proclaim some of them to encourage the devotion and compassion of the faithful.

The massive daily expenses for guarding the castle of Saphet

For the honour therefore of Our Lord Jesus Christ and to show the devoted strength and immense need of the holy knights of the Order of the Temple, and to encourage devotion and compassion and to kindle the charity of the Christian faithful towards the Order and the castle, we will detail the expenses which the house of the Temple made there for building. For as we asked and carefully inquired from the senior men and through the senior men of the house of the Temple, in the first two and a half years, the house of the Temple spent on building the castle of Saphet, in addition to the revenues and income of the castle itself, eleven hundred thousand Saracen bezants, and in each following year more or less forty thousand Saracen bezants. Every day victuals are dispensed to 1,700 or more and in time of war, 2,200. For the daily establishment [*stablimento cotidiano*] of the castle, 50 knights, 30 serjeants brothers, and 50 Turcupoles are required with their horses and arms, and 300 crossbowmen, for the works and other offices 820 and 400 slaves. There are used there every year on average more than 12,000 mule-loads of barley and corn apart from other victuals, in addition to payments to the paid soldiers and hired persons, and in addition to the horses and tack and arms and other necessities which are not easy to account.

The excellence of the castle of Saphet

To show the excellence of the castle so that so much work does not seem useless, burdensome, dispensible and insufficient, or unfit for habitation, it should be noted that the castle of Saphet has a temperate and healthy climate, rich in gardens, vines, trees and grass, gentle and smiling, rich and abundant in the fertility and variety of fruit. There figs, pomegranates, almonds and olives grow and flourish. God blesses it with rain from the sky and richness from the soil and abundance of corn, vines, oil, pulses, herbs and choice fruits, plenty of milk and honey, and pastures suitable for the feeding of animals, glades, trees and woods for making lime-kilns and for cooking plentiful foods, very good stone quarries in the place for building work and irrigation from springs and large cisterns to water animals and irrigate plants, not only outside the castle, but even within where very good fresh water abounds and several great cisterns suitable for any purpose.

There are there twelve water-mills outside the castle and many more powered by animals or wind and more than enough ovens, as is appropriate. Nor is anything lacking for the nobility and needs of the castle; there are various sorts of hunting and various sorts of plentiful fish in the River Jordan, the Sea of Galilee, the Lake of Genasereth and the Great Sea, from other places whence fresh or salt fish can be brought daily.

Among the other excellent features which the castle of Saphet has, it is notable that it can be defended by a few and that many can gather under the protection of its walls and it cannot be besieged except by a very great multitude; but such a multitude would not have supplies for long since it would find neither water nor food, nor can a very great multitude be near at the same time and, if they are scattered in remote places, they cannot help one another.

The usefulness of the castle and the surrounding places which are attached to it

You can realise how useful and necessary the castle is to the whole of the Christian lands and how harmful it is to the infidels by the experience of those who know that before it was built the Saracens, Bedouin, Khwarazmians and Turkmen used to make raids to Acre and through other lands of the Christians. By the building of the castle of Saphet, a bulwark and obstacle was placed and they did not dare to go from the River Jordan to Acre, except in very great numbers, and between Acre and Saphet loaded pack animals and carts could pass safely and agricultural lands could be worked freely. Between the River Jordan and Damascus, on the other hand, the land remained uncultivated and like a desert for fear of the castle of Saphet, whence great raids and depredations and layings waste are made as far as Damascus. There the Templars won many miraculous victories against the enemies of the Faith, which are not easy to recount since a great book could be written about them.[8]

However it should not be omitted that below the castle of Saphet in the direction of Acre, there is a town or large village [*burgus sive villa magna*] where there is a market and numerous inhabitants and which can be defended from the castle. In addition the castle of Saphet has under its lordship and in its district, more than 260 casals, which are called *ville* in French, in which there are more than 10,000 men with bows and arrows in addition to others from whom it is possible to collect large sums of money to be divided between the castle of Saphet and other Orders and barons and knights to whom the casals belong, and from whom little or nothing could be collected before the building of Saphet, nor would it be collected today if the castle had not been built since all were in the possession of the Sultan and other Saracens.

When considering its usefulness, the most important thing of all should not be omitted, that now it is possible to preach the faith of Our Lord Jesus Christ freely in all these places and to destroy and disprove publicly in sermons the blasphemies of Muhammad, which was not possible before the building of Saphet.[9] The Saracens no longer presume, as they did before, to proclaim the blasphemies of Muhammad against the faith of Our Lord Jesus Christ. There can now be visited famous places which are in the district of Saphet, like the well of Joseph, where he was sold by his brothers, and the city of Capernaum which is on the borders of Zabulon and Naphtali, where Our Lord Jesus Christ lived and began his preaching and personally performed many miracles and where Peter paid the tribute of a stater found in the mouth of a fish for himself and for the Lord Jesus Christ and where Matthew sat at the customs, whence he was taken to become an apostle.

Likewise near there on a mountain towards Tiberias is the place where, with five barley loaves and twelve fishes Our Lord satisfied 5,000 men, with twelve baskets of pieces left over. Near there is the place where Jesus showed himself to His disciples and ate with them as is read in the Gospel for the fourth Sunday after Easter and that is the place commonly called the Table of the Lord where there is a church and a solemn pilgrimage. Again nearby, by the Sea of Tiberias, is the village called Bethsaida, where Peter and Andrew, Philip and James the Less were born and where Christ chose Peter and Andrew and the two sons of Zebedee to be Apostles. Again near there by the Sea of Tiberias towards Tiberias City is the place called Magdalon, where it is said Mary Magdalene was born. Places even more holy, like Nazareth, Mount Tabor, Cana of Galilee and many others can be visited more freely and securely because of the building of the castle of Saphet. Because of this, it can be seen how much was diminished and carried off from the infidel Saracens and how much Christianity grew and expanded because of the construction and establishment of the castle of Saphet, because it was done to confound, to weaken and to hold back the infidel and to expand, multiply and comfort the faithful, to the honour of Our Lord Jesus Christ and the exaltation of the church of the Lord God. Amen.

NOTES

1 PROLOGUE TO THE STUDY OF CRUSADER CASTLES

1 J. F. Michaud, *Histoire des Croisades* (7 vols., Paris, 1822) and *Bibliothèque des Croisades* (4 vols., Paris, 1829).

2 *Recueil des historiens des Croisades*, ed. Académie des Inscriptions et Belles-Lettres (14 vols., Paris, 1841–1906) reprint.

3 E. Viollet-le-Duc, *Essai sur l'architecture militaire au moyen-âge* (Paris, 1854); English trans., M. Macdermott, *An Essay on the Military Architecture of the Middle Ages* (Oxford, 1860, reprint Westport, Conn., 1977).

4 M. de Vogüé, *Les Eglises de la Terre Sainte* (Paris, 1860).

5 M. de Vogüé, *La Syrie centrale: architecture civile et religieuse* (Paris, 1865).

6 D. Pringle, *The Churches of the Crusader Kingdom of Jerusalem: A Corpus* I, A–K (Cambridge, 1993), 8.

7 For such biographical details as are available, P. Deschamps, *Les Châteaux des Croisés en Terre Sainte I: Le Crac des Chevaliers* (Paris, 1934), xi n. 1, and H. Bordeaux, *Voyageurs d'Orient* (Paris, 1926), 77–100. Even his name is something of a puzzle since he appears as Guillaume Rey, E. G. Ray, E. Rey and occasionally as Baron E. Rey. He combined his father's surname Guillaume with his mother's, Rey. At one stage he had hoped to inherit the title of Baron Rey which had been held by one of Napoleon's generals but there proved to be a closer claimant.

8 C. du Fresne du Cange, *Les Familles d'Outremer*, ed. E. G. Rey (Collection de Documents Inédits sur l'Histoire de France XVIII; Paris, 1869).

9 G. Rey, *Etudes sur les monuments de l'architecture militaire des Croisés en Syrie et dans l'île de Chypre* (Collection de Documents Inédits sur l'Histoire de France, Paris, 1871).

10 E. Rey, *Les Colonies franques de Syrie aux douzième et treizième siècles* (Paris, 1885; reprint, New York, 1972).

11 C. R. Conder and H. H. Kitchener, *The Survey of Western Palestine* (3 vols., London, 1881–3).

12 C. Clermont-Ganneau, *Archaeological Researches in Palestine during the Years 1873–1874* (2 vols., London, 1896–9).

13 M. van Berchem and E. Fatio, *Voyage en Syrie* (Mémoires de l'Institut Français d'Archéologie Orientale du Caire, Cairo, 1914).

14 T. E. Lawrence, *Crusader Castles*, ed. D. Pringle (Oxford, 1988), 37 n.8.

15 Paris, 1927.

16 2 vols., and 2 vols., plates, Paris, 1925.

17 Deschamps describes his appointment and his work at Crac in *Châteaux* II, vii–xxii (Avant–Propos).

18 For Chastel Pelerin and the excavations, see below pp. 124–7.

19 For Belvoir, see below pp. 58–61.

20 For a summary of this work with bibliographical details, see pp. 23–5 below.

21 D. Pringle, *Red Tower* (London, 1986).

22 See below, chapter 5.

2 FORTIFICATION IN THE WEST AND EAST BEFORE THE FIRST CRUSADE

1 This is not the place for a general bibliography of western European military architecture. S. Toy, *A History of Fortification from 3000 BC to AD 1700* (London, 1955) remains a useful attempt at a general synthesis. The literature on English castles is very well developed: for helpful introductions see for examples R. A. Brown, *English Castles* (London, 1976), C. Platt, *The Castle in Medieval England and Wales* (London, 1982) and M. W. Thompson, *The Rise of the Castle* (Cambridge, 1991), all of which describe the architectural evolution. For other aspects see N. J. G. Pounds, *The Medieval Castle in England and Wales: A Social and Political History* (Oxford, 1991) and for contemporary but different developments in Scotland, S. Cruden, *The Scottish Castle* (Edinburgh, 1960). On French castles see the important study by G. Fournier, *Le Château dans la France mediévale: essai de sociologie monumentale* (Paris, 1976). For an architectural introduction the inadequate J.-F. Fino, *Fortresses de la France mediévale* (Paris, 1970) has been superseded by the excellent J. Mesqui, *Châteaux et enceintes de la France mediévale* (vol. I, Paris, 1991). See also the well-illustrated *Atlas des châteaux forts en France*, ed. C.-L. Salch (Strasbourg, 1977).

2 H. Collin, 'Les plus anciens châteaux de la région de Nancy en Lorraine', in *Château Gaillard* 3 (1966), 26–38.

3 P. Hoffsummer, A. Hoffsummer-Bosson and B. Wery, 'Naissance, transformations et abandon de trois place-fortes des environs de Liège: Chevremont, Franchimont et Logne', *Château Gaillard* 13 (1986), 63–79.

4 M. Bur, 'Recherches sur les plus anciennes mottes castrales de Champagne' *Château Gaillard* 9–10 (1978–80), 55–69.

5 M. Fixot, 'A la recherche des formes les plus anciennes de la fortification privée en France', *Château Gaillard* 9–10 (1978–80), 389–406.

6 For a general discussion see D. Matthew, *The Norman Kingdom of Sicily* (Cambridge, 1992), 257–9; for a brief investigation of three examples, A. J. Taylor, 'Three early castle sites in Sicily, Motta Camastra, Sperlinga and Petralia Soprana', *Château Gaillard* 7 (1976), 209–11.

7 For general surveys of Byzantine military architecture see A. W. Lawrence, 'A skeletal history of Byzantine fortification', *Annual of the British School in Athens* 78 (1983), 171–227, and the interesting but not entirely reliable *Byzantine Fortifications: An Introduction* by C. Foss and D. Winfield (Pretoria, 1986). See also Foss, *Survey of Medieval Castles of Anatolia: Kutahya* (British Archaeological Reports, International Series 261: Oxford, 1985) and the review by R. W. Edwards

in *Speculum* 62 (1987), 675–80. The issue of Byzantine influence on Crusader fortification has been bedevilled by lack of evidence on the Byzantine side. When discussing Byzantine parallels both Deschamps (*Châteaux* I, 45–57) and T. E. Lawrence (*Crusader Castles*, 25–34) were obliged to rely on C. Diehl, *L'Afrique byzantine* (Paris, 1896), refusing to allow themselves to be discouraged by the fact that the fortifications described there were constructed half a millennium before and a thousand miles away and could not possibly have been known to any of the Crusader castle builders. There is still a great deal of uncertainty about Byzantine fortifications. For the walls of Constantinople, see D. van Millingen, *Byzantine Constantinople: The Walls of the City and Adjoining Historical Sites* (London, 1899) and Foss and Winfield, *Byzantine Fortifications*, 41–77.

8 For the siege of Nicaea, S. Runciman, *A History of the Crusades* (3 vols., Cambridge, 1951) I, 177–81 and R. Randall, *Latin Siege Warfare in the Twelfth Century* (Oxford, 1992), 16–25. For the walls of Nicaea, A. M. Schneider, *Die Stadtmauer von Iznik (Nicaea)* (Istanbuler Forschungen, 9; Berlin, 1938) and Foss and Winfield, *Byzantine Fortifications*, 79–120.

9 Runciman, *History* I, pp. 213–35; Rogers, *Siege Warfare*, 25–39.

10 Foss and Winfield, *Byzantine Fortifications*, 13–15.

11 T. Sinclair, *Eastern Turkey: An Architectural and Archaeological Survey* (4 vols., London, 1990), IV, 244–8.

12 See below, pp. 79–84.

13 See below, pp. 84–96.

14 R. W. Edwards, *The Fortifications of Armenian Cilicia* (Dumbarton Oaks, 1987), 161–7.

15 Edwards, *Armenian Cilicia*.

16 Edwards, *Armenian Cilicia*, 65–72.

17 J. B. Segal, *Edessa, 'The Blessed City'* (Oxford, 1970), 236 n. 1 and plate 5b.

18 The best survey of Muslim fortification remains K. A. C. Creswell, 'Fortification in Islam before 1250', *Proceedings of the British Academy* (1952), but this needs to be updated in the light of recent research.

19 Benvenisti, *Crusaders*, 326–31.

20 For a full description, K. A. C. Creswell, *The Muslim Architecture of Egypt* (Oxford, 1952–9) I, 161–217.

21 A. Bazzana, P. Cressier and P. Guichard, *Les Châteaux ruraux d'al-Andalus* (Madrid, 1988).

22 For a general discussion of Muslim fortification in Syria in this period, T. Bianquis, 'Les frontiers de la Syrie au XIᵉ siècle', *Castrum* 4 (1992), 135–49. On Akkar, P. Deschamps, *Les Châteaux des Croisés en Terre Sainte III: la défence du comté de Tripoli et le principauté d'Antioche* (Paris, 1973), 307.

23 Deschamps, *Châteaux* III, 335–6.

24 Deschamps, *Châteaux* III, 339–40 where van Berchem's plan is reproduced.

25 P. E. Cheveddin, 'Citadel of Damascus' (unpublished PhD thesis, University of California, Los Angeles) I, 27–9.

3 CASTLES OF THE TWELFTH-CENTURY KINGDOM OF JERUSALEM

1 Runciman, *Crusades* I, 219, 228; Rogers, *Latin Siege Warfare*, 30–3.

2 Fulcher of Chartres, *History of the Expedition to Jerusalem*, trans. F. R. Ryan (New York, 1969), 150.

3 Runciman, *Crusades* II, 76–7.

4 Pringle, *Churches* I, 223–4.

5 Pringle, *Red Tower* (London, 1986), 40.

6 For the Citadel in Crusader times see C. N. Johns, 'The Citadel, Jerusalem' *Quarterly of the Department of Antiquities in Palestine* 145 (1950), 163–70.

7 Quoted in Johns, 'Citadel', 164.

8 There is no full publication of the castle at Montreal. It is discussed briefly, without a plan, in P. Deschamps *Les Châteaux des Croisés en Terre Sainte II: la défence du royaume de Jerusalem* (Paris, 1939), 42–4. The circumstances of the construction of the castle (but not its architecture) have recently been discussed in detail by Mayer in *Die Kreuzfahrerherrschaft Montreal (Šobak)* (Wiesbaden, 1990), 38–49.

9 Quoted by Deschamps (*Châteaux* II, 42 n. 3) and Mayer (*Montreal*, 47).

10 Deschamps, *Châteaux* II, 43; *Magister Thietmar Pereginatio*, ed. J. C. M. Laurent, in *Peregrinatores medii aevi quatuor* (Leipzig, 1873), 37. The castle belonged to the Sultan of Egypt but the 'vidua Gallica' who put up and helped Thietmar lived in the *suburbana* inhabited by both Muslims and Christians: presumably her husband had been a member of the Frankish garrison in 1188.

11 M. R. Savignac, 'Notes de voyage', *Revue Biblique* 41 (1932), 597: see also Deschamps, *Châteaux* II, 43.

12 Li Vaux Moise (Arabic al-Wu'ayrah) has been the subject of investigation recently by Marino and his team. This work is conveniently summarised in *The Crusader Settlement in Petra* in *Fortress* 7 (1990), 3–11. The castle was rediscovered by M. R. Savignac and published for the first time in 'Ou'airah', *Revue Biblique* 12 (1903), 114–20 and Deschamps, who never visited the site, simply refers to this. The history of the site is discussed by Mayer (*Montreal* passim but especially 188–91).

13 William of Tyre, *Chronicon*, ed. R. B. C. Huygens (Corpus Christianorum, Continuatio Medievalis, LXIII and LXIII A, Turnholt, 1986); English trans., E. A. Babcock and A. C. Krey, *A History of Deeds Done beyond the Sea* (2 vols., New York, 1976). References are to book and chapter, which have the same numbering in both text and translation (up to 21.9 after which the translation is one chapter behind): 16.6.

14 Mayer, *Montreal*, 184.

15 The castle at el-Habis is described, with plans by Hamond, *The Crusader Fort on El-Habis at Petra* (Middle East Center, University of Utah, Research Monograph No. 2, 1970). Hamond believes this is Crusader work but cf. Mayer, *Montreal*, 205–6.

16 Mayer, *Montreal*, pp. 205–6.

17 This issue is discussed with full bibliographical details by Mayer (*Montreal*, 52–4) whose conclusions I am inclined to accept. No trace of Crusader Aqaba has been located but it is worth noting that the southern end of the eastern wall of the surviving Mamluke fort shows traces of older, rougher masonry work. It is possible that this represents a fragment of the Crusader fortress.

18 Fulcher of Chartres, 282 and n. 1. The identification, without any evidence, is given in Rey, *Colonies franques*, 524.

19 William of Tyre, 14.8.

20 William of Tyre, 14.22; see J. Prawer, *The Latin Kingdom of Jerusalem* (London, 1972), 297–9 and M. Benvenisti, *The Crusaders in the Holy Land* (Jerusalem, 1970), 185–9, 205 for the castles around Ascalon and Pringle, *Churches* I, 95 for Bethgibelin in particular.

21 William of Tyre, 15.24.

22 William of Tyre, 15.25.

23 William of Tyre, 17.12.

24 William of Tyre, 20.19.

25 William of Tyre, 15.25.

26 J. S. C. Riley-Smith, *The Knights of St John in Jerusalem and Cyprus 1050–1310* (London, 1967), 435–7; Pringle, *Churches*, 95–101.

27 Rey, *Architecture militaire*, 123–5; see also Benvenisti, *Crusaders*, 205.

28 Quoted from the chronicle of Ernoul by A. Forey, *The Military Orders* (London, 1992), 59–60.

29 D. Pringle, 'Towers in Crusader Palestine', *Château Gaillard* 16 (forthcoming).

30 Pringle, *Churches* I, 150–2.

31 Pringle, *Churches* I, 123.

32 Pringle, *Red Tower*; for landholding in this area see S. Tibble, *Monarchy and Lordships in the Latin Kingdom of Jerusalem 1099–1291* (Oxford, 1989), 103–52.

33 D. Pringle, 'Survey of castles in the Crusader Kingdom of Jerusalem, 1989: a preliminary report', *Levant* 23 (1991), 87–91, 90; Benvenisti, *Crusaders*, 194–6; Tibble, *Monarchy and Lordships*, 45–6.

34 Z. Razi and E. Braun, 'The lost Crusader castle of Tiberias', in B. Z. Kedar (ed.), *The Horns of Hattin* (Jerusalem and London, 1992), 217–27. Galilee and its lordships are discussed in Tibble, *Monarchy and Lordships*, 13–23, 152–68.

35 Deschamps, *Châteaux* II, 100–1.

36 Deschamps, *Châteaux* II, pls. xxviii–xxx.

37 Deschamps, *Châteaux* II, 119–20; Tibble, *Monarchy and Lordships*, 163.

38 William of Tyre, 11.5.

39 Deschamps, *Châteaux* II, 117–18; see also Rey, *Architecture militaire*, 141–2; Tibble, *Monarchy and Lordships*, 13–23; Pringle, 'Survey', 89.

40 There is a full account with plans and illustrations in Deschamps, *Châteaux* II, 176–208. See also Rey, *Architecture militaire*, 127–39, R. C. Smail, *Crusading Warfare* (Cambridge, 1956), 221–2, and Müller-Wiener, *Castles*, 62–3. When I visited the castle in 1964 it was much as Deschamps described. Since then it has been the focus of considerable military activity, especially during the Israeli invasion of Lebanon in 1982, and there seems to be no published information about the present state of the monument.

41 The story is recounted with full references to the sources in Deschamps, *Châteaux* II, 182–7.

42 The building of the castle is described in Mayer, *Montreal*, 115–19. The fullest description of the architecture remains Deschamps, *Châteaux* II, 80–98. See also Smail, *Crusading Warfare*, 218–21 and Müller-Wiener, *Castles*, 47–8. For the most recent comments and additional bibliography, Pringle, *Churches* I, 286–91.

43 William of Tyre, 22.29 (29 in trans.).

44 It is possible that fire signals were used to communicate with Jerusalem but for a sceptical view of this see Mayer, *Montreal* excursus xii, 271–2.

45 William of Tyre, 22.29–31 (28–30 in trans.)

46 Deschamps, *Châteaux* II, 102–16. The best account, with plans and illustrations, is D. Nicolle, 'Ain al-Habis. The Cave de Sueth', *Archéologie Médiévale* 18 (1988), 113–40. I am grateful to Professor B. Hamilton for drawing this article to my attention.

47 William of Tyre, 22.22 (21 in trans.).

48 Deschamps, *Châteaux* II, 210–20.

49 For the beginnings of the Templars see Forey, *The Military Orders*, 6–17.
50 P. 31. See Benvenisti, *Crusaders*, 313–16; Pringle, 'Survey of castles', 90–1.
51 Pringle, 'Survey of castles', 89.
52 For a full discussion of La Fève see B. Z. Kedar and D. Pringle, 'La Fève: a Crusader castle in the Jezreel Valley', *Israel Exploration Journal* 35 (1985), 164–79.
53 Benvenisti, *Crusaders*, 324–5, 327.
54 Pringle, 'Towers'.
55 The evidence for Le Chastellet is presented in Deschamps, *Châteaux* II, 129–33; see also William of Tyre 21.29 and Forey, *Military Orders*, 62.
56 The early history of the Hospitallers is covered in detail in Riley-Smith, *The Knights of St John*, 32–59 and more generally in Forey, *Military Orders*, 17–23.
57 Pringle, *Red Castle*, 56; Tibble, *Monarchy and Lordships*, 67–8.
58 Only preliminary reports of the excavations have been published: R. P. Harper and D. Pringle, 'Belmont castle: a historical notice and preliminary report of excavations in 1986', *Levant* 20 (1988), 101–18 and R. P. Harper and D. Pringle, 'Belmont castle 1987: second preliminary report of excavations', *Levant* 21 (1989), 47–62.
59 Excavations between 1963 and 1968 have made older accounts of the castle obsolete. Unfortunately, the excavations have never been fully published but good general accounts of the building can be found in Benvenisti, *Crusaders*, 294–300 and Prawer, *Latin Kingdom*, 300–7. Note also the recent discussion of the chapel in Pringle, *Churches*, 120–2.
60 The decline of secular lordships throughout the twelfth century is a major theme of Tibble, *Monarchy and Lordships*.

4 TWELFTH-CENTURY CASTLES IN THE NORTHERN STATES

1 Deschamps, *Châteaux* III, 136–7.
2 Deschamps, *Châteaux* III, 293–5, 367–71. W. Müller-Wiener, *Castles of the Crusaders* (London, 1966), 42–3 gives the best plan.
3 William of Tyre, 10.26. For the most recent study of the archaeology of the castle, H. Salamé-Sarkis, *Contributions à l'histoire de Tripoli et de sa région à l'époque des Croisades* (Paris, 1980). Deschamps (*Châteaux* III, 367–71) argued that the Fatimid shrine was in fact an octagon constructed as the mausoleum of Raymond: Salamé-Sarkis has now shown this to be mistaken, although Raymond may well have been buried at the site.
4 Rey, *Architecture militaire*, 115–21; van Bercham and Fatio, *Voyage*, 108–10; Deschamps, *Châteaux* III, 203–15; Müller-Wiener, *Castles*, 64–5.
5 See the discussion of donjons in Pringle, *Red Tower*, 15–18.
6 Deschamps, *Châteaux* III, 297–301.
7 Deschamps, *Châteaux* III, 307–9 is the only account of this castle. There is no adequate published plan. I have not been able to visit because of disturbed conditions in the Lebanon.
8 Deschamps, *Châteaux* III, 313–16; Müller-Wiener, *Castles*, 53.
9 Pringle, *Red Tower*.
10 Deschamps, *Châteaux* III, 317–19; Müller-Wiener *Castles*, 52; Pringle, *Red Tower*, 16–18.
11 See Rey, *Architecture militaire*, 101–2; Deschamps, *Châteaux* III, 327–9 reproduces Rey's section and adds a number of other names to the corpus of small towers in the county of Tripoli. The architecture and distribution of these small castles deserves further research.

12 Van Bercham and Fatio, *Voyage*, 131–5; Deschamps, *Châteaux* III, 311–12. Unfortunately, I have not been able to visit this site.

13 For the best description of the disappointing remains see Sinclair, *Eastern Turkey* IV, 244–8.

14 The history and properties of the family are fully discussed in Deschamps, *Châteaux* III, 191–9. The castle at Margat is described below, pp. 163–79.

15 The castle is described by Deschamps, who never seems to have been there (*Châteaux* III, 345–9) on the basis of work done by G. Saade; neither plan nor photographs are entirely satisfactory.

16 Van Bercham and Fatio, *Voyage*, 241–51; Deschamps, *Châteaux* III, 351–7; Sinclair, *Eastern Turkey* IV, 261–6.

17 Rey, *Architecture militaire*, 105–13 gives the earliest important description with interesting drawings and an inadequate plan. See also van Berchem and Fatio, *Voyage*, 267–83; Deschamps, *Châteaux* III, 217–47; Fedden and Thompson, *Crusader Castles*, 79–84; Müller-Wiener, *Castles*, 44–5; Pringle, *Red Tower*, 18–19.

18 G. Saade, 'Histoire du château de Saladin', *Studi Medievali*, 3rd series, 9 (1968), 980–1016.

19 The story is recounted in Deschamps, *Châteaux* III, 231 who remarks, 'Cet épisode n'est pas un des moins émouvants de l'épopée des Croisades si fertile en événements tragiques.'

20 Crusader castles in the County of Edessa (or the lack of them) are discussed in H. Hellenkemper, *Burgen der Kreuzritterzeit in der Grafschaft Edessa und in Königreich Kleinarmenien* (Bonn, 1976) and Sinclair, *Eastern Turkey* IV, 1–228, neither of whom found evidence of surviving Crusader building.

21 Edwards, *Armenian Cilicia*, 69–70. Edwards discusses other possible Crusader work on pp. 31–3.

5 SIEGE WARFARE IN THE CRUSADER LANDS

1 The hardships suffered by the besiegers at Antioch are described in *Gesta Francorum* (ed. and trans. R. Hill, London, 1962), 30–3, 35, and Raymond of Aguilers, *Historia francorum* (trans. J. H. Hill and L. L. Hill, Philadelphia, 1968), 33, 35. For the problems of thirst at the siege of Jerusalem, *Gesta francorum*, 88, Raymond of Aguilers, 118–19.

2 See below, p. 197.

3 Ibn al-Furat, *Ta'rikh al-duwal wa'l-muluk*, ed. and trans. U. and M. C. Lyons as *Ayyubids, Mamlukes and Crusaders* with introduction and notes by J. S. C. Riley-Smith (2 vols., Cambridge, 1971) II, 127.

4 Pringle, *Red Tower*, 47, 66–7; for a general survey of castle water-supplies, Deschamps, *Châteaux* I, 90–3.

5 Rey, *Architecture militaire*, 101.

6 Abu Shama, Abd al-Rahman b.Isma'il, *Kitab al-rawdatayn* (ed. with French trans., *Recueil des historiens des Croisades: historiens orientaux* 5 vols. (Paris, 1898), IV, 380–1.

7 Baha' al-Din Yusuf b.Rafi' known as Ibn Shaddad, *Nawadir al-Sultaniyah wa'l-Mahasin al-Yusifiyah* (ed. with French trans., *Recueil des historiens des Croisades: historiens orientaux* III, 3–370 (Paris, 1884), 118; English trans., C. W. Wilson, *The Life of Saladin* (Palestine Pilgrims Text Society, London, 1897), 138.

8 See the table in C. Marshall, *Warfare in the Latin East, 1192–1291* (Cambridge, 1992), 243–5.

9 Baha al-Din, 104–6, 119–20.

10 William of Tyre, 14.28.

11 According to William of Tyre (22.29); Ernoul, *Chronique d'Ernoul et de Bernard le Trésorier*, ed. L. De Mas-Latrie (Paris, 1871), 104, on the other hand, says that Raynald of Chatillon, lord of Kerak, knew that supplies were very low.

12 *L'estoire de Eracles Empereur* in *Recueil des historiens des Croisades: historiens occidentaux* II (Paris, 1859), 104–5. The translation is made from the Lyon MS (MS D in the RHC edition) on the importance of which see M. R. Morgan, *The Chronicle of Ernoul and the Continuations of William of Tyre* (Oxford, 1973); Deschamps, *Châteaux* II, 73.

13 See Suger, *Vita Ludovici grossi regis* (ed. with French trans. by H. Wacquet, Paris, 1964), 136–41.

14 For siege warfare, R. Rogers, *Latin Siege Warfare in the Twelfth Century* (Oxford, 1992); for Geoffrey the Fair, J. Harvey, *The Medieval Architect* (London, 1972), 208–9.

15 For siege warfare on the First Crusade and afterwards, Rogers, *Siege Warfare*, 10–89. For eyewitness accounts of the siege of Antioch, Raymond of Aguilers, 30–50, and *Gesta Francorum*, 28–48; for Jerusalem, Raymond of Aguilers, 116–28, and *Gesta Francorum*, 87–93.

16 For the siege of Acre, Rogers, *Siege Warfare*, 212–36; Baha al-Din, 188, trans., 214, 250; Marshall, *Warfare*, 228–9.

17 William of Tyre, 15.18. Usamah b. Munqidh, *Kitab al-I'tibar*, trans. P. Hitti as *Memoirs of an Arab-Syrian Gentleman* (New York, 1927), 102–3.

19 Fulcher of Chartres, 253–4.

19 Baha al-Din, 323–30, trans. 364–5.

20 Ibn al-Furat II, 92–3.

21 Deschamps, *Châteaux* III, 270–2, and below, pp. 177–8.

22 Abu Shama IV, 254.

23 Ibn al-Furat II, 70–1; D. J. Cathcart King, 'The taking of Le Krak des Chevaliers in 1271', *Antiquity*, 23 (1949), 92.

24 Abu Shama IV, 204.

25 William of Tyre, 14.28.

26 See most recently Marshall, *Warfare*, 213.

27 The literature on siege artillery is conveniently summarised (with illustrations) in Rogers, *Siege Warfare*, 254–73. Unfortunately Rogers was not aware of Cheveddin's work which would have clarified some of the problems discussed. See also P. E. Cheveddin, 'The Citadel of Damascus' (University of California, Los Angeles, 1986; unpublished PhD dissertation available on University Microfilms International) I, 277–89.

28 See Cheveddin, *Citadel* I, 278.

29 Ibn al-Furat II, 70–1.

30 Ibn al-Furat II, 73–80.

31 Ibn al-Furat II, 88–95.

32 Ibn al-Furat II, 108–12.

33 Deschamps, *Châteaux* II, 27–8.

34 Marshall, *Warfare*, 237.

35 Rogers, *Siege Warfare*, 212–36.

36 Ibn al-Furat II, 75; Deschamps, *Châteaux* II, 134.

37 William of Tyre, 18.1239; Marshall, *Warfare*, 236.

38 Johns, 'Excavations at Pilgrims' Castle'.

39 Deschamps, *Châteaux* I, 147–50, 164–6.
40 Marshall, *Warfare*, 234; Deschamps, *Châteaux* II, 66.
41 Marshall, *Warfare*, 235.
42 Vitruvius, *The Ten Books on Architecture*, trans. M. H. Morgan (London, 1914), 23.
43 Deschamps, *Châteaux* III, 235.
44 Ibn al-Furat II, 93. The meaning of *sata'ir* is discussed in Cheveddin, *Citadel* I, 194–7 who rejects the idea that wooden hoards were used in Muslim military architecture.
45 Deschamps, *Châteaux* III, 245, pls. xiii b. xvii a, xxviii a.
46 Deschamps, *Châteaux* III, 274, 281, pls. xl d, liv a.
47 Edwards, *Armenian Cilicia*, 15.
48 Deschamps, *Châteaux* III, 238; II, 203–4 and pl. lxix c.
49 See below, pp.124–7, 190–8.
50 Tower P: Deschamps, *Châteaux* I, 185–7, pls. xlvii, xci, xcii.
51 See below, pp. 153–6.
52 Deschamps, *Châteaux* III, 240, pl. xxi c.
53 Deschamps, *Châteaux* III, 319.
54 Johns, 'Excavations at Pilgrims' Castle', 154.
55 Deschamps, *Châteaux* III, 255, pl. xxxv a, c.
56 Deschamps, *Châteaux* I, 256–7, pls. xl, xlii, xcviii.
57 Ibn al-Furat I, 90–1.
58 Ibn al-Furat I, 111.
59 Deschamps, *Châteaux* III, 271.

6 NOBLES, TEMPLARS AND TEUTONIC KNIGHTS IN THE THIRTEENTH CENTURY

1 For the text see Wilbrand of Oldenburg in Laurent, *Peregrinatores Medii Aevi Quatuor*, 166–7. There is a partial translation in T. S. R. Boase, *Castles and Churches of the Crusading Kingdom* (London, 1967), 65. A fuller and more accurate translation will soon be available in Pringle, 'Towers in Crusader Palestine'.
2 For Sidon see Rey, *Architecture militaire*, 153–9; Deschamps, *Châteaux* II, 224–33; Müller-Wiener, *Castles*, 69–71; most recently, H. Kalayan, 'The sea castle of Sidon', *Bulletin du Musée de Beyrouth* 26 (1973), 81–9.
3 Chastel Pelerin was first described by Rey (*Architecture militaire*, 93–100) and subsequently by Deschamps (*Châteaux* II, 24–33), who prints the text of the *Historia Damiatiana* account. However, these, and other early accounts, were made obsolete by C. N. Johns' excavations between 1930 and 1934. The results were never fully published but were partially made available in article form (see especially C. N. Johns, 'Excavations at Pilgrims' Castle, 'Atlit (1932)', *Quarterly of the Department of Antiquities in Palestine* 3 (1934). The excavator also produced a scholarly guidebook, C. N. Johns, *Guide to 'Atlit* (Jerusalem 1947), now extremely rare and all the more valuable because the site is now an Israeli naval base and completely inaccessible. I am grateful to Denys Pringle for letting me see his copy of this guide: there is also a copy in the library of the British School of Archaeology in Jerusalem. Later accounts of the castle are all based on Johns' work. For the most recent discussion with full bibliography see Pringle, *Churches* I, 69–80.
4 The fortifications are most fully described in Johns, 'Excavations (1932)'.

5 For Beaufort under the Templars, Deschamps, *Châteaux* II, 195–7.

6 The description of the building of the castle at Saphet has been edited by R. B. C. Huygens, 'Un nouveau texte du traité "*De constructione castri Saphet*"', *Studi medievali*, third series, 6(1) (1965), 355–87: English trans. H. Kennedy as appendix of this book. The archaeological remains and their interpretation are discussed by D. Pringle in 'Reconstructing the castle of Safad', *Palestine Exploration Quarterly* (1985), 141–9. For earlier accounts, see Lawrence, *Crusader Castles*, 66–9 and Deschamps, *Châteaux* II, 140–2.

7 Montfort was first described in Rey, *Architecture militaire*, 142–51. The excavations were published by B. Dean, 'The Exploration of a crusaders' fortress (Montfort) in Palestine', *Bulletin of the Metropolitan Museum New York* 22 (1927); Deschamps, *Châteaux* II, 138–40 (Deschamps seems to have been unaware of the excavations and merely reproduces Rey's inaccurate plan). The best recent discussion is D. Pringle, 'A thirteenth century hall at Montfort Castle in Western Galilee', *The Antiquaries Journal*, 66 (1986), 52–81. The castle at Judin has recently been surveyed by a team from the British School of Archaeology in Jerusalem: see D. Pringle, A. Petersen, M. Dow and C. Singer, 'Qal'at Jiddin: a Crusader and Ottoman castle in Galilee', *Levant* 26 (forthcoming) which also contains a good discussion of the military architecture, noting the German parallels.

8 Rey, *Architecture militaire*, 69–83 provides the earliest account accompanied by some fine drawings and a plan which includes features which have subsequently disappeared. The fortifications of the town are described in 211–14. Further notes and historical information are supplied in van Berchem and Fatio, *Voyage*, 320–34. See also Müller-Wiener, *Castles*, 50–1 and Deschamps, *Châteaux* III, 287–92. The remains have recently been surveyed and discussed by M. Braune in 'Die mittelalterlichen Befestigungen der Stadt Tortosa/Tartus', *Damaszener Mitteilungen*, 2 (1985), 44–54 and plates 17–21.

9 Rey, *Architecture militaire*, 85–92 and pl. 9 provides a description, a finely drawn cross-section and a plan which includes some outer works no longer extant. See also Müller-Wiener, *Castles of the Crusaders*.

10 I have followed the identifications given in Edwards, *Armenian Cilicia*, 99, 102 n.5. Deschamps, *Châteaux* III, 363–5 offers a different explanation and, as Edwards concedes, 'It is impossible to determine with certainty the Frankish name of Calan' and there is a possibility that it may have been La Roche Guillaume.

11 Müller-Wiener, *Castles*, 48–9, R. Edwards, 'Bagras and Cilician Armenia', *Revue des Etudes Arméniennes*, ns. 17 (1983), 415–55; Sinclair, *Eastern Turkey* IV, 266–71.

12 Edwards, *Cilician Armenia*, 99–102.

13 Edwards, *Cilician Armenia*, 253.

7 THE HOSPITALLERS IN TRIPOLI AND ANTIOCH

1 For the best general account of the Hospitallers in this period see Riley-Smith, *The Knights of St John*.

2 Pringle, *Red Tower*, 41–3.

3 Deschamps, *Châteaux* I, 118.

4 The classic account of Crac des Chevaliers is Deschamps, *Châteaux* I, perhaps the finest account of the archaeology and history of a single medieval castle ever written. For other descriptions see Rey, *Architecture militaire*, 39–67; van Berchem and Fatio, *Voyage*, 135–63; Fedden and Thomson, *Crusader Castles*, 84–90;

Müller-Wiener, *Castles*, 59–62. The name Crac was originally written Crat and seems to have been a Frankish version of Akrad meaning Kurds. It seems to have become Crac by analogy with Kerak in Jordan, also spelt Crac in Crusader sources, which may in turn be derived from the Syriac *karka* meaning a fortress (Deschamps, *Châteaux* I, 112–13) and 'Les deux Cracs des Croisés', *Journal Asiatique* 209 (1937), 494–500. The fortress was known as Crac de l'Ospital in Crusader times and the name Crac des Chevaliers was first used by Rey in the mid-nineteenth century.

5 Deschamps, *Châteaux* I, 122.

6 Deschamps, *Châteaux* I, 125–9; J. De Joinville, *The Life of St Louis*, trans. M. B. R. Shaw (Harmondsworth, 1963), 277; Ibn al-Furat, Ii, 140.

7 Deschamps, *Châteaux* I, 124–5.

8 Deschamps, *Châteaux* I, 129–32; Ibn al-Furat, II, 139.

9 The best discussion of the siege is Cathcart King, 'The taking of Le Crac des Chevaliers in 1271'. This substantially revises the account given in Deschamps, *Châteaux* I, 132–5.

10 Deschamps, *Châteaux* I, 277–8.

11 The issue is discussed by Van Berchem (*Voyage*, 143–4) who wrongly attributes the earliest Muslim examples at Aleppo and Damascus to the time of Baybars after 1260. Cheveddin (*Citadel* I, 275) makes it clear that such box machicolations, which he refers to as brattices, were an integral part of the defensive works erected by the Ayyubid Sultan al-'Adil from 1203 onwards in the citadel at Damascus.

12 Deschamps, *Châteaux* I, 148–50.

13 Deschamps, *Châteaux* I, 290.

14 See Deschamps, *Châteaux* III, 191–9 for a detailed discussion of the extent of these properties.

15 Deschamps, *Châteaux* III, 265.

16 Ibn al-Furat, II, 146–7.

17 Deschamps, *Châteaux* III, 267.

18 Deschamps, *Châteaux* III, 267.

19 The fullest account is in Deschamps, *Châteaux* III, 259–85. See also Rey, *Architecture militaire*, 19–38, van Berchem, *Voyage*, 188–94, Müller-Wiener, *Castles*, 57–8.

20 For the frescoes at Crac and Margat see J. Folda 'Crusader frescoes at Crac des Chevaliers and Marqab Castle', *Dumbarton Oaks Papers* 36 (1982), 17–210.

21 Tour de l'Eperon; the name is given in contemporary sources (Deschamps, *Châteaux* III, 271 n. 1).

22 Deschamps, *Châteaux* III, 270 n.8.

8 MUSLIM CASTLES OF THE TWELFTH AND THIRTEENTH CENTURIES

1 See above, pp. 18–20.

2 Cheveddin, *Citadel* I, 267–8.

3 Müller-Wiener, *Castles*, 65.

4 Müller-Wiener, *Castles*, 56.

5 Van Berchem, *Voyage*, 177–88; Müller-Wiener, *Castles*, 56.

6 C. N. Johns, 'Medieval Ajlun', *Quarterly of the Department of Antiquities in Palestine* 1 (1931), 21–33; Müller-Wiener, *Castles*, 58–9.

7 Cheveddin, *Citadel* I, 51–6, 62–3.

8 For important earlier studies of the Damascus citadel, J. Sauvaget, 'La citadelle de Damas', *Syria* 11 (1930), 59–90 and 216–41; D. J. Cathcart King, 'The defences of

the Citadel of Damascus', *Archaeologia* 94 (1951), 57–96; for the most recent work see H. Hanish, 'Der Nordwestturm der Zitadelle von Damaskus', *Damaszener Mitteilungen* 5 (1991), 181–231, who argues that the citadel as reconstructed by al-'Adil originally extended further to the northwest to make it a more regular rectangle.

9 Cheveddin, *Citadel* I, 274–90.

10 Cheveddin, *Citadel* I, 277.

11 Cheveddin, *Citadel* I, 20–9.

12 Creswell, 'Fortification in Islam', fig. 15.

13 Müller-Wiener, *Castles*, 67–8.

14 Müller-Wiener, *Castles*, 54–5.

15 This castle is considered as Crusader work, at least in part, by Deschamps (*Châteaux* II, 145–74) and Müller-Wiener (*Castles*, 45–6). This argument depends on the identification of Subeibe as the citadel of the nearby Crusader town of Banyas, which is mentioned in the chronicle sources for the twelfth century. However I am convinced by the arguments recently advanced by R. Ellenblum ('Who built Qal'at al-Subayba?', *Dumbarton Oaks Papers* 43 (1989), 103–12) who holds that this is an Ayyubid fortification, subsequently enlarged by the Mamlukes, and has no Crusader work at all.

16 The literature on the Citadel at Aleppo is disappointing compared with its counterpart in Damascus: see van Berchem, *Voyage*, 210–18; Creswell, 'Fortification in Islam'; Müller-Wiener, *Castles*, 66–7; H. Gaube and E. Wirth, *Aleppo* (Wiesbaden, 1984).

9 CRUSADER CASTLES AND THE WEST

1 F. M. Powicke, *The Loss of Normandy* (Manchester, 1913), 290.

APPENDIX

1 This translation is based on the text edited with a good introduction by R. B. C. Huygens 'Un nouveau texte du traite "*Du constructione castri Saphet*"', *Studi Medievali* 3rd series, 6 (1) (1965), 355–87. I have been guided at several points by D. Pringle's review article, 'Reconstructing the castle of Safad', *Palestine Exploration Quarterly* 16 (1985), 139–49, which includes an important discussion of the archaeological evidence.

2 The futile expedition of 1239 is described in Runciman, *History of the Crusades* III, 21–5. The site of Saphet, in Muslim hands since December 1188, was returned to Christian control in the summer of 1240 under the terms of a truce between the Crusaders and Sultan Isma'il of Damascus.

3 I have translated *balestarii* as crossbowmen but they also handled larger crossbowlike engines and the term may be used to describe the men who operated all kinds of siege engines.

4 The shrine and monastery of the Virgin at Saidnaya, much rebuilt, still thrives about 30 km north of Damascus.

5 Qal'at Subeibe on the slopes of Mount Hermon, whose striking ruins were long considered to be partly Crusader but which is now thought to have been built by al-Aziz 'Uthman (the 'nephew of the Sultan' mentioned here) in 1228–30. See above, pp. 184–5.

6 The Templars.

7 This is one of the few recorded examples of the use of slave labour in the building of Crusader castles. The practice is not known from the twelfth century but slaves (captured Muslims) were used by the military orders in the thirteenth, when Crusader manpower was in very short supply. According to a Muslim source, Ibn al-Furat, there were a thousand Muslim captives. Seeing that there were less than 200 Franks at work on the project, they resolved to revolt but the plan was betrayed by Sultan Isma'il who alerted the Franks and the prisoners were all put to death (see Deschamps, *Châteaux* II, 141).

8 A comment more hopeful than realistic but it follows the generally optimistic tone of the whole pamphlet: there were very few Crusader military successes of any kind at this stage.

9 The intention of the author in this final section was to show that the area round Saphet, though not including Jerusalem or Bethlehem, was nevertheless truly Holy Land and therefore worthy of support by the faithful.

BIBLIOGRAPHY

Abū Shāma, ʿAbd al-Rahmān b. Ismaʿīl, *Kitāb al-rawḍatayn*, ed. with French trans. in *Recueil des historiens des Croisades: historiens orientaux*, vols. IV–V (Paris, 1898)

Anon., *Gesta Francorum*, ed. and trans. R. Hill (London, 1962)

L'estoire de Eracles Empereur, in *Recueil des historiens des Croisades: historiens occidentaux*, vol. II (Paris, 1859)

Baha' al-Din Yusuf b. Rafiʿ, known as Ibn Shaddad, *Nawādir al-sultāniyah wa'l-maḥāsin al-yūsufiyah*, ed. with French trans. in *Recueil des historiens des Croisades: historiens orientaux*, vol. III (Paris, 1898): English trans., C. W. Wilson, *The Life of Saladin* (Palestine Pilgrims Text Society, London, 1897)

A. Bazzana, P. Cressier and P. Guichard, *Les Châteaux ruraux d'Al-Andalus* (Publications de la Casa de Velazquez, Madrid, 1988)

M. Benvenisti, *The Crusaders in the Holy Land* (Jerusalem, 1970)

M. van Berchem and E. Fatio, *Voyage en Syrie* (Mémoires de l'Institut Français d'Archéologie Orientale du Caire, Cairo, 1914)

T. Bianquis, 'Les frontières de la Syrie au XIᵉ siècle', *Castrum* 4 (1992), 135–49

T. Biller, 'Die Johanniterburg Belvoir am Jordan: zum frühen Burgenbau der Ritterorden im Heiligen Land', *Architectura: Zeitschrift fur Geschichte der Baukunst/ Journal of the History of Architecture* (1989), 105–36

T. R. Boase, *Castles and Churches of the Crusading Kingdom* (Oxford, 1967)

H. Bordeaux, *Voyageurs d'orient* (Paris, 1926)

J. Bradbury, *The Medieval Siege* (Woodbridge, 1992)

M. Braune, 'Die mittelalterlichen Befestigungen der Stadt Tortosa/Tartus', *Damaszener Mitteilungen* 2 (1985), 44–54 and plates 17–21

R. A. Brown, *English Castles* (London, 1976)

M. Bur, 'Recherches sur les plus anciennes mottes castrales de Champagne', *Château Gaillard* 9–10 (1978–80), 55–69

R. Burns, *The Monuments of Syria: An Historical Guide* (London and New York, 1992)

C. Cahen, *La Syrie du nord a l'époque des Croisades* (Paris, 1940)

C. du Fresne du Cange, *Les Familles d'Outremer*, ed. E. G. Rey (Paris, 1869)

D. J. Cathcart King, 'The taking of Crac des Chevaliers in 1271', *Antiquity* 23 (1949), 83–92

'The defences of the citadel of Damascus', *Archaeologia* 94 (1951), 57–96

P. E. Cheveddin, 'The citadel of Damascus' (2 vols., unpublished PhD thesis, University of California at Los Angeles, 1986: available on University Microfilms International)

C. Clermont-Ganneau, *Archaeological Researches in Palestine during the Years 1873–1874* (2 vols., London, 1896–9)

H. Collin, 'Les plus anciens châteaux de la région de Nancy en Lorraine', *Château Gaillard* 3 (1966), 26–39

C. R. Conder and H. H. Kitchener, *The Survey of Western Palestine* (3 vols., London, 1881–3)

K. A. C. Creswell, *The Muslim Architecture of Egypt* (2 vols., Oxford, 1952–9)

'Fortification in Islam before A.D. 1250', *Proceedings of the British Academy* 38 (1952), 89–125

S. Cruden, *The Scottish Castle* (Edinburgh, 1960)

B. Dean, 'A Crusaders Fortress in Palestine (Montfort)', *Bulletin of the Metropolitan Museum of Art* (New York, 1927)

P. Deschamps, *Les Châteaux des Croisés en Terre Sainte I: le Crac des Chevaliers* (Paris, 1934)

Les Châteaux des Croisés en Terre Sainte II: la défense du royaume de Jerusalem (Paris, 1939)

Les Châteaux des Croisés en Terre Sainte III: la défense du comté de Tripoli et de la principauté d'Antioche (Paris, 1973)

'Les deux Cracs des Croisés', *Journal Asiatique* 209 (1937), 494–500

K. R. DeVries, *Medieval Military Technology* (Lewiston, NY, 1992)

C. Diehl, *L'Afrique byzantine* (Paris, 1896)

R. Edwards, 'Bagras and Armenian Cilicia', *Revue des Etudes Arméniennes* n.s. 17 (1983), 415–55

The Fortifications of Armenian Cilicia (Dumbarton Oaks, 1987)

R. Ellenblum, 'Who built Qal'at al-Subayba?', *Dumbarton Oaks Papers* 43 (1989), 103–12

C. Enlart, *Les Monuments des Croisés dans le Royaume de Jerusalem* (2 vols., Paris, 1926–7)

Ernoul, *Chronique d'Ernoul et de Bernard le Trésorier*, ed. L. de Mas-Latrie (Paris, 1871)

H.-P. Eydoux, *Les Châteaux du soleil: fortresses et guerres des Croisés* (Paris, 1982)

R. Fedden and J. Thomson, *Crusader Castles* (London, 1957)

J-F. Fino, *Forteresses de la France mediévale* (Paris, 1970)

M. Fixot, 'A la recherche des formes les plus anciennes de la fortification privée en France', *Château Gaillard* 9–10 (1978–80), 389–406

J. Folda, 'Crusader frescoes at Crac des Chevaliers and Marqab Castle', *Dumbarton Oaks Papers* 36 (1982), 177–210

A. Forey, *The Military Orders* (London, 1992)

C. Foss, *Survey of Medieval Castles of Anatolia: Kutahya* (British Archaeological Reports, International Series 261: Oxford, 1985)

C. Foss and D. Winfield, *Byzantine Fortification: An Introduction* (Pretoria, 1986)

G. Fournier, *Le Châteaux dans la France mediévale: essai de sociologie monumentale* (Paris, 1976)

Fulcher of Chartres, *History of the Expedition to Jerusalem* (trans. F. R. Ryan, New York, 1969)

H. Gaube and E. Wirth, *Aleppo* (Wiesbaden, 1984)

P. C. Hamond, *The Crusader Fort on El-Habis at Petra* (Middle East Center, University of Utah, Research Monograph No. 2, 1970)

H. Hanisch, 'Der Nordwestturm der Zitadelle von Damaskus', *Damaszener Mitteilungen* 5 (1991), 184–231

R. P. Harper and D. Pringle, 'Belmont castle: a historical notice and preliminary report of excavations in 1986', *Levant* 20 (1988), 101–18
  'Belmont castle 1987: second preliminary report of excavations', *Levant* 21 (1989), 47–61

J. Harvey, *The Medieval Architect* (London, 1972)

H. Hellenkemper, *Burgen der Kreuzritterzeit in der Grafschaft Edessa und im Königreich Kleinarmenien* (Bonn, 1976)

P. Hoffsummer, A. Hoffsummer-Bosson and B. Wery, 'Naissance, transformations et abandons de trois place-fortes des environs de Liège: Chèvremont, Franchimont et Logne', *Château Gaillard* 13 (1986), 63–79

R. B. C. Huygens, 'Un nouveau texte du traité "*De constructione castri Saphet*"', *Studi Medievali*, third series, 6(1) (1965), 355–87

Ibn al-Furāt, *Ta'rīk al-duwal wa'l-mulūk*, partial ed. and trans. U. and M. C. Lyons with introduction and notes by J. Riley-Smith, *Ayyubids, Mamlukes and Crusaders* (2 vols., Cambridge, 1971)

C. N. Johns, 'Medieval Ajlun', *Quarterly of the Department of Antiquities in Palestine* 1 (1931), 21–33
  'Excavations at Pilgrims' Castle, 'Atlit (1932)', *Quarterly of the Department of Antiquities in Palestine* 3 (1934) 152–64
  Guide to 'Atlit (Jerusalem, 1947)
  'The Citadel, Jerusalem', *Quarterly of the Department of Antiquities in Palestine* 14 (1950), 163–70

J. de Joinville, *The Life of St Louis*, trans. M. B. R. Shaw (Harmondsworth, 1963)

H. Kalayan, 'The sea castle at Sidon', *Bulletin du Musée de Beyrouth* 26 (1973), 81–9

B. Z. Kedar and D. Pringle, 'La Fève: a Crusader castle in the Jezreel valley', *Israel Exploration Journal* 35 (1985), 164–79

A. Kloner and D. Chen, 'Bet Govrin: Crusader church and fortifications', *Excavations and Surveys in Israel* 2 (1983), 12–13

J. C. M. Laurent, *Peregrinatores medii aevi quatuor* (Leipzig, 1873)

A. W. Lawrence, 'A skeletal history of Byzantine fortification', *Annual of the British School in Athens* 78 (1983), 171–227

T. E. Lawrence, *Crusader Castles*, ed. D. Pringle (Oxford, 1988)

L. Marini *et al.*, 'The Crusader settlement in Petra', *Fortress* 7 (1990), 3–11

C. Marshall, *Warfare in the Latin East, 1192–1291* (Cambridge, 1992)

D. Matthew, *The Norman Kingdom of Sicily* (Cambridge, 1992)

H. E. Mayer, *Die Kreuzfahrerherrschaft Montreal (Šobak)* (Wiesbaden, 1990)

J. Mesqui, *Châteaux et enceintes de la France mediévales*, vol. I: *Les organes de la défeuse* (Paris, 1991)

J. F. Michaud, *Histoire des Croisades* (7 vols., Paris, 1822)
  Bibliothèque des Croisades (4 vols., Paris, 1829)

D. van Millingen, *Byzantine Constantinople: The Walls of the City and Adjoining Historical Sites* (London, 1899)

M. R. Morgan, *The Chronicle of Ernoul and the Continuations of William of Tyre* (Oxford, 1973)

W. Müller-Wiener, *Castles of the Crusaders* (London, 1966)

D. Nicolle, 'Ain al-Habis. The Cave de Sueth', *Archéologie Mediévale* 18 (1988), 113–40

C. Platt, *The Castle in Medieval England and Wales* (London, 1982)

N. J. G. Pounds, *The Medieval Castle in England and Wales: A Social and Political History* (Cambridge, 1991)

F. M. Powicke, *The Loss of Normandy* (Manchester, 1913)

J. Prawer, *The Latin Kingdom of Jerusalem* (London, 1972)

D. Pringle, 'Reconstructing the castle of Safad', *Palestine Exploration Quarterly* (1985), 141–9

    'A thirteenth-century hall at Montfort Castle in Western Galilee', *The Antiquaries Journal* 66 (1986), 52–81

    Red Tower (London, 1986)

    'Survey of castles in the Crusader Kingdom of Jerusalem, 1989: a preliminary report', *Levant* 23 (1991), 87–91

    The Churches of the Crusader Kingdom of Jerusalem: A Corpus vol. I, A–K (Cambridge, 1993)

    'Towers in Crusader Palestine', *Château Gaillard* 16 (forthcoming)

D. Pringle, A. Petersen, M. Dow and C. Singer, 'Qal'at Jiddin: a Crusader and Ottoman castle in Galilee', *Levant* 26 (forthcoming)

Raymond of Aguilers, *Historia Francorum*, trans. J. H. and L. L. Hill (Philadelphia, 1968)

Z. Razi and E. Braun, 'The lost Crusader castle of Tiberias', in B. Z. Kedar (ed.), *The Horns of Hattin* (Jerusalem and London, 1992), 217–27

G. Rey, *Etudes sur les monuments de l'architecture militaire des Croisés en Syrie et dans l'île de Chypre* (Collection de Documents Inédits sur l'Histoire de France, Paris, 1871)

    Les Colonies franques de Syrie aux douzième et treizième siècles (Paris, 1885; reprint, New York, 1972)

J. Riley-Smith, *The Knights of St John in Jerusalem and Cyprus 1050–1310* (London, 1967)

J. Riley-Smith (ed.), *The Atlas of the Crusades* (London, 1991)

R. Rogers, *Latin Siege Warfare in the Twelfth Century* (Oxford, 1992)

S. Runciman, *A History of the Crusades* (3 vols., Cambridge, 1951)

G. Saade, 'Histoire du château de Saladin', *Studi Medievali* third series, 9 (1968), 980–1016

H. Salamé-Sarkis, *Contributions à l'histoire de Tripoli et de sa région à l'époque des Croisades* (Paris, 1980)

C.-L. Salch, *Atlas des châteaux forts en France* (Strasburg, 1977)

J. Sauvaget, 'La citadelle de Damas', *Syria* 11 (1930), 59–90, 216–41

M. R. Savignac, 'Ou'airah', *Revue Biblique* 12 (1903), 114–20

    'Notes de voyage', *Revue Biblique* 41 (1932), 581–97

A. M. Schneider, *Die Stadtmauer von Iznik (Nicaea)* (Istanbuler Forschungen 9: Berlin, 1938)

J. B. Segal, *Edessa, 'The Blessed City'* (Oxford, 1970)

T. A. Sinclair, *Eastern Turkey: An Architectural and Archaeological Survey*, vol. IV (London, 1990)

R. C. Smail, *Crusading Warfare* (Cambridge, 1956)

The Crusaders in Syria and the Holy Land (London, 1973)

Suger, *Vita Ludovici grossi regis*, ed. with French trans., H. Wacquet (Paris, 1964)

A. J. Taylor, 'Three early castle sites in Sicily', *Châteaux Gaillard* 7 (1975), 209–11

M. W. Thompson, *The Rise of the Castle* (Cambridge, 1991)

S. Tibble, *Monarchy and Lordships in the Latin Kingdom of Jerusalem, 1099–1291* (Oxford, 1989)

S. Toy, *A History of Fortification from 3000 BC to AD 1700* (London, 1955)

Usamah b. Munqidh, *Kitāb al-i'tibār*; English trans., P. K. Hitti, *Memoirs of an Arab-Syrian Gentleman* (Beirut, 1964)

E. Viollet-le-Duc, *Essai sur l'architecture militaire au moyen-âge* (Paris, 1854); trans., M. Macdermott, *An Essay on the Military Architecture of the Middle Ages* (Oxford, 1860; reprinted Westport, Conn., 1977)

Vitruvius, *The Ten Books on Architecture*, trans. M. H. Morgan (London, 1914)

M. de Vogüé, *Les Eglises de la Terre Sainte* (Paris, 1860)

La Syrie centrale: architecture civile et religieuse (Paris, 1966)

William of Tyre, *Chronicon*, ed. R. B. C. Huygens (Corpus Christianorum, Continuatio Medievalis, LXIII and LXIII A, Turnholt, 1986); English trans., E. A. Babcock and A. C. Krey, *A History of Deeds Done beyond the Sea* (2 vols., New York, 1941; reprint New York, 1976)

INDEX

Bold type indicates the main description of each site